WROUGHT IRON IN ARCHITECTURE

An Illustrated Survey

Old Quarter in Naples   G. K. G.

Where wrought iron was used almost as freely as masonry

WROUGHT IRON IN ARCHITECTURE

An Illustrated Survey

GERALD K. GEERLINGS

DOVER PUBLICATIONS, INC.
NEW YORK

Copyright © 1929 by Charles Scribner's Sons.
Copyright renewed © 1956 by Gerald K. Geerlings.
All rights reserved under Pan American and International Copyright Conventions.

Published in Canada by General Publishing Company, Ltd., 30 Lesmill Road, Don Mills, Toronto, Ontario.
Published in the United Kingdom by Constable and Company, Ltd., 10 Orange Street, London WC2H 7EG.

This Dover edition, first published in 1983, is an unabridged and unaltered republication of the work originally published by Charles Scribner's Sons, N.Y. and London, in 1929, under the title *Wrought Iron in Architecture: Wrought Iron Craftsmanship; Historical Notes and Illustrations of Wrought Iron in Italy, Spain, France, Holland, Belgium, England, Germany, America; Modern Wrought Iron; Lighting Fixtures and Knockers; Specifications.*

Manufactured in the United States of America
Dover Publications, Inc., 180 Varick Street, New York, N.Y. 10014

Library of Congress Cataloging in Publication Data

Geerlings, Gerald K. (Gerald Kenneth), 1897–
    Wrought iron in architecture.

    Reprint. Originally published: New York : Scribner, 1929.
    Bibliography: p.
    Includes index.
    1. Architectural ironwork. 2. Wrought-iron. 3. Decoration and ornament, Architectural.   I. Title.
NA3950.G4   1983   729   83-5220
ISBN 0-486-24535-7

DEDICATED TO THE
SCHOOL OF ARCHITECTURE
UNIVERSITY OF PENNSYLVANIA

CONTENTS

CONTENTS

RAISON D'ÊTRE

T HE companion book to this volume, "Metal Crafts in Architecture: Bronze, Brass, Cast Iron, Copper, Lead and Current Developments," was originally planned to be a part of this one. Consequently much of the preface of this book will repeat what has been previously stated in its predecessor, which treats of the decorative metals used in architecture, wrought iron excepted. To include all the material in one volume made it unwieldy in thickness, and, in addition, it seemed advisable to separate the cast metals from wrought iron because generally the latter is so faultily designed in terms of the former. By segregating wrought iron in this book it is earnestly hoped that readers will be less apt to make the common and expensive error when designing, of confusing work beaten at the anvil with that cast in sand moulds.

In starting out with the project of collecting in one volume a concise history of wrought iron in the various countries of Europe and in the United States, supplemented by illustrations of the most representative work, the author felt that in the architect's office of to-day it would be an advantage to have a book that would act as an illustrated key-index, serving as a designer's guide for at least preliminary sketches, as well as giving the layman or architect a bird's-eye vista of the development of the craft in various countries, and the information contained in the chapters on "Craftsmanship" and "Specifications." It was realized from the start that probably only a small proportion of the illustrations of historic examples would be unfamiliar to the initiated, but it was felt that it would nevertheless serve a useful purpose to gather in one volume the outstanding chefs-d'œuvre as a ready reference book for comparing one style with another, and for determining which period or style would best suit a designer's purpose by readily turning from one chapter to another. One hundred and fifty pages of illustrations will be as guilty of omitting some of the thousands of masterpieces as the text may sometimes be lacking in important names, dates, and facts. Some illustrations which were desired could not be procured. Others were excluded because of work ably designed but badly executed, and vice versa. Of some examples which should be allotted their place of honor, the author may not even have known, in which case he tenders his humblest apologies to craftsmen past and present.

It is hoped that the brief historical sketch which begins each chapter will be valuable in the sense that, if a problem calls for a design after the manner of fifteenth-century Italian work, for example, by turning to the text dealing with that period one can become acquainted with at least a few of the chief characteristics and notable examples as a background before beginning to draw. By separating the various illustrations into chapters according to their countries and not according to subject-matter, it is intended to encourage design which does not haphazardly fling together various motifs from all sources and periods without regard for their historical associations. For example, one of the popular quatrefoils is that of the Scaligeri Tombs, Verona (page 40); in fact it has even been listed by certain books as typifying its century; actually it was simply a playful device prompted by the name of the Scala family—employing a ladder instead of stairs. It is to be hoped that modern designers will be as ingenious as he who designed the Scaligeri Tombs quatrefoil, and will not find it necessary to copy that which has no modern significance.

It will be indulgently forgiven, the author hopes, if certain historical facts or outstanding monuments have been unintentionally overlooked; fifty pages of text which attempt to portray a bird's-eye vista of territory which might cover thousands are bound to be guilty of near-sightedness here and far-sightedness there. The author read practically all the available material in the English language (and struggled with a little French and German) at the main library of New York City, as well as the documents in several private collections. However, it is obviously impossible to select with infallibility all material which would universally be accepted as of the foremost importance, particularly in view of the great condensation here necessary.

The books on wrought iron are many and varied. No single one could begin to supplant them all. Some treat of one style, some of one country, but no single one attempts to include the best examples of each country (including American and twentieth-century work), supplemented by brief historical data, and—more important still—a consideration of the limitations and possibilities natural to the metal with which the designer should be familiar. Some handbooks on the craft, notably the German ones, give such complete accounts of the tools and methods necessary to perform anvil operations that one could almost begin forging iron after a perusal, but even these do not attempt to correlate the work of the smith with that of the architectural designer. Up to the present the subject of the architect's drawings and specifications has not been treated elsewhere, very likely because any suggestions brought forward are sure to arouse criticism in certain quarters. However, the information contained in the chapters on "Craftsmanship" and "Specifications" should serve as a guide to architects who have not previously had extensive experience in the metal, but who are desirous of procuring the best products of the craft.

This book does not attempt to cover the same territory as others which deal exclusively with only a portion of the field; the bibliography at the end of the book makes a point of designating sources where more complete information can be obtained concerning the various styles. But, for the architect or layman who is building up his library on wrought iron documents, it is meant to provide a catalogue for the books most worth his while investigating and acquiring as his interest—and means—increases. Each chapter is so arranged that the illustrations which are chiefly of historical interest are grouped with the text, while those of special application to design follow; the information pertinent to each illustration is concisely given under it to obviate the necessity of turning overleaf to track down important facts.

In the pleasant meanderings of the author through the shops of various craftsmen, he became increasingly impressed with the fact that unless the artisan takes definite pride in his work he is in the wrong field. Unless there is a personal gain accruing from the joy of creating, then the metal game must be a severely disappointing one. If any one is intent on mere financial profits it must be galling indeed to try to make them in wrought iron, for how bitter to know the cost of each hammer blow! No different of course, and no more productive of art, is the architect whose organization moves on a cost-sheet basis, and whose completed plans and details are not determined by arriving at a thoughtful and successful effect, but by a schedule of drafting costs which prearranges the date when certain work must be finished for blue-printing, regardless of æsthetic results. Both such persons, while pathetic in having the wrong jobs, are nevertheless culpable for much of the eye-misery foisted on the helpless public. Some philanthropist should endow all "business-getters" in the architectural and metal craft fields who have not the artistic welfare of a job at heart, supplying them with stock-market tickers plus plenty of tape and capital.

The genuine architect is coming to realize that the genuine metal craftsman is a vital part of his organization, since he himself has too many other responsibilities to be able to fill the rôle of metal designer and craftsman. He is learning that he must know how to think and draw in terms of metal, but that the actual effect, for good or bad, is dependent upon the imagination and personality of his confrère, the craftsman. The information on craftsmanship is meant to give the architect some insight into the manner in which the work is carried on, so that he will have a sounder conception of how to design. But, more than that, it is hoped to stimulate sufficient interest in the metal crafts so that the architect will see and enjoy the pageantry of iron in the making, for only by so doing can he come to a riper understanding of what may be expected and what can be achieved.

The author first became interested in the subject of wrought iron when, in the employ of York & Sawyer some years ago, he was working on the interior details of the Federal Reserve Bank, New York City. Mr. Samuel Yellin kindly invited him to his shop on a number of occasions in order to visualize what was, and what was not, feasible and characteristic in iron. Before our going abroad during 1924-25 Mr. Yellin suggested collecting material on wrought iron which would make a practical book in the architect's library and drafting-room. After returning to the United States, the author was encouraged by Mr. Russell Whitehead, Editor of *Pencil Points*, to write a number of articles which appeared in seven instalments during 1926-27 in that magazine under the title, "Wrought Iron Precedent."

The main idea underlying this book, as well as that of its preceding fellow, seemed gradually to shape itself into pointing out that metal work, in order to be beautiful (in the Greek sense), must serve a purpose, and be so designed as to take advantage of the natural endowments of the material. Just before going to press with "Metal Crafts in Architecture," the author was given a reprint of a lecture called "Right Making," by B. J. Fletcher, Director of the Municipal Art Schools, Birmingham, England, delivered at the London School of Economics, Aldwych, January 14, 1925. Because the lecture is apropos of the aim of this book, and because it sounds the keynote of genuine craftsmanship, three excerpts are quoted.

As regards *fitness of purpose*, the first tenet necessary to genuine craftsmanship, the lecture states: "It is a mistake to think that art is hampered by structural or utilitarian requirements; on the contrary: it is from these that it receives its reason and inspiration. The beauty of the perfect forms of natural things comes of necessity. From consideration of the simple shapes of leaves or seeds, to the complex and beautiful shapes and modeling of bones, we must conclude that the inevitable rightness of design is due to the insistent claims of use and purpose; each line or twist is there to fulfil some definite work and duty. . . . On the other hand, it is salutary to remember that where artists and craftsmen have had entire freedom of conditions, some of their worst work has been done. . . .

"As outstanding mistakes, imitation of one material by another will be remembered: paper made to look like cambric, tiles or terra-cotta made to look like stone or marble, iron made to look like bronze, cotton to look like silk. The stupidity of these needs no comment; art is never artifice. With such we shall make no mistake. It is with the just-possible technique, the nearly-good or the clever handling which is not quite sympathetic with its medium, that we go wrong, and in the whole range of fine craftsmanship it is this adjustment of treatment to material which is most often in error. As a skilful violinist makes the utmost of the characteristic quality of his instrument, so will the good craftsman deal with his material. . . .

"Some good and beautiful materials have their individual character degraded in a foolish attempt to make them imitate things which are more expensive. These, and all other shams, are dead against appreciation of beauty or art. By working *with* a material, not against it, we may get beauty.

"This matter may possibly be made clearer by taking a parallel from a totally different source. We would have dogs of pure breed and not mongrels; a strain of spaniel discredits a greyhound. We should know and appreciate the characteristic qualities of brass or wood and feel when the treatment is alien to the material as certainly as we pick out an alien strain in a fox terrier. But in articles of brass and wood we are so used to the presence of treatments proper to stone or marble that we do not see that the treatment is alien and the result a mongrel. It is possibly true to say that of the miles of cast-iron railings which have been made during the past century none has repeated the good cast metal tradition which died about 1840, or made beauty in any other manner from emphasis of the qualities and nature of cast iron. Most of it imitates wrought iron. It is interesting to notice in this connection that errors of treatment are most frequent and greatest in those materials which are most easily modeled or moulded. There is, for instance, in modern times, little terra-cotta or plaster work which shows the characteristic qualities of these two materials. On the other hand, in refractory materials like wrought iron, or hard stone, the suitability of the treatment for its material is more often seen. Materials difficult to work keep the craftsman in hand, make him search for essentials, get most profit from his labor, and force him to work with, and not against, his material."

IN ACKNOWLEDGMENT

THE author is so deeply indebted to a number of his friends, and persons whom he has met, or been in correspondence with since beginning work on this book, for their assistance, counsel and research, that an acknowledgment of twenty pages will be as inadequate as one. It is impossible to know whom to thank first—to do so chronologically will be to gratefully acknowledge Mr. Samuel Yellin's interest in the project for many years, his encouragement of the author to collect material while abroad, and his invaluable instruction at his shop, in correspondence, and in many conversations. Were it not for Mr. Yellin the author would never have interested himself in the project of this book nor its predecessor, "Metal Crafts in Architecture."

Since the author first began work on the book he has been very greatly aided in securing illustrations by Mr. Carl Weiler. The reproductions from the excellent series on French wrought iron, through the courtesy of the Paris publisher, Frédéric Contet, was arranged by Mr. Weiler. The library of the J. G. Braun Company, which Mr. Weiler has collected, has very generously been at the constant disposal of the author.

To Richard Koch, our good friend, and companion of travel along the high-ways and by-ways of Spain, we are indebted for the photographs and information concerning his mellow old city of New Orleans. Unfortunately the chapter on American Wrought Iron had to be so condensed that many of the charming illustrations by his camera had to be omitted. They themselves would have made an entire book.

Mr. Charles ffoulkes, author of "Decorative Ironwork," very graciously loaned his personal negatives for illustrating the chapter on the Lowlands (pages 110-112).

Mr. Alexander H. Burgess, president of Jno. Williams, Inc., loaned the author everything desired in his library (for over a year), and good-naturedly permitted his wrought iron department to be photographed at a time when it was inconvenient (Figures 7, 8, 9, and 10). Mr. Henry Renner, of Renner & Maras, has been of assistance in the compilation of specifications, in the prescription of protecting iron without painting it, and in a number of suggestions incorporated in the chapter on "Craftsmanship." Mr. Charles G. Kemp, of Richmond & Kemp, has given us the benefit of his investigations concerning certain ornaments supposedly wrought iron which proved to be lead. Mr. Milton Wend made a number of suggestions of intrinsic value regarding economic forge operations, as opposed to expensive ones not suitable to the material. Mr. Paul Hermann kindly loaned two measured drawings, pages 61 and 70. The Allied Building Metal Industries of New York City contributed a number of suggestions for the chapter on "Specifications," while to York & Sawyer thanks are due for permission to quote the wrought iron specifications of the Federal Reserve Bank of New York City.

The Victoria and Albert Museum, London, the Metropolitan Museum of Art, New York City, and the Pennsylvania Museum, Philadelphia, have co-operated to the fullest degree in the matter of furnishing illustrations.

Pencil Points published seven articles by the author under the title "Wrought Iron Precedent" during 1926 and 1927; for their permission to use many of the illustrations in this book, and for the encouragement given the author in writing the articles, his sincerest gratitude is expressed.

Chronologically the last and largest measure of gratitude is due my wife, B. F. Geerlings. All the portions of the measured drawings which are intricate or ornate have been drawn by her, first in Europe in all sorts of weather at all times of the day, and then redrawn in ink in their reproduced form. To her also is due the credit for reading all the pages of the manuscript and making the rough places smooth, from the first rough stages to the galley-proof. More noteworthy still, she has not complained about the deflated family-leisure and exchequer during the many months when the book usurped most of the natural working days and the majority of evenings, holidays, Sundays and such other times when one's husband is normally sociable.

In Sir Lawrence Weaver's well-known book, "English Leadwork," he comments in the preface that contrary to the generally accepted belief concerning publishers, he found that working with B. T. Batsford, Ltd., was most pleasurable. We have found not only that we are indebted to his publishers for certain illustrations—and the satisfaction which accrues from pleasant correspondence, but that the publishers of this book and its companion volume have not only done everything in their power to make this a craftsmanlike example of printing, but have made relations so pleasant that the long-looked-for day when the book would be betwixt its covers will not be so much a burden off our shoulders as the termination of a most happy experience.

G. K. G.

February 1, 1929.

WROUGHT IRON
IN ARCHITECTURE
An Illustrated Survey

WROUGHT IRON CRAFTSMANSHIP

BY WAY OF INTRODUCTION

IN the next era, when histories have us properly catalogued and pigeon-holed, we will no doubt be condemned for causing bitter diversion of opinion in being relegated to an exact age. Perhaps we shall be favorably compared with the Stone Age—or the Golden. Fragments of discovered bank and "movie" building reports will be quoted to prove we belong to the first, and radio company dividends submitted to assign us to the second. But some hawk-eyed archæologist, greedy for fame, will attempt to settle the dispute by producing a Fifth Avenue fragment of our monumental débris. With a becoming gesture he will declare we belong to neither, but dub us creators of the "Cast Stone Age," or the "Age of Imitations."

As a matter of fact, we in the building profession (architectural or otherwise), may as well admit in a stage whisper to each other, that we spend a good share of our energy making things "look like what they ain't." A flimsy curtain wall is palmed off on the unsuspecting public as an honest-to-goodness Florentine palazzo made of real stuff. The walnut panelling in its lobby is nothing more than plaster with enough faked worm-holes to house a million mythical colonies. The ashlar sandstone in the monumental halls has been poured from sacks labelled "Caen Stone," without an idea that there is such a place loaning its name to that creamy stone which makes Loire architecture immortal. The rubber floors are given vibratory color treatment to make Botticino marble turn verd-antique with envy. All to what purpose? Our archæologist is certain he is correct—we are in the Age of Imitations.

Yet, in spite of all our concentrated efforts, but little success has attended the imitation of wrought iron. For all its good nature and accommodating spirit, wrought iron asserts a seeming puritanical conscience by looking and acting only what it is. Nor can anything steal its copyrighted traits. We may fashion plaster like Caen stone, rubber flooring like marble, composition sawdust like carved wood, but, in the craftsman's use of the term "wrought iron," we can make nothing intelligently imitate it. In commercial efforts to be "arty" and turn out

hand-made articles in quantity production with the much-vaunted "American efficiency," one sees such pathetic attempts as to make imitation wrought-iron bridge-lamps out of cast iron. Thumb-marks on applied putty are supposed to represent hammer marks, while a silver-and-black finish completes the texture. By the time that process be perfected for discriminating customers, the cost will no doubt exceed that of the genuine article. But no matter. We enjoy our little jokes.

Until recently, wrought iron was mentioned only in a footnote in the social register of building materials. In the best circles it was regarded as existing but not really counting. Its European ancestry was acknowledged as being duly ancient, but was thought to be of unfashionable origin. Only in the last decade has it again been permitted timidly to present itself now and then in halls of state, in salons and counting rooms. Bronze was the fashion of the day when there was money to spend. When there was not, cast iron was the apologetic substitute. But wrought iron, no!

Since the middle of the nineteenth century the general public was scarcely aware of wrought iron until photographs of imaginative Californian and Floridian architecture became widely published. Shops specializing in wrought-iron knick-knacks, hardware, and lighting fixtures also helped to press-agent its virtues. At the present writing even many architects are suspicious, wary, or doubtful about wrought iron, and have been but little interested in considering its historic accomplishments or investigating its modern possibilities. But since Mr. and Mrs. Client have begun to ask for wrought iron, a market is being stimulated.

Wrought iron is gradually coming into its own. It has become a matter of habit on Tudor doors. The old "H-and-L" hinges of Colonial ancestry are being taken for granted. The country's leading architects in domestic work have attained effects with wrought iron which no other material could have made possible. In the realm of large buildings it has scored an outstanding success in such an example as the Federal Reserve Bank of New York City (page 172). The architects, York & Sawyer, employed it instead of bronze because of its greater harmony with the early Florentine type of architecture, being used exclusively for all exterior doors and grilles, as well as all interior grilles, heating and ventilating registers, bank counter screens and lighting fixtures.

Apparently we have no such definite information about wrought iron as distinguished from cast iron, as we have concerning the distinctions between stone and terra-cotta. The differences of the latter are well understood both in the manner of detailing and the contrast in price. But in the case of wrought versus cast iron, we assume the former to be more expensive, decide without good reason that it is apt to be an indefinite quantity which might jeopardize the client's interests, and specify cast iron instead. Not that anything is wrong with cast iron, any more than anything is amiss with terra-cotta, but just as stone can gain effects which terra-cotta cannot because of natural endowments, so also with cast iron's cousin, wrought.

To define "wrought iron" is at once a simple and a complex matter. In this sense it is simple —its name is self-explanatory. "Wrought" iron is "worked" on the anvil by hammering while it is hot, cooling, and sometimes cold. "Cast" iron, on the other hand, is "cast" in moulds and not worked beyond the point of being poured.

The more complex task in further defining wrought iron lies in explaining *how* it can best be "worked," and in what capacity it makes itself most advantageous and adaptable to the architect's needs. In this age when architectural design is fettered from base to cornice by building regulations, and the architect is pressed for doing his best artistically with but meagre funds, it becomes an advantage to him to understand how iron is wrought. A design appropriate to what may be accomplished at a forge will look infinitely better than a *motif* costing ten times as much which had rather be in bronze or cast iron. The salient aspect is not, "how much does this wrought iron design cost?" but, "how will it look?"; if the estimate exceeds the allowance, the design has to be altered (bearing in mind the while that it must be for a *forged* metal), until the cost of execution comes within the appropriation. It is no compliment to an architect that his client has been inveigled into spending $50,000 for entrance grilles, when from their appearance it is evident that if cast they would have looked quite as well, and cost only one-

quarter as much. It is a plume in his cap, however, if with $1,000 he can so intelligently design wrought iron that the building appears $50,000 better. To do so he must be familiar with how iron is wrought, and while a reading knowledge is helpful, it cannot by any stretch of the imagination replace actual visits to a forge. For that matter, who would want to read about wrought iron forging when with a little more trouble he can see the sparks hop, the iron glow all the colors of the rainbow—and more, behold, at the end of the rainbow a virile, impressionistic result!

If building materials had emotions it could readily be forgiven wrought iron if it went into a corner and cried itself into a state of irreparable rust over the lamentable lack of interest accorded the ornament and design which are natural to its temperament. Always to be dressed up in the manner of bronze, and to appear the worse for it, is sorrow enough to justify any tears. Without slighting the abilities of present-day designers, it can be said with a fair margin of safety that less is known about wrought-iron ornament, from both historical and practical standpoints, than about the enrichment of any other building material. When a design cannot be executed in stone because of expense, it may be executed in terra-cotta by a note to the modeler not to "undercut," and, after a little additional attention to the models, the final result may be a very creditable job. But to change from a cast to wrought design, or vice versa, is not such a simple metamorphosis. To illustrate: ever since the day when Vignola sent his treatise on architectural forms to press, the architectural profession has been composing cornices more or less according to formula. The given height is divided into four or five sections, which in turn are reduced to cyma-rectas or cyma-reversas with fillets, facias, modillions, dentils, and bed-moulds tossed in according to the architectural Hoyle. When a problem presents itself in wrought iron, such as a bank-screen cornice, out of force of habit it is designed from a series of stock forms. Whether these elements can be made on an anvil is barely considered. The mere fact that the drawing is labelled "wrought iron" and that Vignola has been faithfully followed, cannot be expected to make the cornice genuine wrought iron either in letter or in spirit.

It might be possible industriously to hunt up isolated cases to prove that somewhere among the best examples of wrought iron work there has been a Vignola-nese cyma profile hammered into immortality. But it is the painful truth, nevertheless, that he who would create a design in strict accordance with the best wrought iron precedent and (equally important in these days) keep within the reasonable bounds of cost, must shelve most of the good old standby mouldings for some mill or foundry to execute in their respective materials. In plying his craft a wrought iron workman has no more tools than a glorified, artistic blacksmith who must work the metal while it is at a glowing heat. When he beats one side of the bar the opposite side is certain to be flattened by its contact with the anvil. An interesting cornice he can make, to be sure, but he would much prefer to do it in the native language of his material rather than force it to stutter foreign idioms. Wrought iron does not talk eloquently in terms of cymas.

It is of interest to consider what the wrought iron vocabulary has to offer instead of such accepted mouldings as the cyma-recta and cyma-reversa: *1-a* of Figure 1 is a profile of what might be desired in a wrought design. To pound out a cyma for any great length could be done only with the most devoted endeavor. Visualize the process of heating only about 8 inches at a time, manipulating it on the anvil, and, with a series of swages, chisels and sundry tools, attempting to approximate the desired profile with its double curve. Assuming this to be satisfactorily done, it would be no mean task to complete another unit of the same length with the identical profile. The results in beating out a long, double-curved moulding would probably appear haphazard and clumsy, even with the greatest care to keep the lines running true. However, if the effect of a double-curved moulding is felt to be indispensable, profile *1-b* (in the same figure) is suggested as a substitute. The cove can be pounded from a square bar, first flattened on one side at an angle of 45 degrees and then introducing the curve by means of a swage. The quarter-round can also be made from a square bar by rounding one of the edges when hot. This diagram, showing how a common moulding for a cast material can be approached, is not meant to convey the impression that where one would ordinarily use a double-curved moulding in a cast design, this *b* in Figure 1 should be substituted in wrought iron instead. It is shown here merely to illustrate some of the forms natural to wrought iron.

In the same diagram *2-a* represents one of many common devices at the necking, middle

or base of a miscalled "wrought iron" baluster. In bronze or cast iron it means a normal casting; in wrought iron it demands abnormal craftsmanship and expense. The same feature translated into a more characteristically wrought form is shown alongside at *b*. What is here shown is merely one of hundreds of possibilities, but it does stay within the normal attainments of anvil, swages, chisels and hammer.

A disinterested observer in architectural fashions would probably decide that the present mode dictated panelled surfaces wherever possible. If panels it must be, *3* indicates the relative difference between the usual cast form

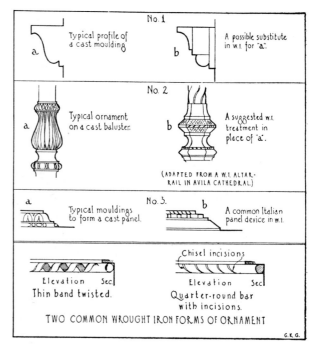

FIG. 1.—CAST AND WROUGHT CONTRASTS AND TWO COMMON WROUGHT-IRON FORMS OF ORNAMENT

and a well known Italian wrought stile, such as frequently was employed in the over-all pattern grilles of Florence and Siena (pages 43 and 51). In Italian work the dentil established itself as an accredited wrought iron expression to enhance stiles and rails. It is needless to mention that there is not the nicety in mechanically accurate spacing as there would be in a material like stone or clay. Since wrought-iron dentils are made by cutting out rectangles along the edge of a plate while it is red hot, it is natural that less discipline exists among their ranks than the orthodox eye is accustomed to see.

Two simple means of ornamentation are shown at the bottom of the above diagram. The one at the left is a thinnish piece of iron twisted around a round bar, hot if it is thick and cold if it is thin, and kept in place by iron "nails." Its brother to the right is shown as a quarter-round bar with incisions made by a chisel; it may be of any cross-section area or shape and may have any pattern in chisel marks which suits the designer's fancy, so long as it is not too complicated. Both devices are particularly adaptable for ornamenting any inner angle which would usually fall to the lot of a bed-mould. Instead of the quarter-round, a simpler gesture is the plain bar with a 45-degree face, often used in Italian work.

One of the greatest difficulties of the wrought iron craftsman is the unbelievable ignorance, even in some of the best architectural offices, as to what wrought iron really is and what it can achieve. Stair railing designs are commonly drawn with twisted bars and classically moulded tops and bases. The entire thing is labelled either "cast" or "wrought iron." One is as nearly correct as the other, yet neither entirely so. The twisted bars could be made in cast iron only with the same difficulty that the classically moulded tops and bases could be wrought. Yet such drawings are blue-printed and issued every day. If the contractor be conscientious he notifies the architect that he can cast the extremities but must have the twisted bars wrought unless he charges an "extra." "All right," says the architect, "make it any way you choose, just so you don't put in an 'extra.' We'll paint the whole thing anyway." Some offices have an entire design wrought at considerable expense, only to paint the finished product finally to simulate bronze. It is like importing Carrara marble (white), then staining it ochre and drilling holes into it in order to imitate travertine. But why the effort to make one material appear like another when it finally looks like neither?

When the architect elects to use wrought iron it should be for very definite reasons. He should know it is not a substitute for another material, but distinctive for its own qualities. As he embarks on his initial wrought iron ex-

FIG. 2.—WROUGHT-IRON FLAG-HOLDER, PIAZZA POSTIERLA, SIENA. (FIFTEENTH CENTURY)

FIG. 3.—BRONZE KNOCKER, PALAZZO DEL MAGNIFICO, SIENA. (GIACOMO COZZARELLI, 1508)

These two comparable forms, one in wrought iron and the other in bronze, exhibit the specific characteristics which are natural to each material, and the type of ornament to which they are best suited. Where the iron has incised ornament, irregular plain twists, and yapping dragon's head, the bronze has double-curved mouldings with regular ornamentation, regular twists with minute scales, classic scroll and acanthus

perience, it augurs well if he takes himself good-naturedly in hand and soliloquizes: "We've been doing this dried-out, formula architecture about long enough! How about going outside the pale of hackneyed forms, by making color, texture and craftsmanship work for us this time? Wrought iron has all the variations in color that lie between jet-black and silver. Its high-lights change like those of panne velvet when you turn it. Its texture has a human quality, full of ups and downs. We will inject a little humor into this sober old problem with some funny little doo-dangle wrought-iron heads of three-legged snakes. When the finished product leaves the forge we know that every molecule will not be rigidly held in leash as in a decorous cast article. But what of it?—a little play is what we are after. Variation and imagination this time! After the wrought iron has been on the job a year or so we expect it to show a slight sign of rust here and there on exterior work. When that happens no doubt the owner will either die of apoplexy or he will sue us for breach of confidence in introducing a bogus material which the painter forgot to paint and which consequently rusted.

"If the owner survives the initial shock with his reason not too badly shattered, we will explain that the rust gives an added, pitted texture which is an advantage when some steel wool or emery cloth has polished off the golden glow. A thin coat of wax mixed with a little boiled linseed oil rubbed on the iron will prevent further rusting for some time to come. Not enough oil to ruin any one's clothes of course, but sufficient to forestall the heinous rust as long as a coat of paint would, anyway. If we are lucky to explain matters that far, we may be able to save up enough breath to add that taking care of wrought iron as it should be done is not more expensive than veneering cast iron with paint."

That may be a long-winded, and rather unreasonable supposition. Probably—for the rare cases where wrought iron is fittingly used and appreciated for its color and texture conclusively prove that the term "wrought iron" is but little understood, and the actual product even less.

The designer of wrought iron should conjure up the village smithy (even though he has never seen one) in order to understand how his designs are to be executed. Combine the raw iron, forge, anvil, array of hammers, tongs, swages,

Fig. 4.—Cast-Iron Balcony, 232 South Third Street, Philadelphia, with Typical Cast Features

fullers, and other tools (page 14), with a smith having a vigorous imagination, an artistic sense, and a love for his work—and there is the sum and substance of the creation of wrought iron. The smith must be something of a strategist, too, with his operations as carefully planned as though he were to wage war against Napoleon. Once the battle begins there is no truce. The iron is heated in the forge fire, which is made to burn briskly at will by means of a bellows; when it is taken out at a lemon glow it demands immediate action or it cools and becomes stubborn. The operation in hand must be thought out in advance so that there are no false starts, or operations to be repeated because the best sequence was not followed. The smith has ever to bear in mind that any blow made by the hammer on one face of the iron means that the anvil underneath is exerting an equal force on the face opposite, which is the equivalent of saying that unless he is careful, one blow may wipe out the effects of another. He must be a quick thinker, an adept impressionist. Modeling is done at arm's length, yet close up the results must have the charm of jewelry. The genuine iron artisan is to be respected as an artist working in one of the most difficult of mediums, and his job should be appreciated as such. When he is forced outside the realm which his iron can naturally achieve, it is unfair to him and his material. The various types of *motifs*, bars, and ornament are considered later, with the reasons for the adaptability of each. Ornamental possibilities are more or less confined to chisel marks, floral forms, grotesque heads, *repoussé* work, and various textures, if the iron is to exhibit the charm characteristic of it.

The best iron work of the past has this

similarity with the best of to-day: the designer and the craftsman was one and the same person. The work of Il Caparra in the Italian Renaissance, the Spanish *coro rejas* by nationally known artists, Quentin Matsys in Belgium, Jean Tijou, and the English smiths like Robinson, Blakewell, Partridge, Buncker, are outstanding examples. To-day Edgar Brandt in France, and a score of outstanding names in this country, repeat the same story. When the architect not only dictates the style of the design, but specifies the size each bar must be, it indicates either that he has no faith in the craftsman or that the latter is merely a mechanical manipulator of smithing tools. In our current architecture the most admirable results are those in which the architect has had a workable knowledge of wrought iron and has taken his preliminary scale details to the iron-worker for his criticisms and suggestions, or otherwise the craftsman has executed his own interpretation of a rough sketch by the architect. There are exceptions doubtless, and certain architects are familiar with forge work, knowing what to design so that it may be executed within the limitations of wrought iron—but not often.

The drawings of an architect for wrought iron will reveal at a glance whether or not he *knows*. The details show the extent of the knowledge behind them as clearly as a sum in addition indicates the correct or incorrect answer. The converse is similarly true, for the shop drawings submitted by an ignorant iron-worker indicate his ability and show such features as whether he intends to "spot weld" scrolls at their junctions or really knows and intends to weld them under a hammer. In a word, wrought iron is no field in which the architect can bluff his way by merely assuming to know how wrought iron should be designed or detailed. If he does not, it is to his advantage frankly to admit it to a craftsman and visit a forge before he begins designing. He may know the last word on bronze and cast iron designing and yet be entirely unfamiliar with wrought iron, just as a pen-and-ink artist would be utterly unable to do a brilliant water-color if he handled nothing but black ink previously. It is no disgrace not to know, but only in trying to hide it. It is a mistake for any architect, no matter how high and mighty, to assume that by much gusto and vociferation he can hold the respect of his draftsmen or craftsmen, when it is evident that it is merely a blustering veneer to hide an absence of knowledge.

There can be no substitute for visiting a forge and seeing a smith in action, but in order to present some reason for the limitations of designs in wrought iron as set forth later, there follows a brief and cursory description of a few of the characteristics of the metal, tools, and means of working the iron.

PROPERTIES OF WROUGHT IRON

The three kinds of iron vary from each other chiefly in their carbon content, although there are other elements which differ in lesser degrees. For an easy "rule of thumb," it can be said that pig or cast iron has from 2 to 6 per cent carbon; wrought iron, .04 per cent; and machine, open-hearth, or Bessemer steel, .2 to .6 per cent. Their chief characteristics may be said to be due to the amount of carbon present. As far as the architect is concerned in his specifications, if he wishes to procure the quality which would be the least susceptible to rust, he should designate "Norway" or "Swedish" iron. The raw product may sometimes cost 60 per cent more than the American "merchant" bars, but in any job it is not the material which is expensive, but the labor. For this reason many of the better forges provide Swedish iron of their own accord, because it is easier to work, tougher, and more malleable. One of the chief sources of supply is from the bottom of shallow Swedish lakes, where from 4 to 6 inches is deposited in from fifteen to thirty years. In the Swedish or Norwegian production the smelting and refining are combined in one step by the sole use of charcoal.

Wrought iron is fibrous in structure, light gray in color, and when cold or hot can be hammered out, twisted and stretched. The more it is worked the more dense, brittle and hard it becomes, but it can be brought back to its original state by "annealing," i. e. heating and then cooling slowly. Excessive cold hammering renders it easily breakable and liable to split. Various stages of its heating may be described as dark blood red or black heat; dark red, at which it should be finished; full red; bright or light red, at which the surface scales if worked and should not be finished at this heat; yellow heat; light yellow heat, good for forging; and white or welding heat, beyond which the iron will burn.

TEXTURE, LEGITIMATE AND OTHERWISE

The mediæval craftsman obtained his ingots in crudely shaped miscellaneous forms. From these he beat out the rods or plates according to his needs. Present-day production provides a large assortment of stock bars, rods, sheets and plates. The task for the smith now begins where for his predecessor it would have been prefaced by the laborious fashioning of rough pigs into regular shapes. This factor brings up two interesting and much discussed features, first, concerning how much "texture" should be administered stock forms, and second, the reason old iron resists rust.

The ideal of the mediæval craftsman in producing a bar or rod was to beat it until it was perfectly round, square or whatever shape he desired. The truer the edges and the fewer the flaws, the better the piece of craftsmanship. It was a tedious process from the rough, crude ingot to the finished bar. What imperfections remained were due to lack of time and effort, or perhaps, they were purposely left. At all events the craftsman did not first produce a perfect bar, and then, because he imagined himself "artistic," give it to his novice helper to maltreat and hack. At present the craftsman begins with all the preliminary work finished. He is not compelled to make square bars out of round ones, or round ones out of pigs. He does in many cases however, work backwards, trying to approach the point from which the mediæval smith started, by scarring the face of the iron by indiscriminate blows. Just as some smiths have a habit of pounding the anvil four times for each time they strike the iron, and cannot tell why they do it, in the same way perhaps the hacking of the face of iron is a habit of unknown cause. It would be more flattering if that were true, rather than, as we suspect, a supposed means of guaranteeing that the product is "hand hammered." Many an inexperienced iron-worker, unable properly to carry on the traditions of his craft, has found that on the uninformed public he can palm off a hacked piece of iron as being of special value because it is thought to be either an "antique" (worn so by time perhaps!) or is "hand hammered," and therefore particularly meritorious. It is of course not any different from the practice of a cabinetmaker in producing a piece of furniture, then turning it over to some destructively inclined boy or a "foot-rubbing" machine in order to imitate an antique, also "elbowed by time." It is a curious state of affairs, whereby the public, in order to be assured that it is getting a hand-made product, is willing to purchase an article which any machine could stamp out, after another machine covers up the tracks of the first by denting and scarring the surface in order to make it appear "hand hammered." To pay an additional sum for an out-and-out "fake," to wilfully aid the insincere producer, to admire a disfigured article, is beyond the realm of reason. By the same line of reasoning, moth-chewed carpets and chipped crockery should soon be immensely valuable.

At the outset there should be a distinction drawn, and thoroughly understood, between wrought iron *texture* and wrought iron *disfigurement*. The former is the result of necessary work on the anvil; the second, an outcome of a fancied demand by the public for an obvious guarantee that hammers have been used. If

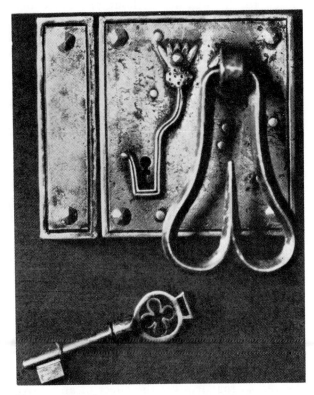

FIG. 5.—RIM LOCK DISPLAYING NATURAL WROUGHT-IRON TEXTURE FROM WORK ON THE ANVIL

The uneven texture has been assimilated naturally from beating when the iron was hot; the stem of the flower is delightfully whimsical, and the irregular bolt-heads admirable. Designed and executed by the Iron-Craftsmen

the deadly monotony of stock bars is to be overcome it can be done by a process similar to that of the mediæval craftsman, viz., by reducing a bar from a stock cross-section area to a smaller size: if a ⅝-inch square bar be desired, to start with a ¾-inch stock bar and "draw" or beat it out until it be reduced to ⅝. This would result in its having texture characteristic of the best wrought iron lineage; to merely hack a stock ⅝-inch bar at random is an insult to the public's improving intelligence. If there be not sufficient funds available to reduce a ¾-inch bar to one ⅝, something might be said in favor of judiciously beating a stock ⅝-inch bar over its *entire* surface—not denting it like a piece of cord-wood being chopped by a novice woodsman, but all-over surface beating. While this seems useless in one way, it is excusable in another sense, in that it makes the surface of the iron more dense, which in turn will make it more resistant to rust. As noted before, this is the second phase of importance in the difference between mediæval and modern forging.

Old iron in many places in Spain is still vigorously healthy although it has been exposed to the weather without any trace of a paint complex. The reason, we are told, is that the bars were beaten out of crude pigs and were a long time in the process of forging, and that all the while they were being beaten the structure became more dense, particularly on the outside. At any rate it seems a proven fact that the more iron is worked under the hammer, the more resistant it becomes to rust action. There is, therefore, some excuse for surfacing stock members when hot by beating with a hammer *all over*. The public is constantly gaining more intelligence and it is well for any craftsman to keep abreast of his time, and if possible, a step or two in advance.

Every architectural designer knows that the simpler the surfaces, the more need for careful study, and that hackneyed use of pilasters and ornament always offers easy egress from hard work. So too with the artistic iron-worker, who would use plain surfaces unbroken by ornament and still make them interesting. A good example is the work of Brandt (page 180) where the entire surface has been carefully beaten so that it gives the effect of an all-over pattern. Deeper accents are added intelligently and belong to a category entirely unlike the crude butchering so frequently done in this country by iron-workers who treat their metal like so much pine being clumsily hand-adzed.

In the surfacing of plain areas there are a number of resources at the command of the artisan which can be legitimately used, without any of the objectional scarring by the ball-peen hammer: the iron could be finished at almost a scaling heat, beaten on an anvil face not perfectly free from scale, scoured with a wire brush when still at a white heat, or even beaten on a slab of rough granite instead of the anvil.

If an inferior smith is to execute the work, a precaution which the designer may take in order to prevent plain surfaces from being needlessly hacked in the effort to ornament them, is to permit only relatively small or narrow spaces to extend unbroken in either direc-

FIG. 6.—WROUGHT-IRON DOOR GRILLE
Residence of Dr. F. W. Pratt, Bronxville, N. Y. (8 by 15 inches)
P. V. Stout, Architect   Executed by the Iron-Craftsmen
The texture is particularly meritorious and honest; it is at once evident that the surface variation is the result of necessary labor; swellings of welds frankly show

tion. If the problem be an inexpensive railing, it would cost but little more than plain bars if the uprights were twisted. If there be a frieze, it can be broken up into various planes (page 75), and these in turn ornamented with inexpensive chisel-mark decoration (Figure 68). With a little thought and ingenuity the details can be so worked out that, although through open competition an inferior iron-worker might have to be awarded the contract, the design would eliminate to a great extent any occasion for vandalistic dents of hammer marks. If the client does not have the foresight to select a capable craftsman, such as the architect might have chosen, it will be decidedly to the latter's advantage to know how iron should be wrought Also, he does well personally to inspect the work at the shop while it is being forged, and then and there reject faulty portions, rather than await its arrival at the building when his client will not tolerate waiting for new iron to replace unsatisfactory workmanship. A good craftsman has too much pride in his work wilfully to produce what he knows to be unworthy results (although even the mighty occasionally tumble), but the iron-worker who would be a better woodchopper will be the one whom the architect cannot afford to leave to his own devices. Constant supervision may result in a fair job in spite of habitual poor work.

TOOLS AND TERMS

An introduction to the principal tools of the craftsman will give the designer a better appreciation of the limitations within which his requirements should confine themselves. There will be no pretense at technical descriptions leading to "self-taught" forging, but only enough of a recital to acquaint the layman with the weapons in the smith's armory. Any reader interested beyond the scope of this chapter can with profit turn to an ably written text on "Plain and Ornamental Forging," by Ernst Schwarzkopf.

HAMMERS
Ball-peen and
Set-hammer

ground off to a convex curve in order to be used, while its other end is responsible for much of the damage referred to in previous paragraphs in the attempt to administer texture. The sledge hammer, No. 1, should not pass without mention, for its employment is necessary not only in heavy work, but in welding, straightening, cutting off, etc.; it usually is manned by the smith's helper. No. 7 is a set-hammer, used in forming sharp shoulders and drawing material between narrow spaces.

Among the principal tools, first and foremost is the anvil, the most general type being known as the English, No. 10, Figure 7. The village smithy and his anvil with its pointed prow are simple enough to conjure up, but the importance of the tool hole at the heel end is but little recognized by the average layman; a number of necessary tools for ornamental forging fit in it as will be described later.

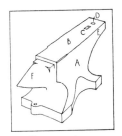

ENGLISH ANVIL
A.—Body
B.—Face
C.—Tool hole
D.—Pritchel hole
E.—Heel
F.—Horn

In the line of hammers the smith has several varieties of this important weapon, two of the most necessary being the cross-peen, No. 9 in the same illustration, and straight-peen. The ball-peen is not pre-eminently a smithing tool, having a flat-surfaced face which must be

HAMMERS
Cross-peen and
Straight-peen

After the anvil and hammer, which are of prime importance, come a group of secondary tools necessary to the making of the common wrought forms—scrolls, curves, prickets, leaves, spikes, etc. Referring to photographs of various forge views (page 16), it will be noticed that at the edge of the water tank alongside the forge fire is a row of tongs hung on a wood strip. Various types are necessary for sundry operations in gripping different shapes of bars: the flat-jawed, hollow bit or bolt, anvil or pick-up, bill, clip, and link tongs. In Figure 7, No. 27 is a link tongs, and 28 a hollow bit or bolt species.

Two necessary tools are the top and bottom fullers, Nos. 11 and 20 the top, and 17 the bot-

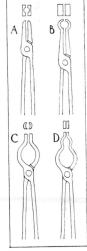

TONGS
A.—Flat-jawed
B.—Link
C.—Hollow bit
D.—Anvil or
pick-up

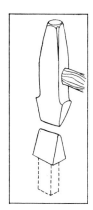

FULLERS
Top and bottom

tom fuller. They are particularly useful in "drawing" any material, i. e., beating it so as to increase its length, or for making shoulders, grooves, depressions and the like.

Top and bottom swages enter into a large part of ornamental smithing, often being specially made to produce a bar of a desired profile. In Figure 7, Nos. 2 and 3 are top swages, and 16, 22, and 30 bottom swages, all of the latter fitting into the tool hole of the anvil. The marginal diagram shows how, when a hot bar is placed on the bottom member and the top swage is being beaten down by

SWAGES
Top and bottom

a hammer, the shape of a bar is changed for better or for worse. It can be appreciated that only a short length at a time can thus be moulded, and that it is difficult to maintain a perfectly true edge. The first section of the bar will conform readily to shaping because of just being withdrawn from the forge fire, the next section less easily because of cooling. To true up a bent rod having a moulded profile is a difficult task, for a blow struck on one face which would rectify matters there, will flatten the side opposite. The result may be to straighten the bar in general, but the local conditions along the length of the rod will vary its profile. If only simple, single curves as the cavetto, congé, scotia, or ovolo are desired, these are possible, but the double-curved profiles, such as cyma-recta and cyma-reversa, are unfair mouldings to ask the smith to make. If the material is to appear wrought and the client is paying for that effect, it will defeat its own purpose to make the iron take on cast characteristics.

The flatter, No. 6, used for surfacing flat

FIG. 7.—WROUGHT-IRON SMITH'S TOOLS

1.—Sledge. 2 and 3.—Top swages. 4 and 5.—Twisting bars. 6.—Flatter. 7.—Set-hammer. 8.—Scroll starter. 9.—Cross-peen hammer. 10.—English anvil. 11.—Top fuller. 12 and 13.—Hot chisels. 14 and 15.—Bottom scroll forks. 16.—Bottom swage. 17.—Bottom fuller. 18.—Mandrel. 19.—Bottom swage. 20.—Top fuller. 21.—Scroll fork. 22.—Bottom swage. 23.—Heading tool (bottom toward front). 24.—Special twisting bar. 25.—Dividers. 26.—Twisting bar. 27.—Link tongs. 28.—Hollow bit or bolt tongs. 29.—Scroll form. 30.—Bottom swage. 31.—Scroll form. 32.—Special tool. 33 and 34.—Twisting bars or scroll forks. 35.—Bending tool used in vise. 36.—Punch

areas only, is employed on the anvil when the iron is at a dark red heat (never at the higher temperatures or the surfaces will scale). The flatter, anvil and the iron must all be free from scale in order to obtain a smooth surface.

The smith's punches are of the round, square, flat and hammer variety; the most frequent in use is the first, No. 36. It is employed by driving it two-thirds through from one side of the heated iron and the remainder from the opposite side of the iron, the burr being forced through the pritchel or tool hole in the anvil.

The heading tool, No. 23, is shown with the bottom of the tool toward the front; it is used in shaping shoulders on tenons, making bolt-heads, and in preliminary steps of flower work. The round hole tapers in diameter from front to rear face, so that the iron is more easily withdrawn.

The hardie, another tool which fits into the anvil's tool hole, is used for both hot and cold cutting. It is made of tool steel, with a tempered cutting edge. The iron to be cut is held against the edge of the hardie and then struck with the hammer directly above so as to form an indentation; this is repeated on opposite sides until bending back and forth over the edge of the anvil breaks the iron in two. Other cutting tools are the hot and cold chisels, used in conjunction with the hardie.

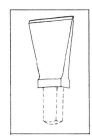

HARDIE

They are similar to each other except that the cold chisel must naturally be the stronger; Nos. 12 and 13 in Figure 7 are hot chisels. The marginal diagram indicates their differences. Cutting edges are curved convexly so that the iron will not cling in the case of a hot chisel, and so as to strengthen the cold chisel.

CHISELS
Cold and hot

The mandrel, No. 18, serves a variety of purposes. It fits into the anvil tool hole and is useful for anything of circular form which can be beaten against it.

The marginal diagram indicates how the scroll form is used and tells a part of the story in the formation of one of the most popular forms since the beginning of forging. A series of scroll forks are necessary, as well as the scroll starters and forms, often

SCROLL FORM

FIG. 8.—TWISTING A LARGE BAR WHEN HOT
The anvil is at the left, the forge in rear centre, and vise at right

made especially for the occasion. In Figure 7, No. 8, the scroll starter is used as its name indicates; a scroll is made by beating the end of a bar into whatever form the inner part of the scroll is to be, hooking it into the end of the starter's inner twist, and hammering the bar around the outside curve of the tool. From this stage the embryo scroll graduates to the scroll form, Nos. 29 and 31 in Figure 7, being beaten and bent to conform with the aid of top scroll forks, Nos. 21, 33, and 34. In the marginal diagram the scroll form is shown dotted in section and the scroll itself in outline. Many tools are similar to the top scroll forks, and can also be utilized for bending, as Nos. 4 and 5 in Figure 7; No. 24 is a special bending tool; Nos. 14 and 15 are bottom scroll forks.

Twisting is one of the simplest exercises for the smith. For light work it may be done cold, and for the sake of keeping the rod or bar straight, a pipe is usually slipped over it. Cold twisting makes for a uniform job, but it is questionable whether that is particularly desirable except in certain meticulous designs. For heavy members hot twisting is necessary (Figure 8), but in this case it is not possible to keep the bar straight by a pipe sleeve. It must be uniformly heated and kept true by water cooling applied from a bottle. If texture be desired, it is essential that the bars be at least at red heat, while a scaling heat will result in even rougher texture because of the surface scaling off. In Figure 8 the workman is using a twisting-bar similar to No. 26 in Figure 7.

Welding is a term generally understood—signifying the cohesion of two similar pieces of

FIG. 9.—FORGING A LAP WELD   FIG. 10.—FORGING A FAGOT WELD

The means which the smith has at his command are shown, the anvil firmly secured, the forge fire with water trough, tool rack and vise alongside

heated metal by means of steady hammering. For a successful operation, the two or more parts must be equally heated, sufficiently plastic for complete union, and the surfaces free from any foreign matter. The virtue of a hand-hammered weld is that it looks its part, and, by the slight swelling at the juncture and general irregularities, adds a charm which an acetylene torch or electric weld cannot attain. The most unfortunate feature about the last two means of welding is that impossible wrought designs are made possible: any two pieces of iron can be laid side by side, a flux added, and the heat turned on. Members can meet haphazardly, fuse, and look ridiculously flimsy. A hand weld satisfies common sense and structural stability in appearance, whereas with a gas flame fantastically uniting parts without effort of brain or brawn, designs more characteristic of embroidery than iron are too often the outcome. The torch should be used with discretion, and in the hands of an intelligent smith it may serve for heavy work with passable credit, but naturally its results always lack the personal touch of the hammer. Its action may be as strong as a hammer weld, but its results never look as convincing. Usually the more inferior the craftsman, the greater the use of the torch, and the more obnoxious the results.

There are various types of welds, some of the more common being the lap weld, two pieces being joined end to end (Figure 9); the fagot, comprised of a number of members (Figure 10); the right angle; the T; the cleft or fork; the split; and the butt weld.

Alongside the forge the smith has some sort of tank for water. This may be used for local cooling of parts of a member, or for submerging an entire unit to cool and harden it.

The term "upsetting" is sometimes used to the architect's confusion. It merely refers to any treatment of the end of a member which will increase its cross-section area, as a blow on the end of a heated bar. To "shoulder" a bar is to decrease its cross-section area at a given point; to "draw" it would be to lengthen it by decreasing its cross-section area; to "spread" it would be to increase its width.

ARCHITECTURAL DESIGN, MOTIFS AND ORNAMENTATION

It would sound like the proverbial fairy-tale to relate that once upon a time there lived an architect who drew for his client a set of drawings, whereupon the client said to him: "Go forth and hire me contractors who will build me this building as you have drawn it." It would seem like a tale within a fairy-tale if the same owner added: "Have you specified the ornamental iron work to be wrought? . . . Excellent, my worthy knave, so be it!"

The modern architect rather expects to draw up two sets of plans. He puts forth his best efforts in the initial drawings, but is fearful the while that they will serve only for the contractor's estimate and the owner's rejection. The second set consists of the architect's fallen hopes and his draftsmen's erasures, along with a generous sprinkling of makeshift substitutes in design and material. Scarcely a single, humbled "w. i." notation dares raise its head. The "w"'s are all replaced by "c"'s because estimates were too high.

Yet this wrought iron weeding need not necessarily occur. When it is demanded that all wrought-iron designs disappear under a rubbing-machine because of unexpected costs, it is frequently because the *motifs* have been drawn for a cast material rather than a wrought. Quite naturally the estimate is unreasonably high. Practically all building materials are either cast or carved; iron alone is wrought on an anvil when hot. Thus, in approaching a wrought problem for the first time it is only natural that the designer should make use of those forms with which he is accustomed to work, and merely label the result "wrought iron." The lack of appreciation of the nature of wrought iron is well illustrated by the fact that some offices specify that an alternate bid be taken for cast and wrought iron on the same set of details. A little bit like staging a race between goldfish and canaries!

In any building where the high cost of wrought iron might exclude its ultimate use, it is good generalship to give thoughtful consideration to the design of each item. The estimate will undoubtedly be lower if the designer visualizes the execution at the forge of what he draws on paper. He must not expect a blacksmith to achieve in iron what a carpenter could attain in wood, a sculptor in stone, or a foundry in cast bronze.

One of the many appeals which wrought iron should make to both architect and client is that the finished product depends in a large measure upon the structural members for its decorative qualities. Another way of expressing this would be to say that wrought iron presupposes there is a practical need for its employment, and in giving it a job the most direct and simple means are best. The essence of good design in iron is to compose structural members in such relative positions and of such proportions that they in themselves are a decorative asset; beyond that point they may be decorated to varying degrees in varying manners. For example, a grille may be of plain, twisted, or ornamented bars, but

the consideration of their sizes is equally important in all cases. Too often the designer seems to regard ornament as a cure-all for his lack of study, and instead of designing a light and graceful grille, as one would expect in wrought iron, he hangs bushels of scrolls and rosettes on piano legs for balusters and thinks it a wrought-iron design. In turning through simple types of railings or grilles for various periods in various countries preceding the High Renaissance, one becomes aware that the leading characteristics are: a nice discrimination in the cross-section sizes of the various parts, the metallic appearance expressed by parts being no heavier than necessary, and structural members being combined and contrasted in a decorative manner. In the best of the old work one does not mistake an iron design for a wood one, nor is one surfeited by flimsy appendages intended to be ornamental.

The poorest of modern iron work is that which serves no purpose. If the architect is using iron merely to be "arty," he has the wrong material. Wrought iron is genuine, and while it enjoys being played with and delights in caricature by moulding itself into amusing grotesques, it never is insincere. One architect displayed with puffing pride a photograph of a series of iron convolutions surrounding a fountain, serving no apparent use and looking like the combined pluckings of several junk-pickers. "It is wrought iron," he said, by way of necessary explanation. "It's decorative, isn't it?" Fortunately it was one of those questions not expected to be answered, for until the end of time the answer could be none other than an explosive "No." Until designers understand what is decoration and what is architectural twaddle, there can be no genuine wrought iron. Pre-fifteenth-century work possesses eternally commendable qualities because the iron-worker was his own designer, and he was genuine to the core; it was when the architect, unfamiliar with the limitations and toil of the forge, dictated designs, that the unwrought qualities of the Renaissance came into being. However, even at its most decadent period it is doubtful if any European ever committed the folly which is so repugnant in our present-day excrescences, as exterior balconies to which there is no access and the railing only six inches from the blank wall; large first-floor windows without a vestige of a grille while some little slit of an opening on the second floor (through which no burglar's infant could force himself) is protected with a mighty grille; or lunettes heavy enough to withstand shells from a "Big Bertha," while the doorway below is without any provision for protection from the imaginary onslaught.

If wrought iron does not perform some useful task it is far better eliminated. It can be richly decorative as perhaps no other metal, but it becomes so only when that which it decorates is serving some employment. If there are grilles they should be serving as screens, not merely bolted to a blank wall. If within the grille there are ornaments, quatrefoils, scrolls, etc., they should be integral parts of the grille itself, so that at a glance it is evident that they are not merely stuck on for the sake of being pretty-pretty. There are hundreds of legitimate uses for iron in lighting fixtures, brackets, balconies, gates, grilles, fences, railings, and scores more inside and out, so that it is worse than stupid to employ iron without giving it a job. No client relishes paying money for a useless item, and no architect has any right to employ iron merely for the sake of using it, when there are plenty of practical applications where it will be a decorative asset.

On first thought it might seem that the architect's wrought iron vocabulary were decidedly limited. His alphabet consists of square or round bars, and plates thick, thin, and of various widths. On paper he can strive to form them into words and sentences, but whether or not they speak eloquently depends on the smith's black magic at the anvil to awaken the gift of tongues in them. There are limitations to iron smithing, Vulcan be praised, but the designer will not find his style cramped by them so much as by the client's purse, which may not want him to say a single word in wrought iron. If the client be finally persuaded to use wrought iron, it may be in no cheerful spirit, and if the estimates exceed the allowance, he may seize the occasion to reverse himself as to the use of that material. It is therefore necessary for the architect not overly keen about doing several sets of wrought-iron details, to have some conception of those forms which are natural to the capabilities of forge work, to understand what operations are most expensive and why, and to be sufficiently conversant with forging so that he can distinguish intelligently between fact and fiction in the contractor's conversations.

The human element in the fashioning of wrought iron is at once an advantage and a disadvantage. It may bring about either a thing of beauty or a desecration. Wrought iron can be made so to beautify a wall that an ugly radiator recess may become an artistic asset, but a poor craftsman can so maltreat the iron and abuse his opportunity that even a door handle may lower the morale of an otherwise beautiful entrance. In short, there is no halfway point in the quality of execution. Either wrought iron should be done by a first-class craftsman or not attempted at all. Badly executed wrought iron is no more enjoyable to see than a musical instrument out of tune is to hear.

Just as a wrought-iron *motif* is best employed when it serves frankly and obviously, in the same degree the component parts of the design are most successfully wrought when they too are ingenuous. If the architect be unfamiliar with wrought iron design he may be inclined to hide all joints and the means of connecting parts, whereas one of the most decorative and simple means of joining portions of a design is by collaring (pages 55 and 72). Briefly described, this consists merely of wrapping a thinnish piece of hot iron around two members which are to be joined, forming a small "collar," and pounding down the over-lapping top end.

Another means at the command of the smith, and also one of the time-honored devices for joining parts, is by "welding," *i. e.*, heating two parts until they are a white-heat, and then beating them with a hammer until in a moment or two they have become fused as one (page 16). This is used frequently where a leaf or small scroll diverges from a larger member (page 123) and in German work where the design consists of a number of volutes, curves, animal heads, etc. (page 137). If the two members be at all large, more than one smith will be needed to perform the operation (Figure 9, page 16).

A third constructional means of combining parts is by "piercing" or "threading," which consists of one bar's penetrating another. The bar to be pierced is heated and laid on the anvil; at the point where another rod is to penetrate it, a punch or chisel is pounded until it has made a hole large enough for the intruding bar. The sides of the bar naturally swell because of the iron's being forced out by the action of the punch; it is this quality which is desirable and bespeaks that the operation was done while the iron was hot, and not cold punched by a power-drill or power-punch in the modern commercial prac-

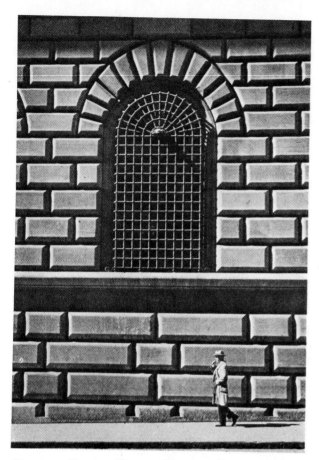

FIG. 11.—BASKET GRILLE, FEDERAL RESERVE BANK, NEW YORK CITY

York & Sawyer, Architects   Samuel Yellin, Craftsman

frequently a baffling problem. The old crafts-men, in setting a grille in place, bent back the ends as shown in the marginal diagram, and when all was in readiness, heated and turned them into prepared holes in the stone jambs; these were filled with molten lead, but even with-out this precaution the grille was secure. This is a worth-while bit of ingenuity, particularly on a circular-headed grille, for if this is not done it requires com-plicated locking devices for each bar. With the modern blow torch it is a simple matter to heat a bar and turn it back into the jamb-hole.

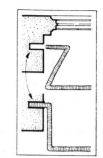

Bars piercing the top and bottom members of a rail or grille usually can be made to do so without the use of machine screws and with better results. A bar can pierce another and then have its protruding end flattened back against the bar it has pierced (marginal sketch and Figure 252), as though it had one end rivetted when hot. This is the natural wrought iron way to accomplish such a joint, as is evident by any comparison with a job done as though it were a wood spindle, which depends for its strength solely upon small screw threads. For a cresting the same treatment may be employed, except that if more gaiety be desired the bar after pene-trating the top member can be converted into a cresting (marginal sketch).

The magnificence of monumental Euro-pean iron has not been particularly beneficial to the artistic engendering of lesser works in this country. Designers visiting Spanish meccas have given their chief attention to the majestic *rejas* of the cathedrals, while the lesser lay work has been taken for granted in the conglomera-tion of pungent odors, vagrant goats and bull-fight posters. Architectural memories have too tenaciously rivetted themselves upon the glory of the monumental rather than the charm of the informal, with the result that often a too audacious and expensive design has brought in such an overwhelmingly high estimate that the chance of using wrought iron in the building is lost for good and all. It were better if the attention of travelling architects and students were not concentrated so much on *partis* which clients will likely never be able to afford, but rather on the quality of the details and their

tice. If a bar is to penetrate another in a hole made as just described, it is run through as soon as possible, because the cooling of the iron will shrink the aperture. This threading or piercing of one set of bars by another set at right angles, is the means of executing the so-called "basket" grille (figure 11), always a fa-vorite. Very often the horizontal bars are to be pierced and therefore are flat and wide, while the verticals or bars to do the piercing may be any shape; at other times both sets of bars may be square or round. When the Baroque and Rococo ushered in forms invented by the archi-tect which were unnatural to wrought iron, the craftsman was driven to employing the tools of the carpenter in order to make tenon joints, "halving" them, and screwing and bolting parts together as any cabinetmaker might. English work after the seventeenth century is particu-larly guilty of this, but because of the design cannot be made differently (page 130).

The manner of terminating ends of grilles in the basket type is interesting because it is

execution, and a searching inquiry wherein the charm of the domestic iron work lies.

A case in point is the Spanish window grille and balcony rail. They are purely utilitarian in such an unassuming ·little town as Ronda (page 94), yet they are most successful decoration. One is naturally driven to ask on seeing them, why, if the Spaniard had the excellent sense to transform a practical and necessary feature of his simple domicile into a handsome advantage, should we with our world wealth and imagined taste insist on barricading ourselves in our cliff dwellings (sometimes

FIG. 12.—WROUGHT-IRON GRILLE ENCLOSING FIRE-ESCAPE, BEVERLEY PROFESSIONAL BUILDING, LOS ANGELES, CALIFORNIA
Obviously without this grille the façade would virtually have been ruined
Harry B. Werner, Architect   Lowith Iron Works, Craftsmen

rightly termed "apartments") behind a maze of maliciously ugly fire-escapes. Goodness knows we need them, but why the insistence that they be hideous! Perhaps the fire-escape designer is a poor, underpaid individual, a victim of the sad maxim that "art follows the dollar." Should we deign to try to resuscitate the fire-escape, no doubt we could work as miraculous changes in it as have visited the automobile. There are no "cribs" within easy reach, but surely some one some day will come smilingly along with philanthropic zest, brilliant ideas, and a fire-escape design which will make his alma mater so famous she will flourish forever without annual endowment drives.

It always seems a pity that we do not realize the potential charm which may be ingrafted upon the simplest forms, and that such items as inexpensive railings and grilles we presuppose must be ugly and leave them to the mercies of an unimaginative draftsman. In reality the simplest combination of bars can be infused with zest if some thought be devoted to them. More effort spent on the possibilities of vertical bars, plain and twisted, would make for better and wider usage of wrought iron than meticulous pains with expensive day-dreams such as the profile of a moulding which cannot reasonably be followed on an anvil. In disregarding the wealth of opportunities inherent in a series of bars, the designer loses an immense opportunity, for nothing in wrought iron is less expensive. The Spanish discovered this centuries ago and, as a result, enriched the dwellings of the peasants as well as the palaces of grandees. As inspiration for modern work, the window grille of the Casa del Conde de Toledo serves as a good example (page 92). This *reja*, built with a minimum amount of work and material, embodies at once a very efficient protection from the sometime troublesome citizens of Toledo, as well as a design above reproach. The only adorning features are the two simple scroll-brackets below and the cresting above, wrought from flat bars having imaginative little quirks, swellings, and leaves to make them genteel. It was all a simple matter on the anvil. This grille consists only of square bars with their faces turned to an angle of 45 degrees with the plane of the wall—constituting the do-re-mi of the wrought iron scale, let us say.

The next note up the clef of square bar usage is illustrated in the simple balcony rail, Figure 113, where the verticals are all twisted.

Variety in the twists is here responsible for an unusually pleasing appearance. In a cast material the models and moulds for these sundry twists would be so expensive that a single type would probably have to suffice, whereas in the wrought product it would be difficult to turn out ten bars exactly alike. In the rail a bar with a few twists is placed beside one with many, or else made envious by a neighbor with a few twists, a straight run, and a few more twines. The actual labor involved in thus turning out a variety was not a mill more expensive than if each bar had been absolutely like every other one. In fact it would be costly indeed to guarantee that all would be uniform.

If the contractor be not interested in his work beyond making all the money possible, he would very likely make a higher charge in estimating a grille with a variety of twists than for one with only a single type of bar. But if such a wrought iron worker becomes the successful bidder on the work and seeks to take advantage of the architect's lack of knowledge by increasing the price of the article when he should really do the reverse, then most emphatically it had been better if the job were cast iron! Wrought iron is one of the most human of materials, and it requires a human being with enthusiasm and genuine interest to produce happy, spontaneous results. Good work cannot be pounded out on a commercial basis by mere money-seekers.

Until one has become engrossed in the wide range of dormant possibilities in even the humble stock wrought-iron rods, it is impossible to comprehend what may be done by a little ingenuity and effort. The various bars drawn in Figure 13 give only some idea of the countless ways of twisting bars, and show a few of the sections which can be used. One of the most easily wrought, and one which contributes very appreciably to any series of bars, is No. 2 of the figure. It is merely a square bar which has been hammered on one of its edges when

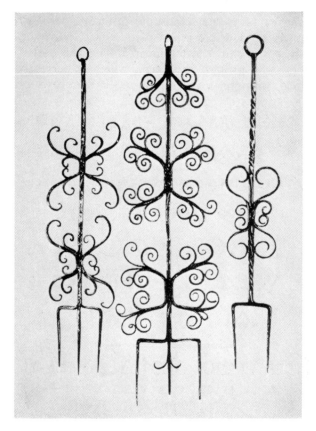

FIG. 14.—THREE TYPES OF SPANISH HEARTH FORKS
The two at the sides are from Granada, the centre one from Madrid. The handle of the fork on the right is rectangular in section, which accounts for the interesting twist. The highlights, although touched up in this reproduction, are even more glistening in reality.

hot; the edge opposite has been equally flattened by the anvil. When twisted it gives the effect of a bar with an intricate section, yet the operation is so simply done as to be almost negligible as to time and cost involved. But unless the architect knows how simple and inexpensive this form is, he is either loath to show it on a drawing, or, after the contract is awarded, is easily convinced that his full-size detail is a "radical departure" from the scale drawing and is bullied by the contractor into believing that a huge "extra" would be due if the design were executed as shown.

Bars oblong in section do unexpectedly pleasant things when twisted. Round bars given an incision along their length will also perform surprisingly, although it is needless to point out that without the previous chisel incision twisting would do little good. Nos. 5 through 9 show more ambitious treatments of the bar before it is twisted; the Spanish alone excelled in this admirable embellishment. The splitting of square bars for a part of their

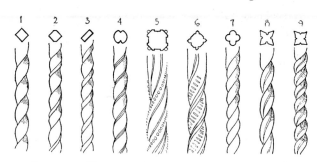

FIG. 13.—TWISTED BARS. (1–8 FROM AVILA)

length, as in the handsome grille on page 67, opens up a whole realm of design. The Spanish were again the foremost among the craftsmen who utilized this form, which is perfectly good wrought iron technique, is readily done

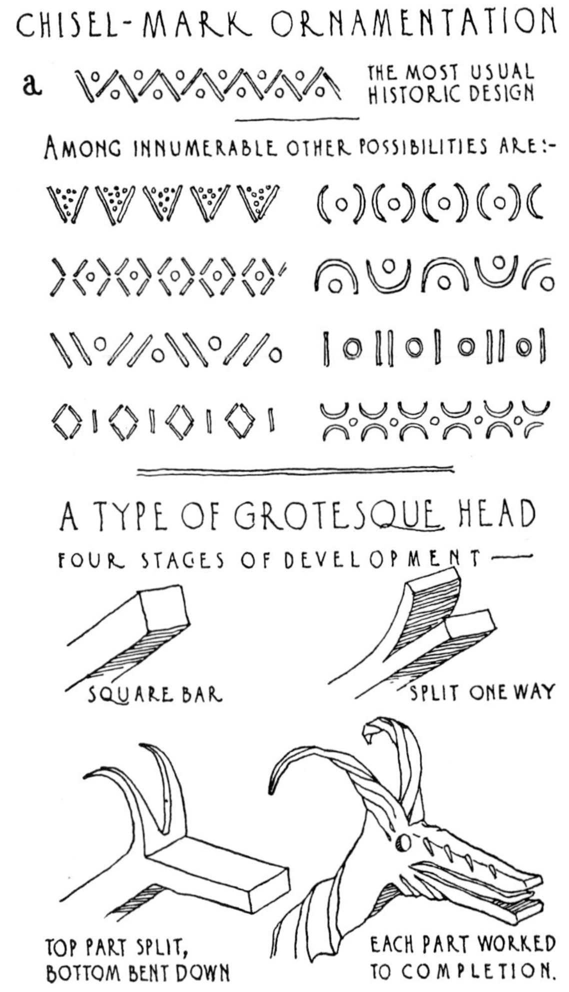

CHISEL-MARK ORNAMENTATION

a   〰〰〰〰   THE MOST USUAL HISTORIC DESIGN

AMONG INNUMERABLE OTHER POSSIBILITIES ARE:-

A TYPE OF GROTESQUE HEAD

FOUR STAGES OF DEVELOPMENT —

SQUARE BAR   SPLIT ONE WAY

TOP PART SPLIT,   EACH PART WORKED
BOTTOM BENT DOWN   TO COMPLETION.

FIG. 15

by a craftsman, and in combination with welding offers one of the main fortes of Spanish design.

A wrought-iron surface is automatically ornamented by the treatment it assimilates on the anvil. It suffers martyrdom while the hammering lasts but it comes out smiling, with high lights and black spots in a free-for-all mosaic which no sophisticated design could approach. "Texture" must therefore be jotted down as surface ornament number one (pages 12 and 176), but second to it and "very popular in all models" and nationalities of wrought iron work, come chisel marks. Figure 15 indicates at *a* the most common chisel-mark ornamentation, and,

following that, some of the many possibilities in other shaped chisels and arrangements. The designer may here go as far as he delights in studying combinations and groupings of marks made by straight, curved or circular chisels on the red hot iron. The pattern should not be too complicated, because it must be remembered that the craftsman has no pencil or chalk mark to follow on the glowing metal. He is compelled to trust to his eye for spacing the surface incisions. He cannot be hindered with too many chisels in hand or too complicated a design in mind. The result, moreover, would be less satisfactory than a simple procession of zig-zags easily hammered.

A favorite means of ornamenting a running band or the elements of a floral cresting, is by the so-called *repoussé* work. Briefly, this consists of pounding out thinnish plates or sheets of iron first from the rear, and later on the front face, resulting in the production of an embossed appearance (Figures 6 and 269). The metal may vary from light-cardboard thickness to perhaps $\frac{1}{16}$ of an inch. The design may or may not be pierced; generally it is not. The greater the thickness of the iron, the more urgent the need for heat in beating out the design from the back, while the thinner the metal, or the finer in scale the ornament, the more likely it is to be worked when cooling or cold. When the design is pierced it is often backed up by a sheet of metal and becomes in reality, applied ornament. A great fondness seems to have existed in historic examples for painting the background of such panels with vermilion, or touching up certain modillions or shields with color. The designer is not much concerned with the forge process beyond this brief description, and can get an excellent idea of the complexion and possibilities of *repoussé* work in the illustrations already referred to. The well-known Siena grille (pages 42–3) is one of the best examples of the pierced type of this ornamentation. Another, a Spanish form of this kind of work and widely different in *parti*, is from a grille in San Vincente, Avila (page 76). Both are clearly indicative of the spirit of wrought iron when used in this manner; there is a continuous variety and imagination at play, without an attempt to compete with bronze which would employ a regular, repeating *motif*.

A consideration which the designer should not disregard is whether or not wrought iron will be the appropriate material to use for the most eloquent expression of his idea. Just as one wears a sack suit to business but evening dress to the opera, so wrought iron has all the unbending and informal qualities which fit many occasions like a sack suit, yet there are those special opera-events when its polished cousin, bronze, is the more graceful performer. It is not fair to expect the rigid, accurate repetition which is natural to bronze, in wrought iron. If, for example, a design has repeating panels or ornament which in iron would necessarily have to be beaten out from the back (*repoussé* work), it would become a tiresome exercise for the smith in which he would have undue hardship imposed upon him. Given a number of panels to fill with varying designs he has an opportunity to exercise the natural tendencies of forging by inviting distinct or radical differences as he feels inclined. It seems misspent effort to ask an iron-worker to fashion all panels alike when it would be simpler for him to work from a scale drawing and vary the design as he progressed. At best he cannot compete with a casting for complacent accuracy. The mediæval work so universally admired makes no attempt at repeating any one single *motif* with rubber-stamp precision. Yet in a counter-screen in a prominent New York bank there are wide panels all alike (or meant to be) which must have been a hardship for the smith, with no apparent reason or advantage gained. The client would have paid far less for cast metal, and, since the design is intended to repeat itself regularly, it would have been a more accurate job. Taking the grille in the Palazzo della Signoria, Siena, as a model, the diversely designed panels are the better for their variation in frankly advertising that each is the human product beaten on an anvil, rather than an attempted imitation of a bronze casting. If precise repetition be desired the sensible thing is to have it cast, rather than give a smith an irksome task which is not to his or his tools' liking.

Even a cursory review of several types of *repoussé* panels makes it evident that there is usually a certain Falstaffian, happy-go-lucky spirit present. In the Prato example (page 31) the leaves in the frieze-panel sport a decided bravado in the irregularity of the leaflets; scarcely two pretend to be twins. In the grille surrounding the tomb of San Vincente, Avila (page 76), the lions, their keepers and the separating leaves vary like so many humans. The iron-worker could hardly have made them otherwise. Had he been working from an architect's drawing he might have had every intention of forging each

unit like every other one, but how displeasing if he had! If there be panels it is well to follow the cue of the famous historic examples, where each has a different design intentionally: alike in character but varying in detail.

Besides the *repoussé* panel's not being exactly duplicated, the craftsman's task is lightened if the length be not too great. The average of the Italian grille-panel approximates five feet. If there is to be a minimum of elaboration, moreover, the craftsman would prefer to make two designs for panels and alternate them, rather than to try to make only one type which would repeat exactly. With an interval between panels the irregularities which might offend purists would be diminished because of the greater difficulty in comparison. In height the Italian designs for the *repoussé* panels are often about the same as the repeating quatrefoil, and thus are seldom over 10 inches.

The success of the *repoussé* panel depends almost entirely upon the individuality of the craftsman executing it. The architect may have the scale, or even the full-size, detail handsomely worked out, yet he cannot show on paper the exact elevation of every spot. By shading he can give some idea of what effect he has in mind, the degree of the modeling and the like, but all the little niceties and quirks which will make it an enjoyable *ensemble* depend upon the interest, ability and personality of the man behind the hammer. There is an element of chance in it too, for wrought iron work is somewhat like pastel or charcoal sketching—an unwitting stroke will sometimes strike the most charming note in the composition.

American cities are suffering from a grim decorum forced upon us by brick, concrete and steel, judging from a terse remark that an eminent German made on first seeing lower Manhattan architecture, "Geometry in stone!" Building materials and structural forms are governed by the exigencies of present-day conditions and therefore cannot be radically altered, but in the embellishment of these forms, "geometry originals" if you will, there can be added the needed genial good humor and "comic relief." Of all the ornamental material at the disposal of the architect, none lends itself to frisking ways better than wrought iron, which introduces another means of ornamentation: grotesque heads.

In practically every grille or cresting there are apt to be loose ends, and what is a more delectable *coup-de-grâce* than to hammer these into swallow-tailed fish or open-mouthed dragons? The well-head at Bruck (page 138) shows to what extent a craftsman with a sense of design and humor, or designing humor, may make fascinating creations from the commonplace. With what enlivening variety each panel is graced! Even in the more classic *chefs-d'œuvre* (pages 43 and 75), the cresting *motifs*, when not fiercely arrayed as spikes, parade as fantastic fruits, flowers, leaves or animal heads. These should not be considered extravagances by the architect when he understands that a grotesque head as a termination for a spiral or cresting unit is easily wrought. At such points the metal is not thick and therefore readily moulded. Even a thick bar is easily split at the end into three sections for a distance of an inch or two, in order to form a head of one section and two twisting horns of the two other parts (Figure 15). To the sincere wrought iron craftsman, a specification calling for a series of these humorous heads as scroll terminations, etc., is the equivalent of a genial invitation to enjoy himself. If, however, he has no interest in his forge beyond its monetary returns, he will be incapable of creating these ingenious grotesques. It is therefore of primary importance that the architect determine what types of craftsmen are estimating on his work, for in the end he will generally find that if the lowest bidding forge is a purely commercial enterprise, it cannot be expected to produce true wrought iron. The craftsman must revel in his work; each hammer blow must represent so much satisfaction in creating harmony and humor, or his results are impoverished departures from the traditions of his guild.

ECONOMIC ASPECTS IN DESIGN

Under the notes on Spanish iron work the subject of carved arabesques which were the glory of the Renaissance artist (pages 88–9) are taken up more in detail. Here we are more concerned with considering the method of ornamentation as applied to modern practice. Beautiful as are the originals and marvellous the supercraftsmen who executed them, in our matter-of-contract age we can hardly hope to use them in wrought-iron design. Splendid inspiration for cast designs, to be sure, but to expect them to be wrought is more than most of our pocketbooks will stand or our time-contract buildings permit. However, this purpose is ably served: they proclaim the high esteem in which the master smiths were held by the nation (page 64), and provide a goal toward which future craftsmen may aspire. If an occasion arose where a client were willing to pay the piper for his wrought arabesques, he might find that there were not a score of craftsmen in the country equal to the task; if it were ever completed it would probably be sought by the museums. The architect is rarely confronted with such a patron, but is chiefly concerned by what he may design to the best interests of client and building which can most successfully be fashioned by the craftsmen available. The tastes of the twentieth-century client are governed more by time-limits and investment-costs than by historic associations, so that if the architect feels it advisable to employ wrought iron rather than cast, it must come within the budget allowance or his client will be unlikely to pay an additional sum. And, after all, why not meet the problems of to-day fairly by studying those forms of iron in which it delights in being humored? Then it is simple to forge, pleasing to see, and easy to buy.

Every architect knows how painful it is to see an amateur-built house which is expensively ugly, where labor and materials have lavishly been squandered to constitute a thing of unsightliness, whereas half the sum wisely administered could have achieved a work of artistic merit. So too must the iron-worker feel toward details which are sent him for execution by the architect, who in good faith thinks he is designing a thing of beauty. In reality it may be nothing more than a series of amalgamated forms snatched up here and there, and not expressing wrought iron in the remotest degree. Such an example is shown in the marginal note; it was accompanied by the architect's specification that "all intersections be halved and welded." Useless phrases meaning nothing! The architect may have meant well enough, but, in the first place, the design is better fitted for embroidery than iron, since the scroll so used is without meaning; certainly it is no brace. In the second place, he asks for duplication of joining intersecting members, first by the carpenter's halving, and second by the acetylene torch, neither of which is typical of wrought iron. It goes without saying that it would be impossible to hammer-weld intersections such as are drawn.

Specific instances where the architect means to be as economical as possible, and not only fails to be so but makes the operation still more expensive, are numberless; a few of the more common examples follow. Bars being bent at right angles are usually shown with a sharp corner both inside and outside; whether or not the designer realizes it, this is an expensive requirement and one which, after all, merely makes the iron simulate a casting. The inner corner can be made sharp without undue time and effort, but the outer corner is apt to be rounded as shown in the accompanying marginal sketch, unless great pains be taken. The rounded corner does no great damage in probably nine-tenths of designs, and, moreover, if the architect be desirous for the iron-worker to show that his product is hand-hammered, no better means exist than in not insisting on the sharp right-angle bend.

Where one bar intersects another it should not be shown as the marginal sketch, unless it be for the avowed purpose of imitating wood joinery or a casting. Only with a great amount of useless energy could a smith forge such an intersection. When all was finished and the article looked poorly, the client would 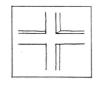 have paid ten times what one of several natural wrought-iron intersections would have cost. As pointed out elsewhere, intersections of bars are most happily managed by piercing one with the other (page 19).

If a wrought operation is to cost the very minimum, naturally stock material will encourage economical success. There is no substitute for calling in a contractor for his suggestions, and determining what material is kept in stock and what variety of sizes are available. The very cheapest work can be worked from round rather than square bars, but the result takes on a soft appearance like much of the German work (pages 137–140). Unless necessity dictates it, good design practice would be not to detail an entire *motif* with them. Combined with square bars, however, round ones may become a valuable asset.

Work that is to be of a utilitarian nature, and yet which the architect wishes to make look as well as possible with minimum cost, may be designed of stock bars or rods, used of course with discretion and variety. It is a mystery why catalogues of fence, fire-escape, and railing companies seem to indicate that all the laws of God and man firmly and forever rule that their products exhibit the monotony of the Sahara desert. Even though the most confirmed stock bars be used by the most prosaic company employing the most blank-minded workers, the architect may still be able to exact some sort of interesting arrangement. In the margin are a few of numberless possibilities on which the designer can enlarge and improve. Square bars turned at 45 degrees to the railing face do not cost a penny more for the fabrication than when they are set parallel, according to estimates from accurate computations by wrought iron companies. Yet, the idea of employing such a simple variation is often considered by the uninformed architect as extravagance. 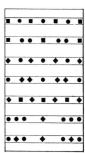 Not only should the vertical bars be given due consideration in their relative size, juxtaposition, and variety of shape, but the horizontal bars as well. If these are flat and not square or round, the operation will naturally be less expensive, and usually more distinctive.

Frequently curved members will be tangent to a straight bar. Instead of some unintelligent use of the torch in welding these together so their adhesion will be a matter of mysterious affinity, it is far better to wrap a collar around them in the typical wrought-iron manner. The torch weld too often leaves the ugly remains of the flux, whereas the collar, even though it be a poor one, at least shows that the underlying idea is right. The torch should be used only by the best craftsmen, for in the hands of an ignorant, unæsthetic worker it may be as destructive to good design, as is a powerful motor car in the hands of a novice driver to human life.

Another item on the cost aspects of wrought iron: hardware for domestic work may in the long run be cheaper than other types, because latches, bolts, hinges, etc., do not have to be mortised into the wood but can be nailed directly to the surface, thus saving the carpenter's time in fitting. Before wrought iron should be rejected because the cost for a hinge or latch is greater than a corresponding cast one, the expense of installation labor for each should be computed.

It is an unfortunate circumstance that wood and stone were habitually designed in certain forms before wrought iron solicited the designers' attention. Iron members are so often made heavy and coarse—when painted they might be mistaken for wood as well as for stone —conveying no metallic idea to any except their prejudiced author. Not only in rails, grilles, stair balusters, etc., is this tendency in evidence, but most frequently when door stiles and rails are made of iron. Designers of bronze doors offend in the same way, in that instead of endeavoring to distinguish between the relative strength of wood and metal by decreasing the stile and rail widths, no such differences are made. In many modern office buildings, bronze and iron doors with 5 inch stiles are so heavy that women can scarcely open them. Why they should be as clumsy as this not even hardware experts know, for there are plenty of stock locks which require only 3 inches for stile width. Again, there is an unintelligent contradiction of hammering the surface of iron to make it appear as such, and yet having it unduly wide so as to be exactly the width wood would be, as though to make it appear like the latter. The fact that wood stiles are made 5 inches wide merely because they will otherwise not be strong enough, never seems to occur to a designer of metal doors.

Beyond describing what forms of bars, plates, and ornament are characteristic to wrought iron, and a brief account of how each is worked at the anvil, it is difficult to give any rules for design which will be of practical use in all cases. The only elements which can be laid down are no different than for any other material: the limitations and possibilities must first be thoroughly understood and appreciated, before it is possible frankly to express ideas in iron. Only after the designer knows what tools he has with which to work can he set about using them, but here again it is well to adhere, at least for the first few designs, to some historic example, and then watch the execution at the forge. When he has seen the process carried out to its completion and feels that he may venture forth *a la* Brandt, more power to him! The latter has had years of forging behind him, so it must not be discouraging if iron innovations are not successful at the outset. From the illustrations hereafter given it must not be assumed that the author has meant to show partiality for any one style, type, or period, but rather to give as comprehensive a survey of the field of wrought iron as is possible within the limits of these pages. It is hoped that the designer will not copy some of the least desirable of wrought traits, like examples of the Baroque and Rococo, but will see for himself where one design expressed beauty and utility in iron better than another.

WROUGHT IRON FINISH

If the finished product must be painted there is but little sense in having it wrought. Making a cast-iron design will be cheaper, and under a coat of paint two of the chief virtues of the wrought product—color and texture— are quite wasted. The client had better be saved needless expense. The advantages of wrought work are presupposed to be sufficiently valuable to the general effect of the design to be worth the extra cost and labor over and above a mechanical casting. There will be variety in the surfacing from its being beaten on the anvil, differences in color due to the high lights where slightly raised surfaces have been made shiny with emery-cloth rubbing, and lack of general uniformity because of the manner in which each part is separately fabricated under varying conditions. What, then, can be the good in submerging some of the chief value of the work under several good thick coats of

paint? The idea of painting every exposed molecule is a splendid tribute to the ability of the advertising agents for the paint manufacturers, but it does no great amount of credit to the architects.

A more desirable finish is secured by burning linseed oil into the iron. The surface should first be scraped or "pickled" until all scale and foreign substances are removed. A heavy coat of linseed or crude oil is then applied and the iron heated, preferably on a charcoal fire. Two precautions must be observed, first, that the iron be uniformly heated so that on cooling the thinner sections will not appear different from the thicker, and second, that the iron be not overheated so as to burn the oil out. The idea is merely to fill with oil the pores of the metal when expanded by the heat. As a final step the iron should be wiped off and gone over with emery-cloth, which will give a silver exposure to the "ups," while the "downs" will remain jet black. It is good practice thereafter to rub a combination of beeswax and boiled linseed oil on the entire surface, which will protect it from the atmospheric conditions for some time, depending on the exposure. Exterior work might require attention in a year, while interior iron would likely last double that time without further treatment. The old argument for painting iron is that the client will not take care of it and oil it sufficiently often to protect it from rust. Assume that the iron does rust a bit: this is usually an advantage in that it adds a bit of texture and can be stopped by rubbing over the offending surface with a little emery-cloth and applying an oil-wax coat. Cast iron needs painting and bronze requires cleaning and oiling; in fact, if the latter is not done once a month it suffers more in appearance than wrought iron does without oiling for a year. If the client does not care to spend the money and effort to keep metal work in proper condition, an initial coat of paint superintended by the architect is not going to help matters.

Perhaps the most ludicrous of all building conditions occurs in painting wrought iron (presumably to protect it from rust) and then adding an "arty" finish coat which extends itself to the uttermost in striving to look like rust. Rottenstone and what-not are added to contribute a rust-pitted surface, and vermilion is carefully painted on and doctored to look like the impish rust itself. Certain iron-workers specialize in just such work and there is a de-

mand for it, so perhaps it is not so much a farce as a pathetic condition hard to associate with an "enlightened age."

Another coating sometimes given, which is less objectionable than paint, is varnish. A tawdry shine is its main drawback, but this may be somewhat obviated by the use of steel wool, or, it is said, certain grades of varnish or shellac which do not dry with a gloss. This, like oil and wax, requires attention after a year or two of exposure.

It may be that the ever baffling problem of preserving the desirable complexion of wrought iron as it comes from the anvil, will succumb to an electrical means now being tried with cadmium. The entire iron composition, or convenient segments, are submerged in a bath and a thin film of cadmium is then deposited. From present results it is impossible to predict how successful this treatment will be, but indications are that it will serve as a rust protector for at least three years on exterior work. Chromium would be superior, but it has a tendency to deposit only on outside surfaces, and distributes unevenly by discriminating against small nooks and crannies, the inside of small scrolls, and the like.

Interior work or semi-exposed iron in loggias survives quite happily with only oil-wax treatment and in general can do very well without the use of the paint brush. The oil is too light a film to come off on one's clothes and offers no tangible objection—except that a time-honored prejudice is discarded.

THE ARCHITECT'S DRAWINGS

To describe how the architect may best draw up wrought iron in the working drawings, is to seem contradictory at the outset. In one sense the details should be so definite at ¾-inch scale that the wrought iron estimator will know exactly what he is to furnish and how much time will be necessary at the forge, according to the degree of elaboration and difficult workmanship required. In another sense there should be sufficient latitude so that, as the iron craftsman later develops the design, he is not hindered by too strict detailing, particularly in the dimensioning of bars. The best practice seems to be for the architect carefully to study his details in conjunction with some wrought iron artisan, so that, when the drawings are sent out for estimate, there will be at ¾-inch

scale: complete information as to what is required, what the nature and extent of the ornament is to be, supplemented by smaller-scale diagrams showing the location of various units. If there be miles of grille work where it seems impossible to determine what size the bars should be without seeing several trial samples in place at the job later, then it is well to mark such bars as being between certain minimum and maximum sizes, asking for estimates both ways.

Of all materials wrought iron defies actual representation on paper more stubbornly than any other. The surfacing and play of light and shade of the finished product baffles reproduction to any satisfactory degree, for to render accurately even a small section of a twisted bar would be both expensive and tedious. Some of the best craftsmen, vitally interested in their work, and to whom it means more than making greater profits each succeeding year, prefer that the architect send them only the scale (¾ inch) details after having a conference, and permit them to do all full-sizing. These drawings are done on heavy, opaque detail paper in charcoal, which, on account of the grain of the paper, will give a rapid and fair representation of iron surfacing. The heavy paper has the advantage of permitting its being hung at the building or in the architect's office at the approximate height and place which the finished product will occupy, as well as standing the abuse of much rubbing out with progressive changes. After approval by the architect, these serve as shop drawings and are obviously more easily read than pale blueprints in the gloom of the shop. The fact that the architect has no duplicate is not a serious disadvantage, for if he needs a record that he has checked certain drawings, this can be filed in a letter. His scale details will locate the work if any question comes up later. When the architect attempts to show construction of wrought-iron members he is worse off than when he tries to indicate cabinet construction for a mill. It is effort wasted on his part, and is likely only to pro-

vide the forge with amusement. The architect's time is spent to better advantage criticising the working shop drawings as submitted by the craftsman. In order that all bidders understand that doing the "full-sizes" comes within the scope of their work, it should be clearly so stated in the specifications, and the manner in which they should be done.

It not infrequently happens that the projected side, front, and plan of a detail is so involved that only a university freshman who has just passed his descriptive geometry examination can understand it. The purpose of working drawings should be none other than to make perfectly clear *what* the contractor is to do and *how*, so that it is often preferable to draw free-hand perspective sketches with dimensions noted, than laboriously to project planes and intersections, which, when all is handsomely (and probably incorrectly) done, would not be as helpful to the craftsman as a rough perspective. One should never lose sight of the fact that iron remains hot and pliable only when it has just come from the fire, and that whatever is to be done, must be accomplished without hesitation; a simple drawing will be a help, an involved one a hindrance.

The subject of specifications is separately considered under the final chapter, page 193.

FIG. 16.—WROUGHT-IRON TORCH AND STANDARD SOCKETS, PALAZZO DEI PRIORI, VOLTERRA
Now, as well as in the fifteenth century, simple snake-heads and chisel-mark ornamentation typify good wrought-iron technique

ITALIAN WROUGHT IRON

THE fanfare of architectural trumpets has ever acclaimed the glories of Italian edifices, paintings, frescoes, and sculpture, so much to the exclusion of the minor arts that the traveller going to Italy by boat or by book has in general paid but passing attention to its iron work. Venice, for example, is too gala a pageant, its color too rich and vibrant, for humble wrought-iron grilles to receive concentrated attention—who would halt his gondolier to study a grille on the Grand Canal when the Ca' d'Oro beckons, a few strokes further? In Verona the Loggia del Consiglio seizes upon all one's time, while the marvels of the wrought-iron Scaligeri Tombs languish around the corner. In Siena the architectural pageantry of the Cathedral, supplemented by the marvels of floor, wood carvings, frescoes, mosaics, pulpit and what not, diminishes to the zero point any lavish attention for the torch or standard holders on the Via de Citta. Or, in the old quarters of Naples (where only carefree architects and their kind wander among the street spaghetti-stands, the intimate sights and the preposterous odors which only the Neopolitans boast), what place in the sun do the fascinating balconies hope to assume, even with their fanciful spirals (see frontispiece).

For all the undoubted wonders of Italian art in architecture, sculpture or painting, those of wrought iron are scarcely a whit less inspirational in their realm. With a little effort it could no doubt be proved analytically that the well-known grille in the Palazzo della Signoria at Siena bears the same relation to the greatest achievement in wrought iron, as the Cathedral façade does to the ultimate in mosaics. The fact that the grille is less widely known than the Cathedral façade should not relegate it to a lower position in proper appreciation. Yet, over and over again in the study of a modern building, it is deemed all-important that the profiles of entablatures be given careful study while the metal work is considered outside the pale of the designer's necessary consideration or knowledge. A haphazard small-scale sketch or two is supposed to suffice for the metal work, and the consequent result often is to mar the potential distinction which the *ensemble* might have had but for the thoughtlessly designed grilles.

The determining factor in the failure of any iron work, particularly Italian, is not that the *parti* may be entirely wrong (with plenty of material to draw upon, this may be a simple problem to settle), but rather insufficient care in selecting and composing ornament and detail. The relation of stiles to the field of ornament (pages 36 and 42), the height of a running band to cresting ornaments, the proportion of solids to voids in pierced *repoussé* panels (pages 39 and 51)—in a word, the *finesse* of the component parts largely determines the success of the design. The same conscientious attempt should be made to achieve a composition of beautiful and distinguished enrichment in wrought iron as would go toward developing an entablature which would do credit to Trajan's Forum. The proper design of an Italian grille is not merely a matter of jotting down the possible *motifs* which appeal to the designer's particular fancy, and then combining them in luckless fashion—such procedure never produces the desired effect. Not that it is desirable to re-use old masterpieces in the identical atomic sequence, for it might easily happen that such a reproduction would look entirely out of place in our modern setback architecture! But, just as Classic or Romanesque *chefs-d'œuvre* are studied and analyzed in order to determine wherein lies their successful composition before applying their *motifs* to a modern problem, in the same fashion it is not only desirable but essential, to the creation of a "modern" grille, that the old precedents be examined and assimilated before attempting to combine their devices in creating an iron design which will harmonize with the architectural setting.

Courtesy of Victoria and Albert Museum

FIG. 17.—SEVENTEENTH-CENTURY VENETIAN RAILING

FOURTEENTH CENTURY

There is no iron work extant in Italy from previous to the thirteenth century, possibly none even before the fourteenth. The Classic forebears of Italy discounted the virtues of iron as an ornamental material in favor of bronze, and never employed it decoratively. Consequently the Renaissance revival had no Vitruvius-text for the guidance of the iron craft. Earlier work in England, France, and Spain probably was unknown to the first Italian craftsmen; certainly they designed and worked the material in an entirely different manner. Whereas the first forms in other countries consisted of the C- and S-scrolls, the initial Italian efforts were bent toward perfecting the more difficult quatrefoil.

From the outset the quatrefoil seems to have maintained a reputation for being the most acceptable form in grilles, screens, balustrades, gates, etc. Although permitting of many varied and rich forms, it was basically the single outstanding *motif* through the fourteenth, fifteenth, and early sixteenth centuries. At the inception of the quatrefoil it was made by piercing sheets of iron, with the broadest faces placed vertically; at first these were thin, but, with increase in skill and rivalry, the sheets or plates became thicker and the perforated design more complicated. These plates formed panels let into rectangular frames. The iron work of the Scaligeri Tombs, Verona (1380), is among the best of early examples (pages 40–1). The panels are extremely large, and, since the repeating quatrefoil units are fastened in a manner comparable to individual links in a coat of mail hung in a rectangular frame, the grille is not rigid but allows the tourist the satisfaction of making it sway as it is pulled or pushed. The type of grille forged earlier by Conte di Lello da Siena in 1337 (page 36), consisting of smaller panels, established the prototype which was generally followed with but little deviation, particularly in Tuscany. Other examples of early fourteenth-century grilles survive at Sant' Anastasias, Verona, and St. Mark's, Venice; Perugia claims an interesting example (1338); and an elaborate and excellent grille in Santa Croce, Florence (1371), assumes a strictly architectural design. From a technical standpoint this early work was beyond reproach. Later in the sixteenth century the quatrefoil was formed of independent scrolls banded together as in Scuola di San Giorgio, Venice (page 44).

In early grilles, coincident with employing repeating quatrefoils in rectangular panels was the development of the top frieze of pierced or *repoussé* work, surmounted by a cresting. Conte di Lello's Orvieto and San Miniato screens already referred to (pages 36–7) are illustrations of a prototype perfected and developed in the work of the succeeding two centuries, and revived in the seventeenth and eighteenth. In early crestings the designers were content with the simple trident, the spike, the bar divided into one vertical and one bent prong, and the simple fleur-de-lis. Later, enriched prickets, leaf-clusters and flowers (the lily a favorite) budded and bloomed. It is difficult to establish a definite date for the introduction of floral forms, but they doubtless blossomed first in the early crestings and unwittingly sowed the seeds for the unfortunate flimsy workmanship following in the sixteenth and seventeenth centuries.

Window grilles were introduced * into Florence by Walter de Brienne, Duke of Athens, during his brief rule in 1343. Their avowed purpose of excluding intruders was proclaimed by their utilitarian simplicity. No decorative possibilities were awakened until the fifteenth century. About the only variation from the gridiron, with bars placed horizontally and vertically, was the occasional Venetian practice of "threading" them diagonally. Constant political and civil disturbances made the window grille a permanent fixture.

* Gardner, "Ironwork," II.

FIFTEENTH CENTURY

By the fifteenth century Italian smiths had triumphantly emerged from the field of experimental endeavor, prepared to attack more sophisticated compositions. The naïveté of early craftsmanship diminished as Classic *motifs* increased their influence on the architectural régime. Although the quatrefoil in grilles changed but slightly, stiles and rails accepted dentils (page 39), crowning friezes were surmounted by simplified entablatures enriched with dentils and moulded forms, and panels assumed the stamp of orderly architectural supervision. The convincing workmanship of the preceding century led to an increased acceptance of iron as a decorative possibility. Craftsmen like Nicolò Grosso (1455–1509) developed technique to a high state of excellence. In his particular case, the financial phase of iron work was elevated to a remarkable plane as well; Nicolò was termed "Il Caparra" by Lorenzo di Medici, from his habit of demanding payment in advance. Vasari somewhat mitigates his Shylockian tendencies by declaring with more enthusiasm than accuracy, that Il Caparra "was unique in his calling, without an equal in the past, and probably not to be excelled in the future." Modern craftsmen may well envy old Nicolò his financial audacity, his publicity agent Vasari, and his sundry torch- and stand-ard-holders, and lamps (Palazzi Strozzi and Guadagni, Figures 67, 296 and 297).

Door hardware never received the distinguished attention in Italy that it did west and north of the Alps. Ornamental hinges and keys were rarely of artistic consequence and the actual "butts" were generally concealed; ornamental locks seldom if ever occurred. Iron was still considered the cheap substitute for bronze. Where doors were not cast of that metal, they were formed of wood panels, sometimes richly carved, and in many cases, particularly in the north, enhanced by nail-heads or ornamental studs (pages 57 and 60).

In screens and grilles the simple bar treatment began to yield to ornamental demands, beginning with round bars "threaded" (one set piercing those at right angles to it) diagonally in the German style, as in the Zucchini Chapel screen of San Petronio, Bologna (1483).

What the fifteenth century in Italy lost in renown in the display of door hardware, it more than regained in the realm of armor. The military productions were of the highest quality, with so general and acknowledged a reputation that at a great Spanish tournament in 1434 only Italian weapons and armor were permitted—and that at a time when the Spanish *rejas* had no peers in workmanship! One whimsically wonders whether the excellent weapons were more than a match for protective door hardware, or if on the other hand the residents welcomed burglars in order to match their skill at arms. Milan was perhaps most famous for its weapons, with Florence and Brescia closely contending.

FIG. 18.—WROUGHT-IRON GRILLE, BAPTISTRY OF PRATO CATHEDRAL. (1348)

The entire grille consists of four vertical sections, each with an upper and a lower division. The upper divisions have four quatrefoils in both width and height (31 inches), while the lower have five in height (39 inches). Stiles are 2½ inches wide; crowning denticular rail 4 inches high; *repoussé* panel 6 inches high with shield painted red and white, and pierced leaves at side, gold

SIXTEENTH CENTURY

In the early sixteenth century iron achievements proudly rode the crest of the wave which, by the end of the century, frothed into the trivialities prefacing the Baroque and Rococo. The early part of the period witnessed a more formal bondage of architectural forms (as the torch- and standard-holders of the Palazzi Strozzi and del Turco of Florence (pages 58–9), and somewhat of a departure from the preceding frank usage of iron as iron, to an imitation of bronze forms. Lanterns, knockers, standard- and torch-holders became the accepted expression for the iron-craftsman, while weather-vanes and exterior finials occurred but occasionally. The smith's abilities were intrigued by brasiers, and sometimes candlesticks, one of particular note being forged in Pistoia. Before the close of the century large gilded lanterns were common accessories of stairs and corridors, not always entirely of iron—nor entirely in good taste. Iron became widely used in furniture: bed-frames and sometimes bed-posts, brackets for desks and tables, lighting fixtures of many usages and sizes, etc. Gilded Venetian lamp-chains of the period are well known.

Venice had always been influenced by the East, and in iron work no less than in other pursuits. Damascening (inlaying one metal in a narrow chiseled groove of another) was probably introduced via her canals to the mainland. Screens, balconies, balustrades, and grilles (even religious ones) take themselves less seriously there than anywhere else and seem willing that, although made of "sterner stuff," they should partake of the festive mode characteristic of Venice. It may be said that while the remainder of Italy was developing according to traditional precedent, Venice inaugurated a new school. The quatrefoil fashioned from pierced plates fell into disuse—as entailing too much labor, say the harsh critics—and banded C-scrolls were substituted. These were at first used only horizontally, then vertically and finally diagonally. A modified and characteristic form of the quatrefoil, composed of C-scrolls and spear-headed accents collared together, is found in grilles such as those of San Giorgio degli Schiavoni. A great fondness for the interrupted scroll developed in Venice. Great rivalry arose between smiths in the creation of lunettes and

FIGS. 19 (LEFT) AND 20 (RIGHT).—DOOR AND DETAIL OF ITALIAN WROUGHT-IRON GRILLE, NOW IN
ISABELLA STEWART GARDNER MUSEUM, BOSTON

grilles of lacy and sparkling virtues. The work of Sansovino in the Zecca (mint) of Venice exhibits a bold virility. This school maintained itself with such commendable vigor that when the remainder of Italy in the seventeenth century had fallen into inconsequential and lazy mannerisms of the poorest traits of the French school, it continued to be nurtured by its own traditions, as the wide var·ety of grilles on the Grand Canal alone testifies.

Outside of Venice early sixteenth-century work includes a series of worthy lunettes at Lucca (pages 48–9). The Palazzo Orsetti has two of note, the Palazzo Micheletti, Piazza S. Martino (page 50), and scattered throughout the town remain a number of simpler ones on unassuming houses, as that on page 47. These ingeniously designed fanlight grilles exemplify what so often occurs in iron work within a community where a craft excels in one particular form of expression, establishes tradition and emulation, but ventures only timidly in other directions.

Venetian influence extended itself to the mainland to an indeterminate yet positive degree—very obviously on such occasions as the first-floor loggia door grilles and the second-floor exterior balcony of the Palazzo Bevilacqua (page 53). Both have the same characteristics of banded C-scrolls, relieved from monotony by being formed of small square twisted rods, and terminating in yapping animal heads of varying ferocity.

J. Starkie Gardner credits sixteenth-century workmanship with being "distinguished for massive but good work, and excellence of design"—a compliment more generous than much of the work of the later part of the century warrants.

To sum up, Italian workmanship up to the mid-sixteenth century closely adhered to the attributes of the metal, and employed only those forms which the hammer could readily achieve. There are but rare occasions of "carving" iron into arabesques, or fashioning difficult capitals and bases, which so frequently and amazingly occur in Spanish work. Neither is the split bar (a favorite of the Spanish *reja*), nor a series of interesting twists, used to any extent. The Italian grille was generally found dividing itself into rectangular panels by stiles composed of dentils on each side of a triangular centre rib (refer to drawings on pages 51–2). Between these stiles and rails the quartrefoil disported itself in a variety of forms, made in Tuscany from a pierced plate, and in Venice with its component parts collared together. This type of grille (exemplified by one in the Palazzo della Signoria, Siena), having its main portion as described above, usually is crowned by a *repoussé* frieze and surmounted finally by cresting flowers, spikes or animal heads.

SEVENTEENTH AND EIGHTEENTH CENTURIES

This period in iron work parallels the decadence in architecture. It is a curious jumble of influences—and results. Certain isolated examples are not without merit, but since the Italian borrowed his ideas from France directly, or indirectly via Germany, the modern designer fares better to hark back to the original French sources for inspiration. Craftsmen became more engrossed in vying with each other from a designing rather than an iron-working standpoint. Some designer seem to have considered the contrast of solids and voids, but for the most part it is "paper designing" executed in the cheapest (and coldest) fashion. The feeble gestures in which the craft attempted expression confined themselves largely to working the metal *cold*—naturally making for cheap and flimsy construction in thin material. Forms are so diversified that they are difficult to trace and to classify, being of opposite extremes: naturalistic and geometric, close and open. Generally, however, work is agog with paint and gilt, but sadly deficient in sound construction. Floral forms which were to the credit of such grilles as earlier ones of Florence and Siena (pages 43 and 51) in relieving the rigid phalanx of repeating quatrefoils, became a regimental rout of conflicting manœuvres. Scrolls were encased with thin, grass-like leaves. Conventional or naturalistic flowers were tacked on as afterthoughts. Vitruvius was no longer a consultant. The honest forging of vigorous beating had become a mere tradition. In some instances so degenerate had the craft become that, instead of rods or bars, ribbon-like twisted bands were used with cast ornaments pinned on, if the design was thought to require such bolstering. Intersecting tracery was borrowed from Germany and the East. Italian workmen were seemingly under Teutonic influence in such examples as the screen in Santa Theresa, Mantua, and the altar rail in San Francesco, Ferrara. Few excellent examples of iron work of this period exist in northern Italy except in Venice. Exceptions are: the screen in the south aisle chapel of San Ambrogio, Milan; the chapel enclosure in San Pietro, Mantua; and the screen in the Palazzo Capodilista, Padua.

Andirons were uncommon in the seventeenth century except in large living or reception rooms. "For the most part they were simple and massive forgings, the front con-sisting of a strong vertical bar, incised with some ornament on two spreading feet, and finishing as in France, in a crook or bronze knob." * Sometimes a spit was held by vertical bars. The richer ones, like some in the Bargello, have delicate pierced work.

Unfortunately the iron work of this period has not rusted away as might be desired, and because it is widely distributed and easy to buy, is best known and most imitated by the local craftsmen of to-day.

* Gardner, "Ironwork," II.

FIG. 21.—THIRTEENTH-CENTURY (?) ITALIAN GRILLE

The grille over-all is 8 feet 7 inches high by 5 feet 8½ inches wide; the circular *motifs* are 5½ inches in diameter; vertical bars are ¾ of an inch wide by ½ inch deep; intermediate horizontal rails are 1⅝ inches wide

FIG. 22.—FOURTEENTH-CENTURY ITALIAN DOOR

This Tuscan door, now in the National Museum, Florence, attains its rich effect through simple wrought-iron means—that of being built up of successive pierced plates and sheets, and by stiles triangular in section

FIG. 23.—WROUGHT-IRON CHANCEL SCREEN IN THE SACRISTY CHAPEL, S. CROCE, FLORENCE.   (1371)

It is astounding that with so little historical background such difficult forging forms should have been so expertly fashioned.   The tracery and inscription are built up of superimposed sheets of iron

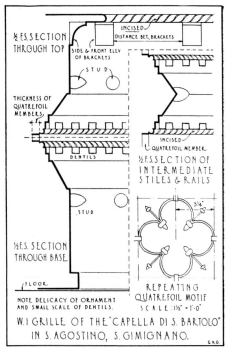

FIGS. 24 (PHOTOGRAPH) AND 25 (DETAIL).—GRILLE, CAPPELLA DI S. BARTOLO,
CHURCH OF S. AGOSTINO, SAN GIMIGNANO

FIG. 26.—CHANCEL GRILLE AT LEFT OF NAVE, ORVIETO CATHEDRAL
(CONTE DI LELLO DA SIENA, 1337)

FIG. 27.—LEFT TRANSEPT CHANCEL GRILLE, CAPPELLA DEI BARDI, S. CROCE, FLORENCE. (FIFTEENTH CENTURY)

FIG. 28.—CHANCEL GRILLE, ORATORIO DEL LORETINO, PALAZZO COMUNALE, SAN MINIATO. (LELLO DA SIENA)

FIG. 29.—WROUGHT-IRON GRILLE WITH THREADED BARS TWISTED, ZUCCHINI CHAPEL, S. PETRONIO, BOLOGNA

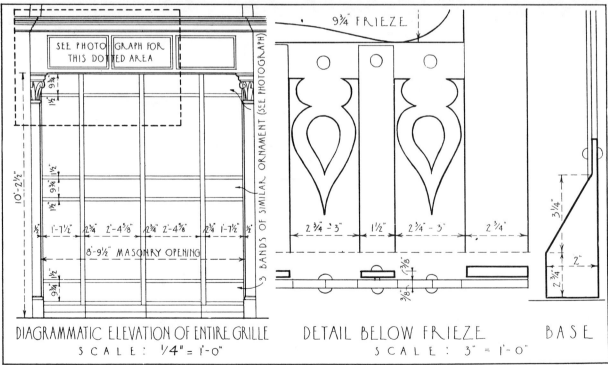

FIG. 30.—GRILLE TO CAPPELLA DEGLI SPAGNOLI, S. MARIA NOVELLA, FLORENCE.   (FOURTEENTH CENTURY)

FIG. 31.—CHANCEL GRILLE OF CAPPELLA BARTOLINI-SALIMBENI, S. TRINITA, FLORENCE. (15TH CENTURY)

FIG. 33.—GENERAL VIEW OF SCALIGERI TOMB RAIL OF MASTINON-II

FIG. 32.—DETAIL OF SCALIGERI TOMB RAIL OF CAN SIGNORIO

The detail at the left is taken from a tomb to the left of the one shown in Fig. 33; details of both are shown on the page opposite. The ladder, which occurs in the centre of both quatrefoils, is a playful device prompted by the name of the family, *Scala*, employing a ladder instead of stairs. It has been copied innumerable times without realization of its significance

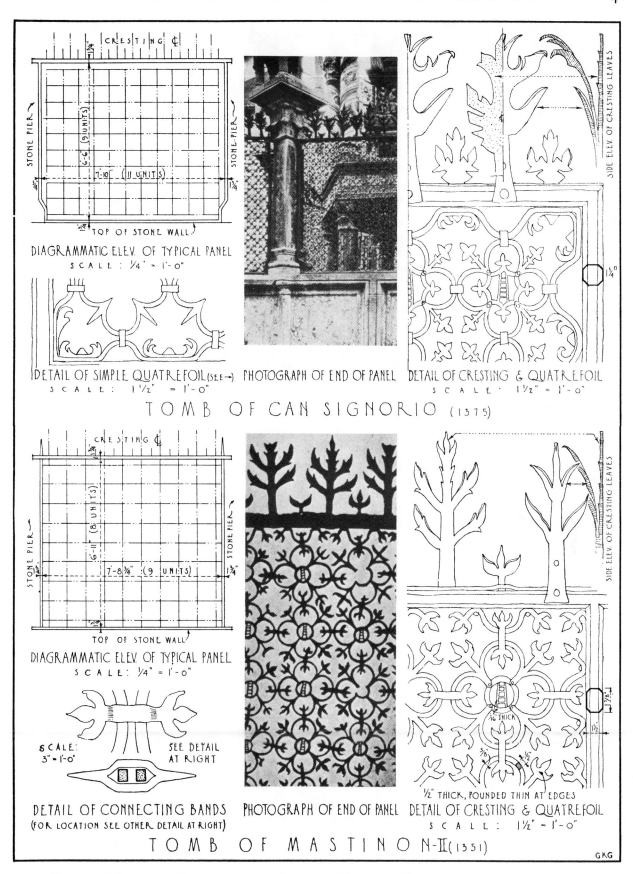

FIG. 34.—MEASURED DETAILS OF THE SCALIGERI TOMBS AT VERONA. (SEE PAGE OPPOSITE)

FIG. 35.—WROUGHT-IRON GRILLE OF THE CAPPELLA SUPERIORE DETTA DEL CONSIGLIO, PALAZZO DELLA SIGNORIA, SIENA. (NICOLÒ DI PAOLO, 1436)

The satisfactory composition of this grille, its pleasing relation of component parts, and its harmonizing quality with the entire chapel, have long made it one of the most admired and emulated works of the iron art of Tuscany. The scale of the field of the grille and the cresting are particularly appropriate to the type of frescoes

FIG. 36.—DETAIL OF WROUGHT-IRON GRILLE, PALAZZO DELLA SIGNORIA.   (SEE PAGE OPPOSITE)

This detail incorporates the most usual and best executed characteristics of fifteenth-century work.   The variety of the cresting and its intelligent vignetting of the *repoussé* frieze is as worth analysis as the relation which the parts of the delicate quatrefoil bear to the typical Tuscan stiles

44

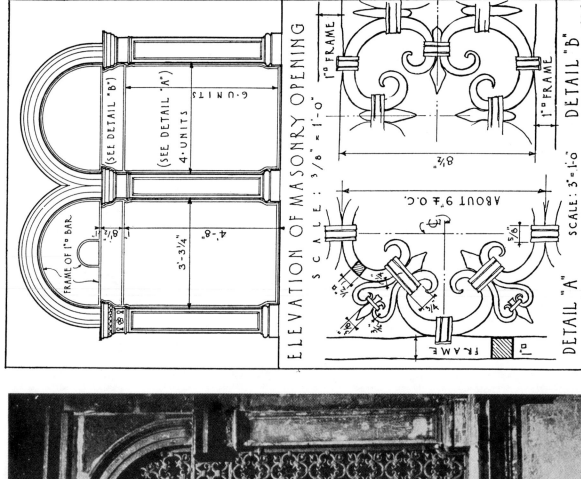

Fig. 37.—Wrought-Iron Window Grille of Scuola di S. Giorgio, Venice

ITALIAN WROUGHT IRON: ILLUSTRATIONS

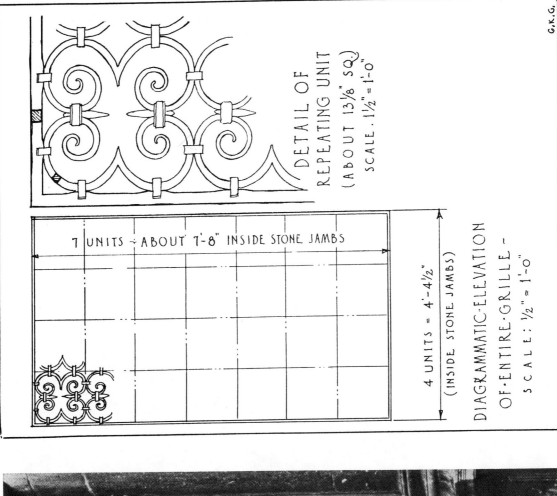

DETAIL OF
REPEATING UNIT
(ABOUT 13⅛" SQ.)
SCALE. 1½" = 1'-0"

7 UNITS · ABOUT 7'-8" INSIDE STONE JAMBS

4 UNITS = 4'-4½"
(INSIDE STONE JAMBS)

DIAGRAMMATIC·ELEVATION
OF·ENTIRE·GRILLE ~
SCALE: ½" = 1'-0"

G.K.G.

FIG. 38.—WROUGHT-IRON WINDOW GRILLE OF ABANDONED CHURCH ON S. GIUSTINIANI CANAL, VENICE

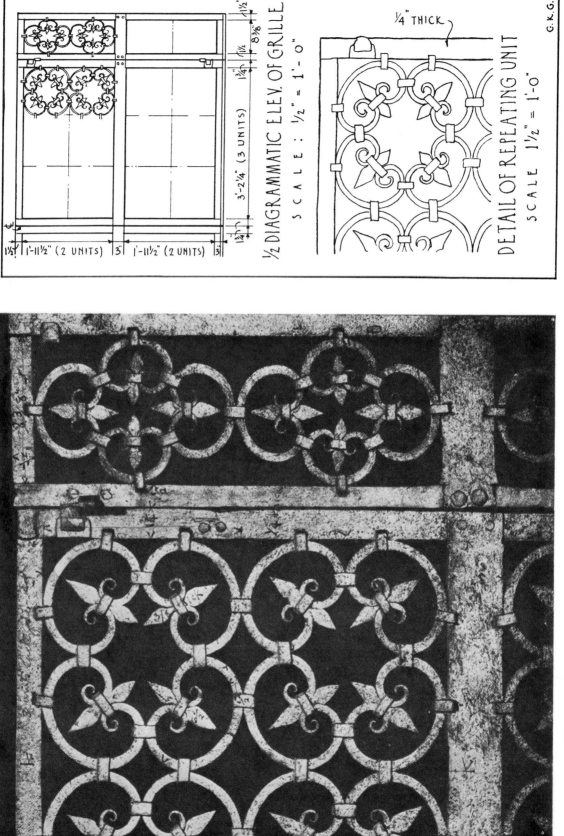

½ DIAGRAMMATIC ELEV. OF GRILLE

SCALE: ½" = 1'-0"

¼" THICK

DETAIL OF REPEATING UNIT

SCALE 1½" = 1'-0"

G. K. G.

FIG. 39.—DETAIL OF WROUGHT-IRON CHANCEL GRILLE, CAPPELLA DEL SACRAMENTO, ST. MARK'S, VENICE

The characteristic Tuscan quatrefoil was cut from a single sheet of iron, while the Venetian favorite was like this example, composed of scrolls banded together, with accents at their juncture. The texture is worthy of attention

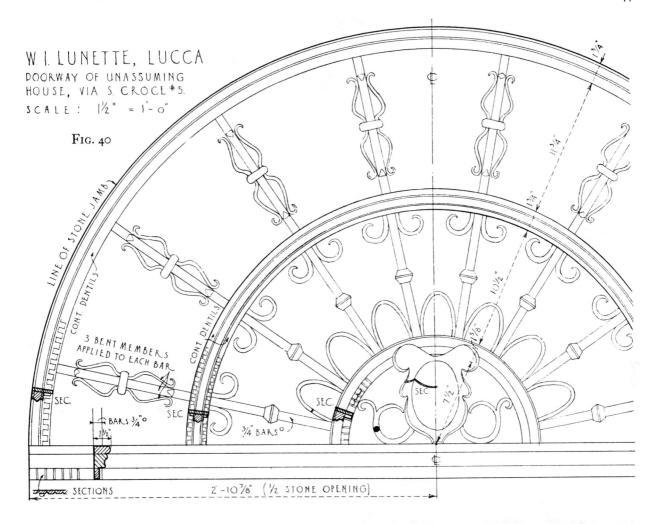

W. I. LUNETTE, LUCCA
DOORWAY OF UNASSUMING
HOUSE, VIA S. CROCE #5.
SCALE: 1½" = 1'-0"

FIG. 40

LINE OF STONE JAMB

CONT. DENTILS

CONT. DENTILS

3 BENT MEMBERS
APPLIED TO EACH BAR

SEC.

SEC.

SEC.

SEC.

2 BARS ¾"◻

1½"

¾" BARS ◦

7½"

5⅛"

10½"

7¼"

11¼"

¾"

SECTIONS

2'-10⅞" (½ STONE OPENING)

LUNETTE IN LOGGIA OF
PRIGIONI, RIVA DEGLI
SCHIAVONI, VENICE.
(ADJACENT TO 'BRIDGE OF SIGHS')
SCALE · ½" = 1'-0"

LINE OF
STONE JAMB

B.F.G.

4'-7¾" (½ STONE OPENING)

G.N.G.

FIGS. 41 (DRAWING, LEFT) AND 42 (PHOTOGRAPH,
ABOVE).—WROUGHT-IRON LUNETTE, LOGGIA
PRIGIONI, VENICE

The illustrations on this and the following three pages typify some of the favorite fanlight mannerisms—in Lucca (Figs. 43, 44, 45, and 47) the same *parti* is followed of radiating arches, with an ornate band either at the centre, the outside, or both, while later in the seventeenth century, particularly at Venice, the inter-rupted scroll banded together was frequent. The most pleasing ones are like those in Figs. 44 and 48, where a thin member is in-troduced within the radiating "arch," gaining variety not only by the difference in thickness, but in alternating plain with twisted bars.

FIGS. 43 (ABOVE) AND 44 (BELOW).—SIXTEENTH-CENTURY FANLIGHTS OF THE PALAZZO ORSETTI, LUCCA
(BETWEEN STONE JAMBS, 7 FEET 8½ INCHES)

FIG. 45.—WROUGHT-IRON FANLIGHT FROM THE MONASTERO DELLE BARBANTINE, LUCCA.   (16TH CENTURY)

Courtesy of Victoria and Albert Museum

FIG. 46.—WROUGHT-IRON ITALIAN FANLIGHT.   (SEVENTEENTH CENTURY)

In earlier work the scrolls would probably gradually become thinner and more graceful
at their terminations.   The width is 6 feet 2½ inches, and the height 3 feet 5¼ inches

DETAIL AT CENTER
SCALE · 3" = 1'-0"

2 FLAT BARS (1·TWISTED)
WOUND AROUND CORE.

SECTION

4¾" R

SPRING LINE

LINE OF STONE JAMB

ELEVATION

SECTION

SPRING LINE

DETAIL "X"

DETAIL OF OUTER PORTION
SCALE · 3" = 1'-0"

DETAIL "X"

2¾"

WOOD DOOR BELOW SPRING LINE   2⅝" 4¾"

7¾"   1'-7¾"   7⅜"

(½ STONE OPENING)   2'-10⅞"

HALF·ELEVATION OF LUNETTE
SCALE · 1" = 1'-0"

GKG

FIGS. 47 (DRAWING) AND 48 (PHOTOGRAPH).—FAN-
LIGHT OF PALAZZO MICHELETTI, LUCCA.

FIG. 49.—GRILLE AT EXTERIOR SHRINE, PALAZZO
DELL' ARTE DELLA LANA, FLORENCE

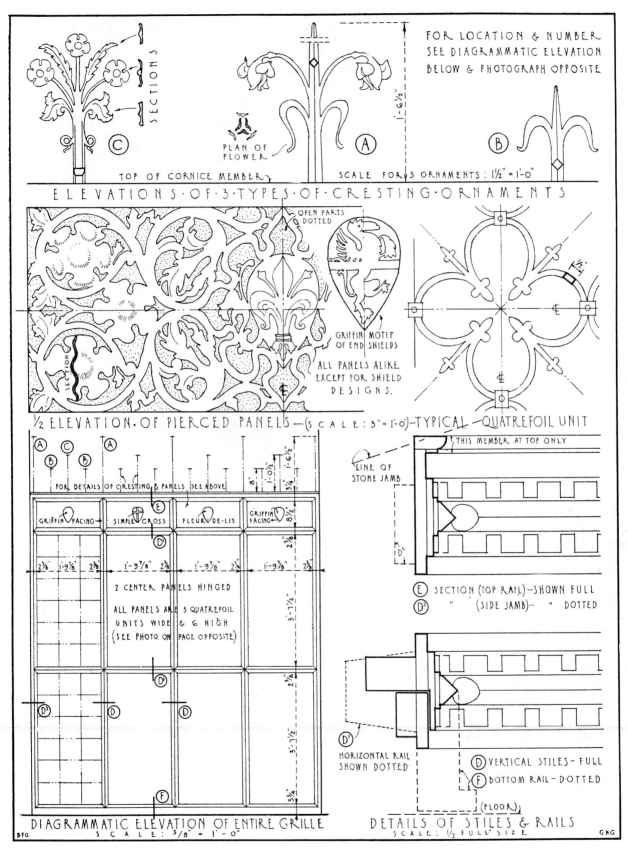

FOR LOCATION & NUMBER
SEE DIAGRAMMATIC ELEVATION
BELOW & PHOTOGRAPH OPPOSITE

SECTIONS

C

PLAN OF FLOWER

A

1'-6½"

B

TOP OF CORNICE MEMBER

SCALE FOR 3 ORNAMENTS: 1½" = 1'-0"

E L E V A T I O N S · O F · 3 · T Y P E S · O F · C R E S T I N G · O R N A M E N T S

OPEN PARTS DOTTED

SECTION

GRIFFIN MOTIF OF END SHIELDS

ALL PANELS ALIKE
EXCEPT FOR SHIELD
DESIGNS.

1½

E

½ ELEVATION · OF PIERCED PANELS · (SCALE: 3" = 1'-0")   TYPICAL · QUATREFOIL UNIT

THIS MEMBER AT TOP ONLY

LINE OF
STONE JAMB

A   C   A
B   C   B

FOR DETAILS OF CRESTING & PANELS SEE ABOVE

1'-6½"
1'-0½"
6"
3/4
8½
2⅜

GRIFFIN FACING   SIMPLE CROSS   E   FLEUR-DE-LIS   GRIFFIN FACING

D¹

2⅜   1'-9⅛"   2⅜   1'-9⅛"   2⅜   1'-9⅛"   2⅜   1'-9⅛"   2⅜

2 CENTER PANELS HINGED

ALL PANELS ARE 3 QUATREFOIL
UNITS WIDE & 6 HIGH
(SEE PHOTO ON PAGE OPPOSITE)

3'-1½"

2⅜

D¹

D   D

3'-1½"

F

3/4

E   SECTION (TOP RAIL) — SHOWN FULL
D²   "   (SIDE JAMB) — " DOTTED

HORIZONTAL RAIL
SHOWN DOTTED

D   VERTICAL STILES — FULL
F   BOTTOM RAIL — DOTTED

(FLOOR)

DIAGRAMMATIC ELEVATION OF ENTIRE GRILLE
SCALE: 3/8" = 1'-0"

DETAILS OF STILES & RAILS
SCALE: ½ FULL SIZE

DFG   GKG

FIG. 50.—WROUGHT-IRON GRILLE IN FRONT OF FOURTEENTH-CENTURY SHRINE TO S. MARIA DELLA
TROMBA, EXTERIOR OF PALAZZO DELL' ARTE DELLA LANA, FLORENCE.   (SEE FIG. 49 OPPOSITE)
The cresting units are inspirational singly but even more so collectively, in the way they supplement and complement each other

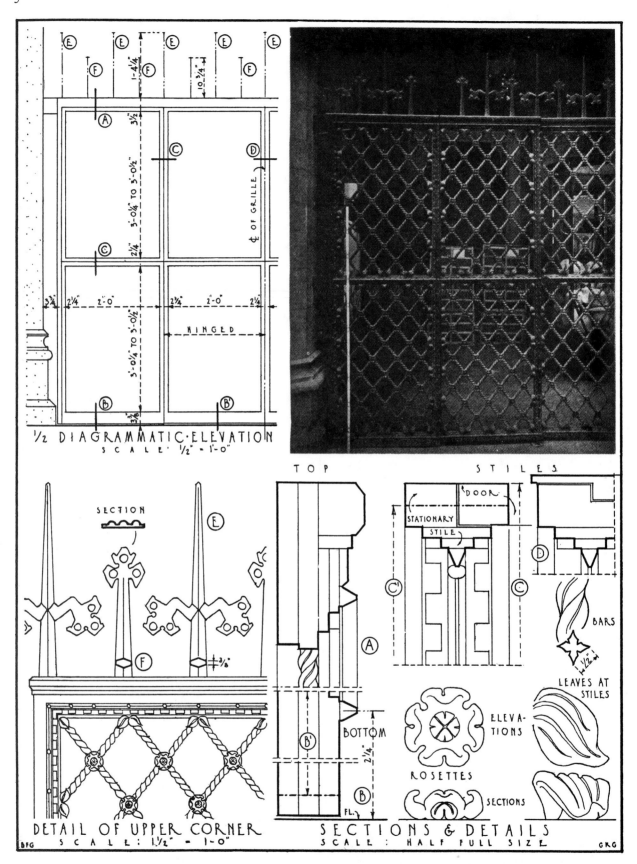

FIG. 51.—WROUGHT-IRON GRILLE, PALAZZO DELL' ARTE DELLA LANA, FLORENCE
This grille should make a modern appeal with its economical design of twisted bars, simple rosettes, and appropriate cresting

NOTE: SCALE OF DETAILS, 3" = 1'-0"

DETAILS AT TOP RAIL

REPEATING SPIRAL UNIT

DETAIL AT CENTER (FRONT ELEVATION)

REFLECTED PLAN OF TOP RAIL

SIDE ELEVATION

½ FRONT ELEVATION

SCALE: ¾" = 1'-0"

GKG

FIG. 52.—WROUGHT-IRON BALCONY, PALAZZO BEVILACQUA, BOLOGNA

One of the unusual features of this balcony is the top rail, which, instead of consisting of a single member only, includes a *rinceau* (see reflected plan in corner); the small insert photograph shows how effective this can be when viewed from below. The type of scrolls and the general design show Venetian influence

FIGS. 53 (ABOVE) AND 54 (RIGHT).—SECOND-FLOOR
INTERIOR DOOR, PALAZZO COMUNALE, PISTOIA

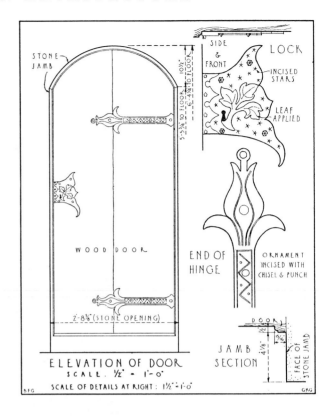

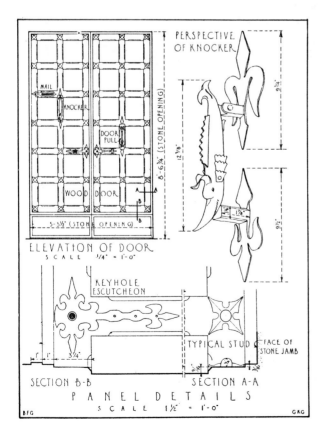

FIGS. 55 (LEFT) AND 56 (ABOVE).—NEW DOOR OF
OLD HOUSE NEAR I FRARI CHURCH, VENICE

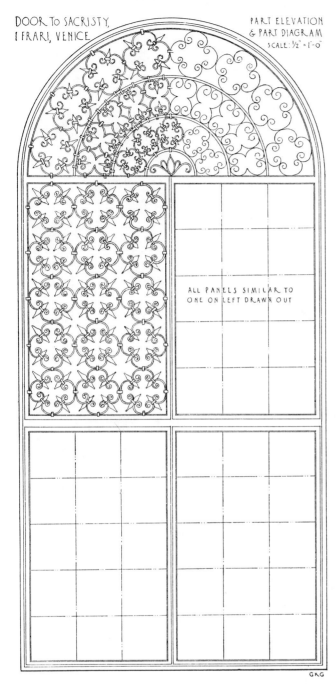

DOOR TO SACRISTY, I FRARI, VENICE

PART ELEVATION & PART DIAGRAM
SCALE: ½" = 1'-0"

ALL PANELS SIMILAR TO ONE ON LEFT DRAWN OUT

GKG

½" THICK   11½"   ¾" THICK

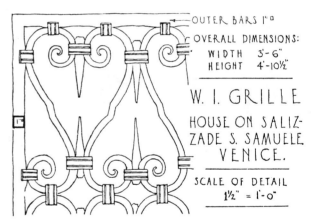

OUTER BARS 1"□

OVERALL DIMENSIONS:
WIDTH   3'-6"
HEIGHT   4'-10½"

1"

W. I. GRILLE

HOUSE ON SALIZ-
ZADE S. SAMUELE.
VENICE.

SCALE OF DETAIL
1½" = 1'-0"

FIGS. 57 AND 58 (LEFT COLUMN).—DRAWING AND DETAIL OF DOOR GRILLE TO SACRISTY, I FRARI CHURCH, VENICE

FIGS. 59 AND 60 (THIS COLUMN).—PHOTOGRAPH AND DETAIL OF WINDOW GRILLE OF HOUSE ON SALIZ-ZADE S. SAMUELE, VENICE

In general the effect of the Venetian grille is not as structural as it is sparkling, nor useful as ornamental. Its parent architecture does not take itself over-seriously, so that the iron work cannot be too strenuously blamed for assuming the same liberty. Seldom in Venice do the rectangular quatrefoils or similar repeating units occur as in Tuscany, but rather there is a great fondness for combining scrolls of different sizes, interrupted S-scrolls, or scrolls with ovals. Generally at the juncture of banded members there is an accent in the shape of a dart or spearhead, while the bands themselves are often ribbed. The I Frari door grille (to the left) behaves Tuscan-like below the spring-line, but the fanlight takes on the sporting characteristics of its native city

FIG. 61.—WINDOW GRILLE, HOUSE ON PONTE e CALLE DELLA OSTREGHE, VENICE

FIG. 62.—BALCONY ON HOUSE OPPOSITE I FRARI CHURCH, VENICE. (DETAIL BELOW)

FIG. 63.—DETAIL OF WROUGHT-IRON BALCONY, HOUSE OPPOSITE I FRARI CHURCH, VENICE

The Venetian craftsman made a valuable contribution to the wrought iron vocabulary when he illustrated some of the limitless possibilities in combining several varieties of scrolls, and in making them do double duty as the large C-scrolls above

FIG. 64.—VIEW OF ENTIRE DOOR

FIG. 65.—DETAIL OF SINGLE PANEL

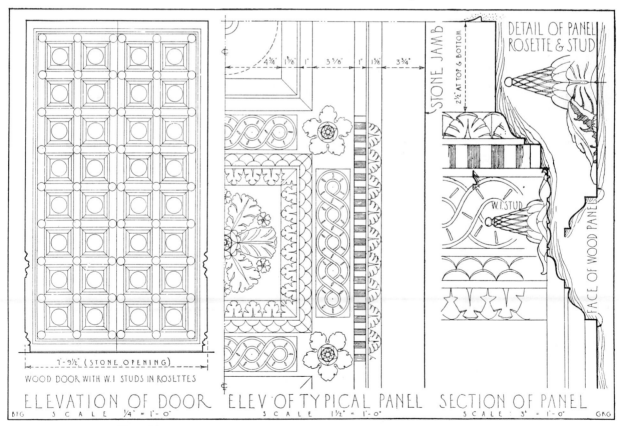

FIG. 66.—MEASURED DETAILS OF DOOR AND WROUGHT-IRON STUDS.
WOOD DOOR WITH IRON STUDS, BAPTISTRY, CATHEDRAL OF PARMA

While the stone and wood carving is beautiful, Fig. 64 shows how the decisive accents of the iron studs enliven the whole

WROUGHT IRON IN ARCHITECTURE

FIG. 68.—STANDARD HOLDER, PALAZZO GRISOLI, SIENA. (14TH CENTURY)

This gallant monitor, frankly assembled for all the world to see his joints, and freely exposed for several centuries to weather, and yet none the worse for either, is an eloquent oration on the virtues of chisel-mark decoration and wit in architecture

FIG. 67.—COURT STANDARD HOLDER, PALAZZO STROZZI, FLORENCE

This outstanding example of wrought-iron modeling, craftsmanship, and composition is prevented from looking like bronze or marble by the flat profiles of mouldings, shallowness of dentils, diminished width, and tool-marks. (By Nicolò Grosso)

ITALIAN WROUGHT IRON: ILLUSTRATIONS

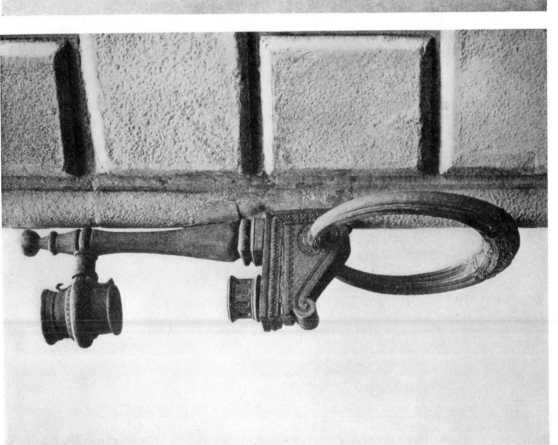

TWO SIXTEENTH-CENTURY WROUGHT-IRON STANDARD HOLDERS

FIG. 69.—PALAZZO DEL TURCO, PIAZZA SS. APOSTOLI, FLORENCE

FIG. 70.—PALAZZO MANCINI, CORTONA

This well-mannered, dignified High-Renaissance composition includes all the refinement and *finesse* which could be desired in bronze, yet the flatness of its ornament stamps it as wrought

The varying twists on the upper necking and ring, the delicate chiseleing on the base-band, and the structural, graceful leaves below the latter, merit careful study

ELEV. OF DOOR
SCALE : ¼″ = 1′-0″

PROJECTION OF VOUSSOIRS

FACE OF BUILDING

SECTION THRU STONE JAMB
SCALE 3″ = 1′-0″

DETAIL OF W. I. STUD
SCALE: ½ FULL SIZE

W. I. STUDS

SECTION THRU DOOR STILE AT JAMB

W I STUD

PANELS 15⅜″ 0″

INCISED ORNAMENT MADE BY CHISELS & PUNCH

SIDE

FRONT

PERSPECTIVE

DETAIL OF W.I. HANDLE
SCALE 3″ = 1′-0″

B.F.G.

G.A.G.

FIG. 71.—WOOD DOOR WITH WROUGHT-IRON STUDS, PALAZZO GUADAGNI, FLORENCE

The iron studs on the stiles and rail are a definite part of the decoration, and serve as a tie between the scale of the rusticated voussoirs and that of the carved wood panels; the knocker is good wrought technique

Courtesy of Metropolitan Museum of Art

FIG. 72.—SEVENTEENTH-CENTURY ITALIAN GATE

The spread lozenge-shaped form which is included between scrolls
is the saving grace for what might otherwise be a mediocre design

From a drawing by Paul Hermann

FIG. 73.—DOOR AND BALCONY, CASA PERI, LUGANO

The pattern of the studs and horizontal joints of the door atone
for some of the flimsiness of the fanlight and balcony design

From a photograph by Paul Hermann

FIG. 74.—IRON-WORKER'S SIGN, STREET IN ASSISI

This lad and his draconic pet speak for themselves—and do
so more volubly than many of their brethren in America

FIG. 75.—CHAPEL "GRATING," ARONA, LAGO
MAGGIORE

This is not so much an example of what to emulate in playfulness as what to avoid in instability and meaningless curves

FIG. 77.—VENETIAN GRILLE. (SIXTEENTH CENTURY)

The gilt roses and lilies project; the height is 9 feet 2 inches, the width 5 feet 6 inches

FIG. 76.—PAIR OF WROUGHT-IRON GATES. (SEVENTEENTH CENTURY)

The round bars and design show strong German influence. The height is 5 feet, the width 3 feet 3¾ inches

SPANISH WROUGHT IRON

BEFORE the designer essays to employ *motifs* taken bodily from Spanish wrought iron he should acquaint himself with the manner in which they are forged, and, equally important, as to the willingness of the client to part with his bank-roll. In the past the tendency too often has been to copy certain stone traits as closely as possible, some from one page and some from another, without realizing that the result is more suitable to cast bronze than wrought iron. The calibre of the Spanish craftsman is not frequently equalled in this commercialized age, when only once in a lifetime is there a demand for carved arabesques in iron, so that even though the Midas-client should be willing to spend limitless funds, it is likely to be disappointing to attempt to secure the successful reproduction of the grand old masterpieces.

Preceding the mid-fifteenth century there are numerous ornamental and structural mannerisms in Spanish iron work which are as applicable to good forge work to-day as five centuries ago, and the designer will find it well worth his while to investigate those characteristics which are natural to wrought iron. Probably no single style offers as many modern adaptations to economic and pleasing effects in iron as the Spanish, but to be able to discern them necessitates a knowledge of what is covered in the chapter on "Craftsmanship." The variety of treatment of the single bar, as well as the striking arrangements of different types, are worthy of application to the modern problem where time and funds are limited. The solid *repoussé* panel, or one pierced and mounted on a vermilion background, and the restrained but intelligent use of gilt and color, are sure to produce more effective results than time spent merely copying arabesque ornament. After all, a designer should be more than an archæologist.

The menu offered by Spanish *chefs-d'œuvre* ranges from milk toast to lobster salad—all delectable dishes to be sure, but some too rich for the blood. It behooves the designer to decide upon his *a la carte* order with the nicety of an expert dietician.

TWELFTH TO EARLY FIFTEENTH CENTURIES

The first Spanish expression in iron was in much the same manner and in many of the same forms as those in France and England of the twelfth century. The grille of Winchester, England (1093), precedes a very similar type in the Santa Cruz *reja* of the Pamploña Cathedral, probably forged in the early thirteenth century. Other early grilles from Palencia are formed of collared C-scrolls placed back to back. Although this period is of greater historical interest than intrinsic value to the designer, such examples as survive are by no means elementary, but offer helpful suggestions for architecture of Romanesque antecedents.

By the beginning of the fourteenth century, shrines and tombs were becoming more and more enriched, necessitating adequate protection from thieving, yet requiring good visibility for worshippers. The earliest accepted type of *reja* which satisfied such practical requirements and included religious propriety as well, was a simple series of vertical bars. The development of these vertical bars forms an interesting phase to be considered later in a separate paragraph.

Although Spain was slowly compressing Moorish power southward toward the Mediterranean, she encouraged many of the swarthy workmen to remain after the "Reconquest," appreciating that the exchange in craftsmanship would be to the decided advantage of her own arti-

FIG. 78.—*REJA* OF THE CAPILLA DE SANTA CRUZ, CLOISTERS OF PAMPLOÑA CATHEDRAL. (1225?)

The iron is said to come from Moorish tent chains captured at the battle of Las Navas

63

sans. As a result there is the blending of the Gothic with the Moorish, creating the so-called "Mudéjar" style. "Plateresque" is the term given the period of the late fourteenth and the early fifteenth centuries, derived from the word *platero*, a silversmith who employs rich chasing and chiselling. During this period the intercourse with Italy was beginning to influence architectural taste. While nothing of great importance in iron was accomplished until the late fifteenth century, the smiths were becoming increasingly adept with a hitherto undeveloped craft. Elaborate locks and hinges, on which the artisans of France, the Lowlands, Germany, and England were concentrating their abilities, attracted but little attention from the Spanish craftsmen. With the passing of the Gothic, the lock dwindled further, until, at the time of the Renaissance, its significance was negligible. The general development of the *reja* elements is considered in the period following (page 66), and the characteristics of the Gothic and Renaissance examples are there described and summed up.

MID–FIFTEENTH THROUGH FIRST-QUARTER SIXTEENTH CENTURY

Spain wrote the most brilliant page of wrought iron history in this period of three-quarters of a century. The influence of the "Italian manner" of the Renaissance took effect on the architecture first and on the iron work later. Among other difficulties the smith was delayed by the necessity of fashioning new tools for a new system of ornament; the results are seeming anachronisms with iron work more *Gotico-florido* than the aperture framing it, even though obviously made for the occasion. The country was suddenly ablaze with prosperity, adventure, success of conquest. The refulgence of the national and individual wealth sought visible utterance, which among other expressions provided cathedrals and churches with iron grilles unequalled before or since. There was no royal encouragement, no patronizing nobility. It was the spontaneous enthusiasm of a people fortunately represented by talented sculptors, silversmiths, architects, clergy, and artists of the highest order—geniuses equally capable of conception and execution in iron. Competitions for the great *rejas*, which were won by submitting full-size models in wood and elaborate drawings, were events of national importance. The progress within this three-fourths of a century is astounding. Not only were all the natural difficulties in iron overcome, but the most exasperating complications were invited; by 1550 every conceivable problem had been solved.

Compared with the architect the iron-worker was beset by problems requiring greater inventiveness: where the former had well defined Italian prototypes to follow which could be modified to suit conditions, the iron-craftsman had his own tools to invent and his own ornamental vocabulary to evolve before even considering the design. In creating the monumental *rejas* he was beginning with rough "pigs" for material and a clean slate in design. Instead of "stock" bars or plates he had but a limitless fund of energy.

There may have been a fondness for a general *parti* for the monumental or minor ecclesiastical *rejas*, consisting of one or more superimposed series of vertical bars or spindles, divided by horizontal bands, and crowned by crestings composed of richly varied flowers or figures. But within those bounds there could scarcely be imagined a greater wealth of varying forged forms: bars with plain and ornamental twists, spindles and balusters almost as similar as though cast from a single mould, pilasters from 1 to 4 inches wide enriched by carved or applied arabesques, capitals of Corinthian parentage with fanciful details, portraits and pantomimes in *repoussé*, luxurious leaves and flowers, bars which divide and, after performing a graceful curve and convolution, rejoin the two parts into a single bar—these are but syllables of the vocabulary which eloquently declaimed the glory of the fifteenth and sixteenth centuries' iron work in Spain.

Such Gothic cathedrals as extended from Burgos to Seville, Santiago de Compostela to Barcelona, might in themselves well have furnished sufficient inspiration and occasion for super-craftsmanship. But in the early sixteenth century a change in the church service doubled the opportunities for iron work display. The priest's choir (*coro*) had been at the east end flanking the high altar, as is still usual in the cathedrals of other countries. The change in ritual moved the *coro* into the nave west of the crossing and facing the high altar (*altar mayor* or *capilla mayor*). The side chapels thus became less imposing and the natural vista from rear of nave to high altar was blocked by the *coro*, so that from an architectural and pictorial standpoint far more is lost than gained. However, it did present the iron craft with tremendously monumental problems, which in all cases were translated into masterful achievements (pages 83 and 9). Additional opportunities were also offered along the entire ambulatory by the chapel fronts and three sides of the *capilla mayor*. The best work was done before 1520; until 1550–60, richer effects were obtained, but by less "legitimate" wrought craftsmanship. Large grilles continued to be produced until the final expulsion of the Moors in 1609.

Although the proudest masterpieces of Spanish workmanship are the great cathedral *rejas*, the design and usage usually transcended the genuine limitations of iron. (The grille surrounding the royal tombs of Ferdinand and Isabella at Granada is considered by Digby Wyatt the best designed and most imposing (Figure 80). Instead of frankly appearing as a metal beaten on the anvil when hot, it became a habit to carve and incise it to attain the effect commonly attributed to a cast metal like bronze. Although from a technical standpoint

FIG. 80.—ROYAL CHAPEL *REJA*, GRANADA CATHEDRAL, BY BARTOLOMÉ DE JAEN, 1523–30. (40 FEET HIGH)

there is nothing further to be accomplished or perfected than the Renaissance *rejas*, yet one is sympathetically drawn to the pre-Renaissance work. The latter was satisfied to manœuvre without shaped spindles, carved capitals or arabesques, and was not too technically awe-inspiring for mental comfort.

It is only natural that in the north, where much of the best architecture was built by French, Flemish, and German workmen, the iron should bear a foreign stamp. Palencia Cathedral is illustrative, where a "screen is lightly constructed of twisted vertical bars with moulded caps and bases, bent at the top into a cresting of ogee arches, each crowned with a single, much-curled and -shredded thistle leaf, and a narrow band of delicately pierced sheet iron beneath, forcibly recalling early sixteenth-century German. Threaded lattice-work, rather massive and of various dates, is not uncommon. It occurs in the gates to the cloisters at Toledo, which, with their band of thistle-like ornament, might well be mistaken for German." * Further indications of foreign influence are manifested in the hexagonal overhanging pulpit in San Gil,

FIG. 79.—*REJA* IN OLD CLOISTERS, BARCELONA CATHEDRAL. (FIFTEENTH CENTURY)

* Gardner, "Ironwork," II.

Burgos, a late-fifteenth-century work of iron overlaid on a wooden frame, of French or Flemish flamboyant design.

The evolution from the simple vertical bar to the highly ornamented baluster or spindle may be taken as a competent indicator of the development of the iron craft in Spain. The earliest bars were flat and placed vertically as at Pamplona, serving merely as supports for the scroll units which formed the real body of the composition. Afterward came the period when scrolls disappeared and grilles were composed solely of plain bars. The Gothic continued to employ bars throughout its régime, but it gradually endowed them with combinations of twists, variety in cross-sections and incised ornamentation (pages 74–77). The Cathedrals of Barcelona and Toledo have a most extensive series of typically Spanish examples of the

FIG. 81.—WINDOW GRILLE IN APSE, COLEGIATA DE SAN ISIDORO, LEON

While this early grille consists simply of C-scrolls united by heavy bands, the small circles in the interstices make it seem highly varied. The width is approximately 2 feet 3½ inches

vertical member in all its stages; Avila too, in the Cathedral and San Vincente, records a fairly complete story. Some Gothic examples in Barcelona are built up of round bars, ½ inch in diameter and from 12 to 15 feet high. The demand for ornamentation encouraged the alternating of plain with twisted bars, then the variety of twists, and finally the moulded caps and bases. These latter became more and more ornate; success in moulded forms such as these may have encouraged the next development: the spindle. But before the bar succumbed the climax was attained with various forms peculiar to Spanish work: the bar was divided about midway between horizontal bands and the split parts fashioned into Gothic tracery forms, with minor accents welded on to perform a duty similar to crockets (page 75). It must be remembered of course, while the perfectly square or round bar appears simpler than the modeled spindle, that to the Spanish smith having to start with crude ingots, the former must have taken more patience, if not greater ability, to forge. The spindle could be accomplished in several sections and then welded together, while fashioning a true, square bar meant tedious beating of a rough "pig." Nevertheless, that *rejas* were composed of countless spindles all practically alike and of necessity beaten out on an anvil, will always provoke technical admiration and awe. While a spindle may be a *tour-de-force*, at least its good taste in design is a compensating factor, and not, for example, like certain German traits of "basket-weaving" in iron, which, though technically difficult, possess no particular architectural merit. Where the Gothic or Transitional Period had a row of equally heavy bars or verticals, the Renaissance grilles interrupted the steady march of spindles by occasional pilasters or piers, these being usually ornamented with arabesques. In forging spindles from the solid the weight of a single one sometimes reached 250 to 300 pounds.

Difficult as was the forging of bars and spindles from crude ingots, it was not without its reward. Many of the grilles so formed have never been painted and, though subjected to the weather, have not rusted. It is no secret that modern iron work would live as healthily if produced similarly: the iron was heated only in a charcoal (not coal) fire, and in being beaten from an irregular ingot to a mature bar or spindle, it thus started on the rigors of its career with its structure dense and its pores closed.

Horizontal bands almost parallel the history

of vertical bars in their process of development. In the Gothic period early grilles had horizontal bars top and bottom for rigidity. When screens rose higher, intermediate horizontal bars were pierced to allow passage for the verticals. Transitional Renaissance work boasted modest horizontal bands which passed in front of the verticals. The cresting from San Vincente, Avila (page 76), is exemplary of thin plates cut to form a crowning or intermediate band. Instead of the later *repoussé* panels it was not uncommon to rivet a pierced sheet over a background plate, or, before applying it, to cover the background with vermilion or gilt paint, or stout textile material. Inscriptions in panels were generally made by piercing a plate about $\frac{1}{16}$ of an inch thick and applying it to a background or allowing it to remain freestanding; when several thicknesses were superimposed it was done so expertly as to appear a single piece. In the Renaissance the skill of the craftsman spared neither pains nor imagination in enriching a frieze with lively arabesques; in the lofty *coro rejas* he was fond of interrupting the spindles at frequent horizontal intervals. More strictly architectural forms were borrowed in increasing quantities as the Renaissance progressed, and, in lieu of mere horizontal bands, there were moulded cornices built up solidly of iron, or veneered iron on wood cores. Even in the best work mouldings made of iron are always crude as compared with the delicately fashioned spindles or crestings, for the obvious reason that to beat out a double curve for even a short length and maintain a true edge is extremely difficult on an anvil, and the task multiplies with each added inch. Iron when cold cannot be deliberately planed as wood or chipped as stone; it is in its final state when the last blow has been struck before the metal cools.

The ardor with which the Spanish Renaissance iron-craftsman filled crestings with portraits and figures might be interpreted as a victorious symbol that the Moorish ban had been overthrown. Although there was extensive use of heraldry, one of the outstanding characteristics of the period was the free use of the human figure in broad *repoussé* panels and freestanding crestings. The great *reja* at Granada, screening the royal tombs, is a noteworthy example (page 65). Small and large portraits are handled in the manner of silversmithing, and curiously enough, pagan and Christian figures are intermingled. This type of work was generally accomplished by rivetting together two *repoussé*

panels having considerable relief—a feat of no mean ability. This troublesome problem involves working with a flat plate only and maintaining the while an equal thickness of iron throughout as the modeling is produced by beating the back of the plate. Success is dependent upon the smith's ability to "move the metal along," a performance which, on an extensive scale, is now regarded as a lost art.*

One is less apt to criticise the *reja* crestings *in situ* than on the bald page unattended by their entourage. In the Spanish cathedral seldom if ever does one see a high *reja* at any distance. Because of the *coro* blocking the nave one is able to regard *rejas* in sharp perspective only—when crestings invariably foreshorten greatly as a result. The actual effect of what may seem a

* Byne and Stapley, "Spanish Iron Work."

FIG. 82.—FIRST-FLOOR LOGGIA WINDOW GRILLE, CASA DEL CONDE DE TOLEDO, TOLEDO

This is typical in *parti* for many domestic grilles: vertical bars divided and rejoined, surmounted by a crowning horizontal pierced frieze and cresting. Its width is 3 feet 9 inches, the height of the vertical bars 4 feet 1¼ inches, the top frieze 6 inches high, the cresting 22 inches high, and the projection from the face of the wall 10 inches. The vertical and intermediate horizontal bars are ⅝ inch square untwisted, the end bars 1⅝ by $\frac{5}{16}$ of an inch, top and bottom bars 1⅝ by ⅝ of an inch

"top-heavy" cresting on paper, in reality seems an interesting silhouette softened by dim lighting. Incidentally, the spiky liliaceous flowers on crestings, and such appurtenances as high church candlesticks, may be said peculiarly to characterize the fifteenth and sixteenth centuries.

In the matter of window grilles the Spaniard used them sometimes because he imagined they absorbed an excess of heat, often because they were necessary, and always because he liked them. They occur in too great a variety to be classified. Invariably they possessed the happy faculty of cajoling the window openings into harmonious scale with the surrounding architectural detail or the human figure. Just as many a Georgian or Colonial house is ruined without muntins, so are countless Spanish façades if robbed of their *rejas*. One finds similar traits in grilles for windows, as for ecclesiastical work— on a lesser scale perhaps, but often with compensating sparkle and originality. The simplest types consist of a series of vertical square or round bars piercing or "threading" those placed horizontally. Others are composed of vertical bars, square ones turned at 45 degrees to the front of the grille, alternating with twisted ones. The next stage in craftsmanship is the split bar and *repoussé* cresting (pages 67 and 70), and finally the modeled spindle. Balconies follow much the same tendencies, and what applies to window grilles is applicable to them also. The window grilles of the Alcalá de Henares may be considered as "popular" Renaissance types (page 87).

Perhaps the same fascination which led the Italian sculptors from Andrea Pisano to Donatello to express themselves eloquently in stone and marble pulpits, is accountable for the Spanish prowess in pulpits of wrought iron. These usually were placed in pairs, one left and one right of the *capilla mayor* beneath the crossing. Avila Cathedral has an iron pulpit in flamboyant Gothic, hexagonal in plan and 10 feet high, bearing the arms of the Cathedral— the *Agnus Dei*, the lion, the castle, all surmounted by a crown (page 85). Tracery is built up of successive layers of pierced plates frankly rivetted together. The frame is an oak core to which the iron is applied. The accentuated rivet heads announce that in no sense is it a wood design, or an attempted imitation executed in iron. The accepted date is 1520.

Avila Cathedral has also a Renaissance pulpit (page 84) entirely of wrought iron except

for wood cores in certain mouldings, which is an eloquent testimonial to the craftsmanship and ingenuity of the Spanish workmen. Almost the entire wrought iron alphabet is recorded, from small *repoussé* panels with rivets and joints frankly displayed, to denticular courses and full-modeled figures of solid iron serving as brackets. As a composition it attains a lightness which no non-metallic material would permit. The base, consisting of a single shaft, would be too frail except, of course, in anything but metal. Not only is its sturdiness satisfying to the eye, but it is playing up to the scale set by the ornament

FIG. 83.—PANEL DETAIL WITH IRON STILES AND PIERCED PLATES, MAIN DOOR, SAN ESTEBAN, SALAMANCA

The panel inside the iron stiles is 12½ inches wide by 17½ inches high; the corner studs project 1¾ inches from the wood face, while the centre one projects 2½ inches. This is an unusual Spanish door treatment

above it. As a study in design it is worth passing notice that interrupting the shaft of the column by horizontals brings it into key with the pulpit proper, whereas had the column remained unbroken, all the applied ornament in Christendom would have availed but little. The entire pulpit has been stifled by gilt for so long that quite naturally it has lost its vivacity. In places some of the gold has scaled off; one wishes that the remaining paint would become ashamed of itself and vanish too. One might wonder at the true cyma-recta mouldings until enlightened by Prentice's drawing (page 84). The ornament is of a good-natured, virile, wrought iron nature, so full of strange quirks among its animal kingdom that even constant association with things holy has not turned its devils into angels. The stair is later, by an inferior hand.

The wrought-iron pulpit remained a favorite to the last, even though it assimilated foreign flavor. One such is in San Salvadore in Cortejana (province of Estremadura), built up solidly of iron without wood framework. It is late seventeenth century, enriched with first cousins of florid German forms.

Spanish doors of importance are Moorish or Mudéjar in tradition and spirit. Nowhere does one see the distinctive type of door hinge which is common throughout France, England, Germany, or the Lowlands. The beautiful doors to the *Patio de los Naranjos* (Court of the Oranges) Cordova, are of Moorish workmanship under Christian direction, and, although of copper in this case, are good examples of the metal-sheathed type. The other favorite *parti* is to space ornamental nail-heads at intervals on doors composed of vertical planks. That these studs are a source of great interest to the collector, being of great variety and easily packed, is unfortunate for Spain. Only doors of remote or privately owned places remain unscarred and maintain their handsome quota of *repoussé*

studs (pages 190–2), made by beating thin plates into a thousand and one geometrical and conventionalized shapes. In the Renaissance, locks were slighted compared to other countries, yet there are occasional pierced lock plates of interest (page 190). Knockers inveigled more attention from the smith, who went to Nature for subjects to adapt and caricature men, animals, claws, heads, etc. An unusual door treatment is that of San Esteban, Salamanca (page 68), which is simple to fabricate and yet sufficiently decorative to recommend itself for modern adaptation.

Among other qualifications as an artist the Spanish craftsman sensed when to use paint and how to apply gilt—a matter in which we moderns have no idea except to hide all virtue of the forging. Paint was confined to heraldic shields for backgrounds of pierced panels, and for accentuating occasional spots of ornament. Gilt was applied in a genuinely forged manner. First a "fixing coat" of diluted and transparent glue was applied to the iron; after it had dried, gold leaves of infinitesimal thinness were dipped in poppy oil and then beaten into the iron, naturally partaking of its texture. Wholesale gilding never seems satisfactory (or ethical), but if iron must be given a foreign color, the least objectional manner would be by this method of beating.

Strange as it seems, the Spanish smiths were not noted for armor.

1525–1600

Many an art has slowly reached its zenith and then faltered through an agonizing death of equal duration, thereby tarnishing much of its earned brilliance. But not so with the crowning achievement of the Spanish iron work—the church *rejas*. Their meteoric rise in less than a century suddenly ended with the abrupt decline in national prosperity and energy. It had taken

the enthusiasm of an entire people and vast sums of money for the performance to continue. When the actors had played their parts and the climax was attained, the curtain was rung down. There was no postlude by inferior artists.

Iron work of this period played a manifestly subdued rôle, in no sense an attempt cheaply to imitate the magnificent past. Any tendency to

Courtesy of Victoria and Albert Museum

FIG. 84.—CRESTING FROM A LATERAL CHAPEL SCREEN, AVILA CATHEDRAL (C. 1490)

The pierced Gothic inscription, translated, reads "Master John Francis, chief master of the works in iron, executed this work." The length is 9 feet 2 inches

an excess of elaboration was checked by the re-action to the Greco-Roman style. After the middle of the sixteenth century church grilles became low, and horizontal rather than vertical. Gardner gives two examples of this type: that of the *coro* of the Plasencia Cathedral, by Juan Bautista Celma (1604), and one in the "new" cathedral, *Nuestra Señora del Pilar*, Saragossa (1574–79), with the same restrained but finer architectural treatment, variously attributed by Ford to the same Juan and credited by Riano to Cela.

SEVENTEENTH THROUGH NINETEENTH CENTURIES

After the sixteenth century the smith turned his hammer to lesser subject matter, and, fol-lowing the lead of architectural taste, to work marked by weaker design. After the Plater-esque came the brief Greco-Roman revival, then the Baroque and Rococo, termed in Spain the despised "Churrigueresque," after the in-fluential (?) architect Churriguera. Weather-vanes and finials in the form of crosses became common. Simple wrought-iron designs were the best products of the period. Balconies became universal in the late seventeenth century. The influence which France exerted on the greater part of the Continent at this time was con-tagious in Spain as well. Design was inferior to that of France under Lepautre and Marot, with a tendency to exaggerate that country's worst features. Some of the best balconies of the period are in Palma de Mallorca (page, 91).

Balconies not infrequently extended across an entire façade, composed of spindles and sup-ported by long, graceful scrolls. Furniture made excellent use of iron in diagonal braces, connect-ing pieces, corner angles, nail-heads and hinges.

By the eighteenth century the great palaces and public buildings, as well as the country in general, lacked adequate wealth for creative ornamentation of any kind. The French style was badly interpreted. There was no occasion for the large exterior gates in vogue in France and England, and no iron work of consequence can be credited to this period.

Through no fault of the smith the iron work of the nineteenth century actually lost ground. Of the fine old iron only the great *rejas* were able to withstand successive devastation by in-vading armies, political revolutions, foreign dealers, and rich collectors.

From drawings by Paul Hermann

FIG. 85.—DOMESTIC WROUGHT-IRON WINDOW GRILLES AT AVILA

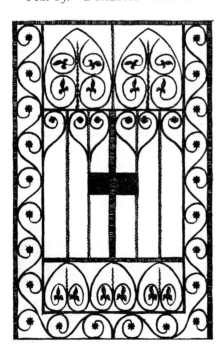

The width of this grille is 4 feet; the others are drawn at the same scale

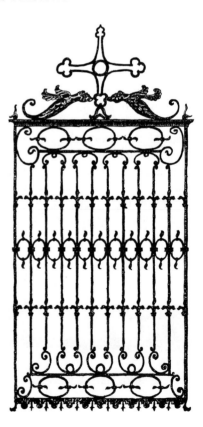

FIG. 86.—GOTHIC *REJA* IN CLOISTER OF BARCELONA CATHEDRAL

In this illustration it appears likely that the original grille consisted of purely utilitarian bars and perhaps a simple row of prickets, but that at a later date the "crockets" at the centre, and the ornate tracery frieze alone, were added

FIGS. 87 (ABOVE) AND 89 (BELOW).—AISLE-ALTAR SCREEN, SAN VINCENTE, AVILA. (THIRTEENTH CENTURY)

Although this is one of the best of early Spanish grilles, and is most admirable for the colorful termination of the large scrolls and the introduction of small ones, it seems to languish in oblivion

FIG. 88.—PORTION OF WINDOW GRILLE, WEST FAÇADE, S. MARIA DEL MERCADO, LEON. (THIRTEENTH CENTURY)

This example loses in contrast with Fig. 87 because of greater scroll monotony and flat bands instead of triangular ones, but the tiny scrolls are a delightful touch and a redeeming feature

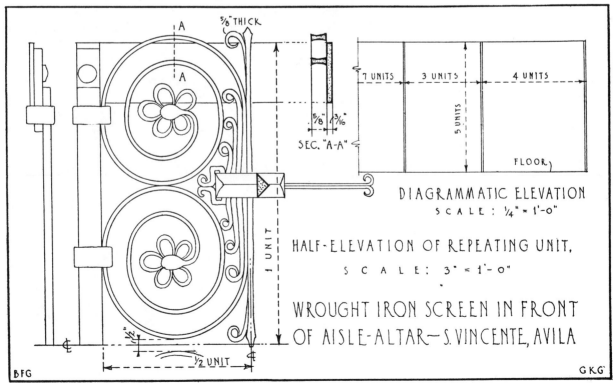

5/8" THICK

SEC. "A-A"

7 UNITS   3 UNITS   4 UNITS

5 UNITS

FLOOR

DIAGRAMMATIC ELEVATION
SCALE: 1/4" = 1'-0"

HALF-ELEVATION OF REPEATING UNIT,
SCALE: 3" = 1'-0"

WROUGHT IRON SCREEN IN FRONT
OF AISLE-ALTAR—S. VINCENTE, AVILA

1 UNIT

1/2 UNIT

BFG

GKG

FIG. 90.—ENTRANCE PORCH GRILLE, MAIN FAÇADE OF BRAGA CATHEDRAL, PORTUGAL

Chronologically in the development of the Spanish grille, following the use of plain round bars comes this alternating of square with twisted ones, and giving them simple bases and necking-bands. The *repoussé* frieze and cresting may have been added at successive periods later. The composition of raising the centre portion of the cresting, as well as the individual cresting units, are noteworthy

FIG. 91.—WROUGHT-IRON SCREEN IN CAPILLA MOZÁRABE, TOLEDO CATHEDRAL

This example typifies the Gothic grille at its best before falling prey to the chiselling of ornament later in the Renaissance. Actually this is a reproduction of the original screen, but it is a tribute to the excellence of modern craftsmanship

SECTION

CRESTING & CORNICE

¢ OF DOOR

¾" THICK

◇ 1½" □   ◇ ⅜" □   ◇   ◇

FLOOR   STONE BASE

BFG   DETAIL SCALE: 1½" = 1'-0"   ELEVATION AT DOOR SCALE: ¾" = 1'-0"   GKG

FIG. 92.—MEASURED DRAWING OF SCREEN IN CAPILLA MOZÁRABE, TOLEDO CATHEDRAL

Almost the whole gamut of favorite Spanish Gothic forms are shown to advantage here: the split-bar in two versions
with small accents welded, alternating plain and twisted bars, simple bases and caps, *repoussé* frieze and cresting

VERMILLION BACKGROUND

ALL GILDED

1/16" THICK

APPLIED ON PLATE

SECTION

GRILLE SURROUNDING
TOMB OF SAN VINCENTE—
CHURCH OF S. VINCENTE, AVILA

1" SQUARE
BARS
TWISTED

1/16" THICK

OCCASIONAL
TWIST
REVERSES

SPIKES ON GRILLE
OVER RIGHT AISLE
S. VINCENTE, AVILA

3'-3"

FLOOR

2 LIKE THIS ON EACH
SIDE OF CENTER

THIS ONE IN CENTER
(HEIGHT ABOUT 24")

SCALE: 3/8" = 1"

A.F.G.   G.K.G.

FIG. 93.—DETAILS OF GRILLE AND CRESTING, CHURCH OF S. VINCENTE, AVILA

The various elements of this grille are sound wrought-iron craftsmanship, and can be inexpensively achieved
(compared to the carved arabesques on the page opposite) because they can be naturally forged by a good smith

FIG. 94.—WROUGHT-IRON SHRINE RAIL, AMBULATORY OF AVILA CATHEDRAL

The carved caps of bars A and D, and the arabesque on A, are more suitable to stone or bronze than to iron which is supposed to be forged at the anvil. The frieze is legitimate in that it is applied pierced *repoussé* work

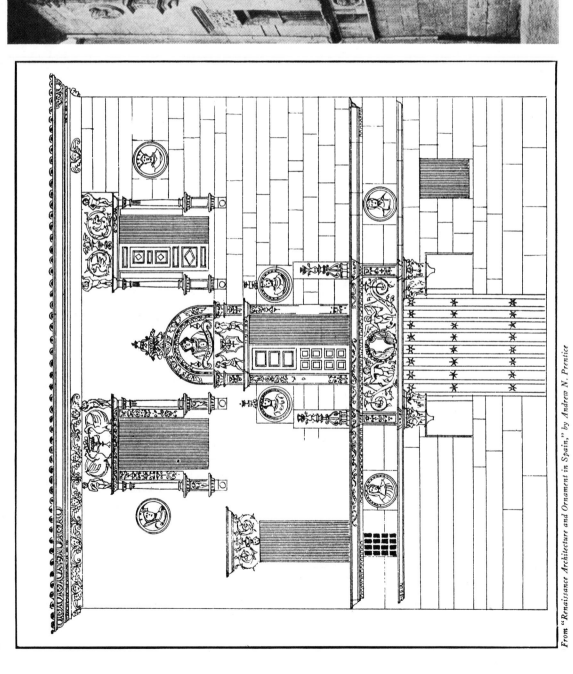

Fig. 95.—Casa de las Muertes, built by Don Alfonso de Fonseca, Salamanca. (Early sixteenth century)

This buff stone façade faces to the north, thereby accepting with good grace the definite contrast and sparkle which the iron balcony and window grilles afford, in lieu of sunlight and shadows. In a city renowned for its Renaissance palaces this has always ranked as one of the most admirable of the smaller type

SPANISH WROUGHT IRON : ILLUSTRATIONS

Fig. 97.—Patio of Santa Cruz Hospital, Toledo

A better effect with less iron and effort is difficult to imagine; the design of the whole, as well as the details, were evidently carefully considered

Fig. 96.—Window Grilles of Casa de las Conchas, Salamanca

This enriched effect was readily attained by natural wrought forms: plain and twisted bars, pierced bands placed in front of the verticals, and *repoussé* shells and shields

FIG. 98.—WROUGHT-IRON *REJA*, CAPILLA BAUTISMAL, TOLEDO CATHEDRAL

From "*Renaissance Architecture and Ornament in Spain*," by Andrew N. Prentice

FIG. 99.—WROUGHT-IRON *REJA*, CHAPEL OF THE HOLY GHOST, TOLEDO CATHEDRAL

From "Renaissance Architecture and Ornament in Spain," by Andrew N. Prentice

FIG. 100.—WROUGHT-IRON *REJA* OF SIDE CHAPEL, CUENCA CATHEDRAL

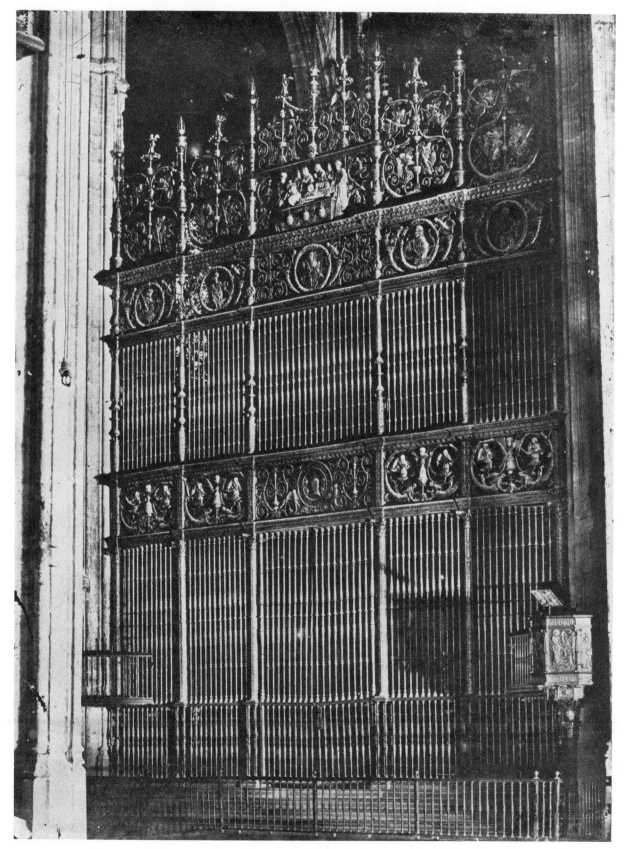

FIG. 101.—WROUGHT-IRON *REJA* OF THE ALTAR MAYOR, SEVILLE CATHEDRAL

Although we may decry the magnificence of such a *tour-de-force* in iron, its wealth in design suggestions for cast metals is not to be denied. It is said to have been covered with beaten gold leaf, but on the approach of Napoleon's army was given a coat of black paint

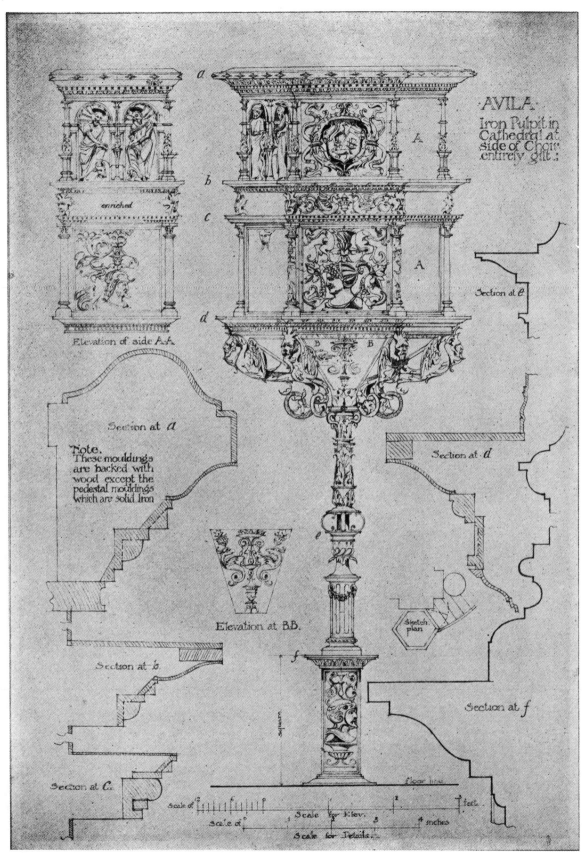

From "Renaissance Architecture and Ornament in Spain," by Andrew N. Prentice

FIG. 102.—WROUGHT-IRON GILT RENAISSANCE PULPIT, AVILA CATHEDRAL

Photograph by L. Ollivier

FIG. 103.—AVILA CATHEDRAL, LOOKING TOWARD *CORO* FROM THE CROSSING

The wrought-iron Gothic pulpit is at the left, while the Renaissance one (page opposite) is out of sight to the right.   The view is
taken from immediately in front of the *reja* to the *altar mayor*, and shows the manner of dividing the priests' choir from the high altar

From "Renaissance Architecture and Ornament in Spain," by Andrew N. Prentice

FIG. 104.—WROUGHT-IRON GRILLE AT BACK OF HIGH ALTAR, CUENCA CATHEDRAL

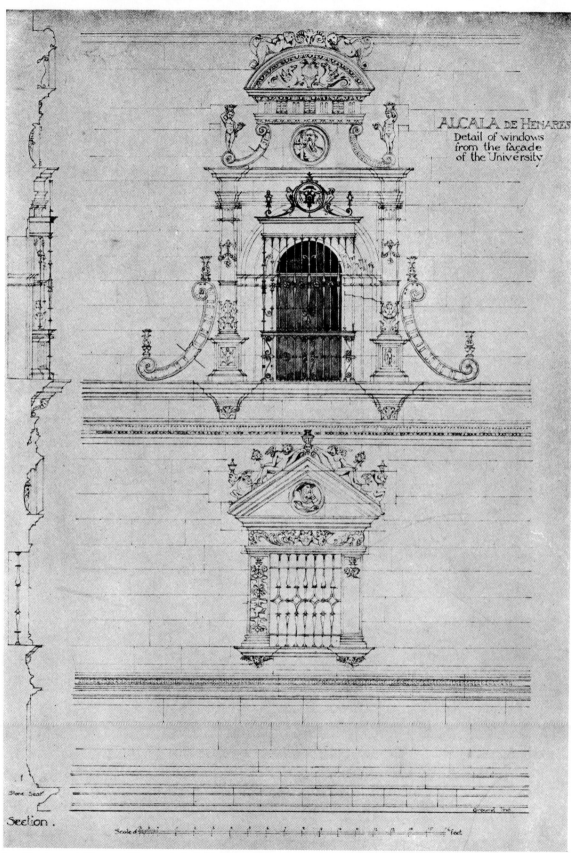

ALCALA DE HENARES
Detail of windows
from the façade
of the University

Section.

From "Renaissance Architecture and Ornament in Spain," by Andrew N. Prentice

FIG. 105.—DETAIL OF WINDOWS AND THEIR GRILLES, ALCALÁ DE HENARES

FIG. 107.—CLOISTER GRILLE, BARCELONA CATHEDRAL

Catalan work of the fourteenth century frankly used iron as iron, and usually limited ornamentation to the dictates of necessity, twisted bars excepted

FIG. 106.—CAPILLA DE LOS CABALLEROS, CUENCA CATHEDRAL

The base of this sixteenth-century grille combines the wrought twisted bar and simple base, with the cast-like Renaissance arabesques and gate base-panel

SPANISH WROUGHT IRON: ILLUSTRATIONS

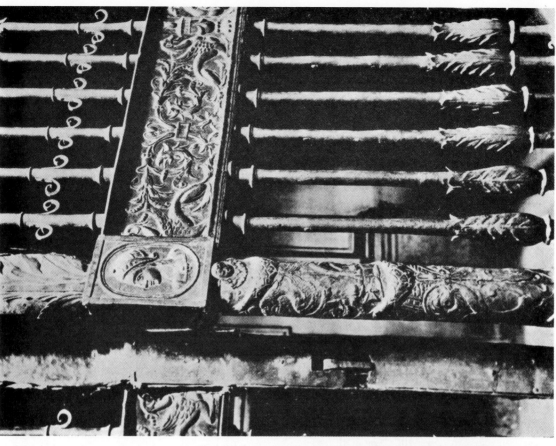

FIG. 109.—GRILLE NEAR TRANSEPT PORTAL, CUENCA CATHEDRAL

This sixteenth-century detail translated into twentieth-century craftmanship would better suit a foundry than a forge, although it is a monument to Spanish prowess

FIG. 108.—CAPILLA DE LOS CABALLEROS, CUENCA CATHEDRAL

This detail is a continuation higher up on the bars shown in Fig. 106, contrasting the genuine wrought forms of the Gothic (on the right) with the cast tendencies of the Renaissance

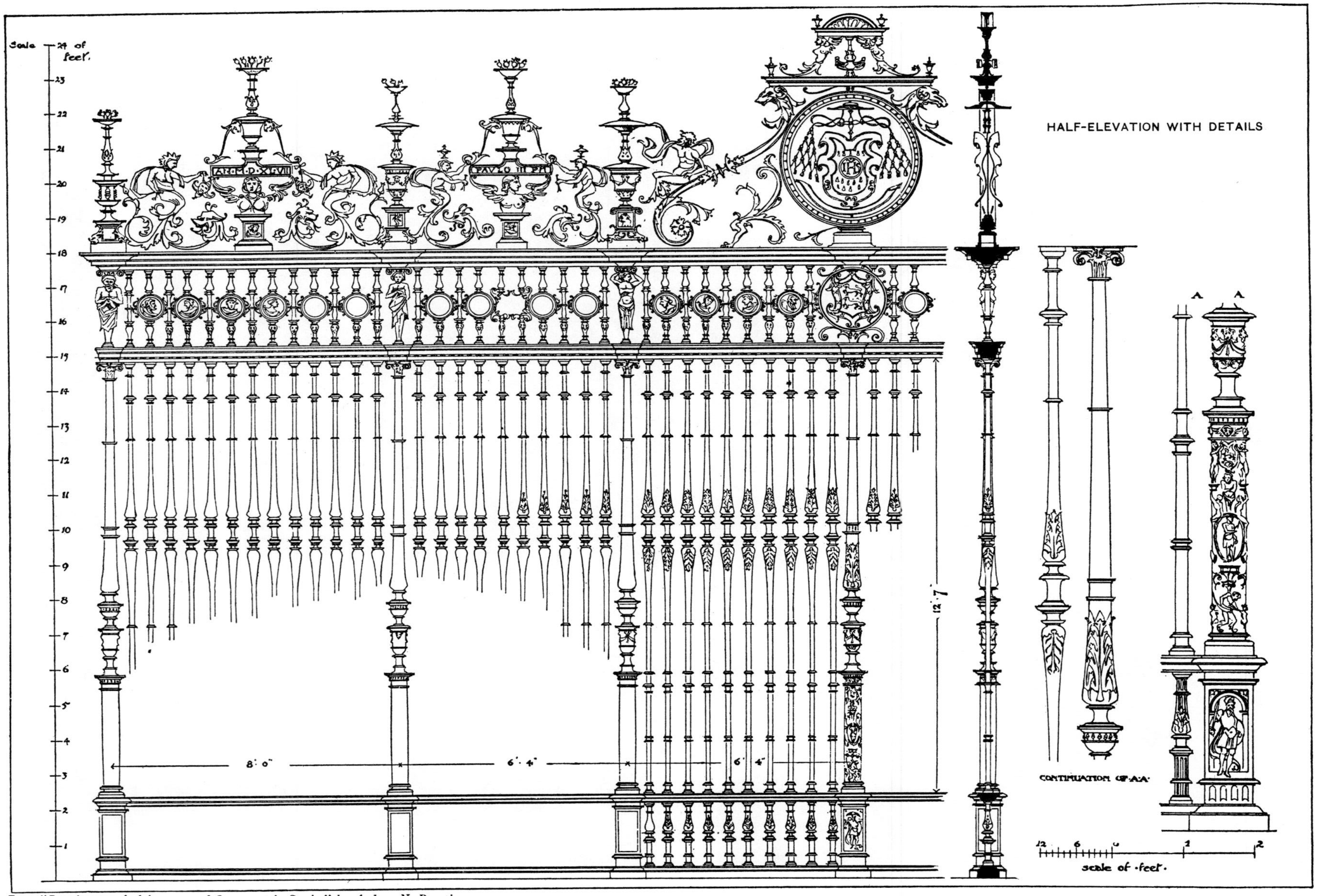

HALF-ELEVATION WITH DETAILS

CONTINUATION OF A-A

scale of feet.

From "Renaissance Architecture and Ornament in Spain," by Andrew N. Prentice

FIG. 110.—"Wrought-Iron and Bronze Screen to Choir," Toledo Cathedral

SPANISH WROUGHT IRON: ILLUSTRATIONS

FIG. 111.—FOUR WROUGHT-IRON BALCONIES FROM PALMA, MAJORCA

"Curious wrought-iron balconies form one of the principal charms to the streets of Palma, and are to be observed at every turning. Four typical examples are here given, the lower design to the right being from the Casa Morell." (Prentice.) These balcony rails were executed at the time of widespread French influence, and, as far as the designs are concerned, are typically French rather than Spanish

FIG. 112.—WROUGHT-IRON WINDOW GRILLE

FIG. 113.—WROUGHT-IRON BALCONY

STREET FAÇADE OF THE CASA DEL CONDE DE TOLEDO, TOLEDO

When iron is designed as intelligently and economically as these examples, it lies within the realm of possibility for even the modest dwelling

SPANISH WROUGHT IRON: ILLUSTRATIONS

Fig. 115.—Balconies and Awning Rod, Typical House, Ronda

Fig. 114.—Patio Window Grille, Casa del Conde de Toledo

Fig. 116.—Typical Andalusian Street with window grilles a feature, Ronda

Fig. 117.—Simple Ronda Houses which achieve distinction with iron work

FRENCH WROUGHT IRON

N surveying the entire realm of iron
work, the eminent authority on the
subject, J. Starkie Gardner, comes
to the conclusion that to the French
goes the "palm in ironworking, for their delicacy of execution, refinement of design and inventive genius." * And not without good cause.
Although at certain periods Italian, Spanish,
and English craftsmanship ascended loftier
summits in iron work than did the French,
nevertheless the latter's influence and superi-
ority continued for longer periods than any of
the others. It increased gradually with the
Crusades, subsided and awaited its chance during the Renaissance, and then, when the craftsmen of other nations (except England) were
retrograding in the revelry of Baroque, Rococo,
and what followed, France asserted her genius
and extended her influence not only to all of
Europe but even to her distant colonies. The
work of Tijou and his followers flavored the
work of England, while the iron work of the
seventeenth and eighteenth centuries in Germany, Italy, Spain, Portugal, and Mallorca
can with propriety be adopted by any French
town. In fact, "never since the destruction of
the Roman Empire has such unanimity in matters of art prevailed among the nations of Europe." *

American courses of study in art too often
treat of French architecture in a deprecating
manner, inviting an unfavorable comparison
between the best of the Italian Renaissance
with the feeblest of the French Rococo. In all
fairness to iron work of the latter period it will
be remembered that, even at its lowest ebb,
Italian craftsmen thought it sufficiently excellent to emulate. The superb workmanship
existing in the entire realm of French iron,
coupled with imaginative design (which up to
the seventeenth century even the Italian purist
must acclaim), should at least merit unprej-
udiced scrutiny by the open-minded designer.
To scoff architecturally at any period of French
iron work is more often indicative of a lack of
knowledge of existing achievements, than evidence of broadly cultured discrimination. If
in many examples of post-Renaissance work
wrought-iron designs are more appropriate to
cast iron or bronze, they at least have admirable *motifs* to their credit; in fact, it is a rare
day when some idea or application cannot be
culled from French iron work of good lineage.

* Gardner, "Ironwork," II.

ELEVENTH AND TWELFTH CENTURIES

The charm of early French work of the
eleventh and twelfth centuries is as contagious
as in any period following—perhaps more so.
The iron work of this period will forcibly recommend itself to any one who feels strongly that
iron should frankly profess its hammer and
anvil origin, and not appear an imitation of a
design more suitably cast. Iron retained its
simplicity until the end of the twelfth century,
content with chisel- and punch-marks for surface decoration. C-scrolls were inclined to coil
up into circular rings, instead of the quatrefoil
of Italy, Spain, and England.

Although there are museum pieces in France
of Roman relics, even antedating any iron work
of English origin, it was not until the eleventh
century that French iron went about the serious business of making history. The first work
which can be termed "French" shows the same
fondness for C- and S-scrolls as does the English "St. Swithin" grille of the same period.
Grilles at Conques (Aveyron) are unique for
France and are among the best of twelfth-century work, consisting of varying C- and S-
scrolls in nine separate screens between the
pillars surrounding the sacristy. They are protective and utilitarian as well as decorative.
The hinges of Angers Cathedral, probably of
the twelfth century, are reminiscent of English
or Norman examples; crosses and crescents
make a pattern over the entire door without
any reference to the actual concealed hinges.
Other twelfth-century work enlivens interest in
Le Puy-en-Velay, Pontigny, Orcival, Cham-
pagnac, and the Abbey St. Jean les Choux.
Perhaps the doors to the cloisters of Durham
Cathedral were produced in France (1135);
parts are not welded as in English work.

95

THIRTEENTH CENTURY

Iron work continued the traditions of the preceding century but added stamped work to its repertoire. The results of this new device chiefly enriched Isle de France architecture or work directly influenced by it, although some traces occur in Auvergne. Stamped work was not, as its name suggests, the sterile product of a soulless machine, but was the personal hammered result of an intelligent smith employing dies. The method required the imbedding of hammers in the heated metal, bearing the reversed modeling of the desired ornament, similar in principle to what is now termed "swage" work. It is a matter of controversy whether the credit for the invention is due to French or English craftsmen. Suffice it here to say that the new method was in vogue but a relatively brief period and produced lesser works in England than France. Its climax culminated in the hinges of the Porte Ste. Anne, Notre Dame, Paris, by the great artisan Biscornet (Figures 125–7). These hinges have been the subject of voluminous discussion, particularly concerning the method of simulating the reeding of the stems. Some theories make them out to be cast, Viollet-le-Duc conceived that small rods were welded together, while authorities such as J. Starkie Gardner decide that the delicate and deep incisions or grooves were tooled on a single flat strip of hot iron. As is usual with extraordinarily fine mediæval iron work, the devil is supposed to be the collaborator, if not the sole author. Other stamped hinges of

early types are to be enjoyed at Rouen, Sens, and Noyon, while a more developed stage was at Braisne (near Soissons) in a decorative grille with stamped conventional leaves and grapes. The change of fashion ushered in by the Louis XV style incited the destruction of most early simple C-scroll grilles, so that only a few of this period survive, such as one in the choir of St. Germer near Beauvais, fragments of St. Denis, Cluny, and a few scattering others. In the thirteenth century the popular *motif* was the vine, but sometimes the trefoil or cinquefoil held the field unchallenged or in conjunction with fruit or rose-like flowers. A repetition often occurring was a tongue between two unequal scrolls for terminations. The arrangement in design was generally geometrical.

France established leadership in the Gothic style by the end of the thirteenth century and extended her influence to England, Belgium, and particularly Germany. Her iron work was emulated, but not to an equal extent with her architecture. The admirable stamped work of the period under such masters as Biscornet (and in England under Leightone) for the time being animated and stimulated the craft. However, stamping, like many another interpretation of a medium, which in the hands of a master was a legitimate and inspiring expression, was later corrupted into a degenerating influence by inferior artisans. No meritorious stamping survived the close of the century.

FOURTEENTH AND FIFTEENTH CENTURIES

Italian traits became assertive in sheet-iron usage both in grilles and hinges, of two and even three thicknesses. The fourteenth-century grille is typified by one in the cloister of Le Puy-en-Velay, composed of vertical bars hammered into caps and bases at the ends, garnished by crockets and terminations of sheet iron welded and rivetted. Grilles in general were of "small vertical bars threaded vertically or diagonally, enriched with pierced plates or borders," * based on geometric forms. Quatrefoil and foliage compositions were imported freely from Italy. One of the earliest examples of "tracery grilles" was in the choir gates

* Gardner, "Ironwork," I.

formerly in Rouen Cathedral. The quatrefoil was diagonally arranged at Langeac (Haute Loire). A field of S-scrolls surmounted with hooked and spiked standards comprises an interesting grille at Troyes Cathedral. Decorative window grilles made some of their earliest appearances at Chabot and Troyes Cathedral. Those in the house of Jacques Cœur at Bourges are distinctly Spanish in the split-bar device.

Plain grilles and tomb rails did not enjoy the same favor as in England at this time. Hinges became severe.

In the fifteenth century French iron work became renowned for "chiselling from the solid locks, keys, bolts, knockers, coffers, caskets, gratings, and screens." * It is regrettable that the direct means of the smith in working the metal when hot was abandoned, yet the high quality of craftsmanship is somewhat compensating. The work was characterized by being mediæval in spirit, flamboyant in detail and minute in scale, with architectural usage of figures, canopies, mouldings, and crockets. Designs were carved chiefly from the solid, "whether elaborate or simple, vertical, compact, and restrained." *

Other phases of iron work developed old tendencies or varied them slightly. Locks became a matter of personal pride with the smith, who fashioned such complicated movements that

*Gardner, "Ironwork," I.

sometimes each required several keys. Sheet iron was increasingly used, either being pierced for tracery or else rivetted together to form panels (within a frame) or hinges. Railings in Toulouse Cathedral modified the treatment of previous standards in the manner of the famous Siena grille in the Palazzo della Signoria. Screens in the Collegiate Church of St. Quentin, at Notre Dame, Paris, and some window grilles at Dijon, are of fifteenth-century origin. One at St. Sernin is ornamented by naturalistic oak leaves and acorns. Caskets (for jewels, etc.) were of two types, being either a steel box 8 or 9 inches long with barrel lid, or a wood box with flat top, both having in common iron bands and plates with pierced tracery or inscriptions.

RENAISSANCE (SIXTEENTH CENTURY)

The smith was hesitant in accepting the new design and ornament, and moreover seems to have been but seldom employed by the architect in the early part of this period. Few great works were executed. Technically there were no radical changes, although *repoussé* was often substituted for the old method of chiselling. Under Henry II artisans were sent to Italy for study, yet they clung tenaciously to hereditary ornament and individuality. Under Henry III emphasis was placed on the trivial and delicate forms of iron, with frequent return to chiselled ornament. Jewelry-like craftsmanship created in abundance such forms as buckles, whip handles, and mounts for purses (*escarcelles*); keys became fashionable and were worn as jewelry. The "Strozzi key" to the apartments of Henry III was one example of the high esteem to which ornamental keys clambered, selling later for £1,200.

The craft seemed content to doze in the

apathetic state which had paralyzed its energies at the end of the fifteenth century. Occasional exertions, however, hopefully indicated that forge fires were not entirely burned out. An early Renaissance grille occurs at the Château Amboise, of vertical bars with occasional lozenge-shaped panels. A defensive park railing was constructed for Louis XI at Plessis-lès-Tours. Domestic requirements created a demand for firedogs, including kitchen types with spits, two or more cressets and swivel brackets. Large courtyard well-heads may be judged by those at Hotel Cluny, Dijon, Beaune, Marcoussis, Nantes, and Troyes. Occasional iron chairs, benches, small coffers, and plaques for furniture were wrought. Cursinet (died middle seventeenth century) was the foremost exponent of damascening gold and silver, an ornamentation of iron beginning to grow in favor. No armor of importance was wrought during the Renaissance in France.

LOUIS XIII (1610–1643)

The Baroque in France ushered in an entirely new conception of the possibilities of iron. Mediæval restraint in craftsmanship was released by the rapidly growing tendencies in architecture, which were to culminate later in the excesses of the Rococo under Louis XV. Gardner sums up the characteristics of the period as favoring designs cut into panels and dependent largely upon the repetition of

scrolls; "scroll work simple and less frequently broken or reversed than under Louis XIV; . . . collars much used; leaves sparingly and generally small, sheathing slightly crinkled and in pairs, with stems often beaded. If large leaves were introduced they were rather crudely modeled acanthus with blunt, unsophisticated lobes; palm leaves were not rare; rosettes were tame and large fleur-de-lis were frequently combined in designs." The period brought in foliated balustrades and railings, composed generally of scrolls and curves.

Among the best-known staircases are those at the Palais Royal and Bibliothèque by Antoine Lemaître, and the Escalier Royal at Fontainebleau to the Galerie d'Henri III. Other examples of the period are the screens to the Chapel de St. Eustache, Rouen Cathedral; grate work about the Château Wideville; rails and gates of the Parc de Carrouges; and the lyre-shaped balustrades and gates of the Porte Dauphine by Achille Poyart (1640) at Fontainebleau.

BAROQUE, LOUIS XIV (1643–1715)

The new order under Louis XIII had gradually developed greater skill, richness, and orderliness of design, leading by degrees to an increased vogue for gates; courtyard, garden, and park rails; screens; staircases and important balconies. The work of this period was "rich and costly, full of nobility and grandeur, executed by a generation of smiths lavishly patronized, and filled with emulation and pride of craft. The best designs were by the best architects." * J. Hardouin Mansart designed the

* Gardner, "Ironwork," II.

screen for the Château Clagny (1678) and that for Meudon; Girard that for St. Cloud (1680); Gittard that for Château St. Maur. The "publishing" craftsmen, Jean Lepautre, Jean and Daniel Marot, Jean Le Blond and Langlois, issued *Livres de Serrurerie*, of their designs for ornamental iron work. Perhaps the most magnificent example of iron craftsmanship, following the Spanish *coro rejas*, are grilles by an unknown hand, brought from Maisons to the Louvre, now serving to close off certain galleries.

ROCOCO, LOUIS XV (1715–1774)

The Baroque under Louis XIV gradually lost what reserve it had unwillingly inherited from the Renaissance, and exuberantly expanded into the Rococo under Louis XV, confusing itself with whimsical curves and lack of symmetry and repose. Details were forged beautifully with exquisite modeling and delineation, yet need to be considered as an entirety accompanied by their rich architectural settings. Viewed coldly and calculatingly, according to twentieth-century commercialized, arid precepts (whereby ornament is an expression of surplus cash-on-hand), the iron work of Louis XV revels in an excess of ornamentation. On the other hand, seldom if ever has the decorative iron of a period mirrored so precisely the traits of current society. The costumes of the day, the frothy social functions, the tortuous machinations of government, were not a whit less extravagant than the iron work.

The characteristics of the period may be judged by the work of Cuvilliès, who flourished about the middle of the century. There persisted a fondness for broken non-structural curves, lack of symmetry, queer cockscombs and endive leaves (distinctive of the Rococo), harmony of fan and shell *motifs*, "broken convolutions, and intertwining lines and elaborate ciphers." * The tendencies of the period varied, of course, because of the size of the country and mixture in population. The South and West workmanship is freest from mannerisms, while that of Burgundy and the East, taking Paris as a gauge, is more heavy and exaggerated.

Iron work was blessed with church and aristocratic patronage to such an extent that under Louis XV "nearly every cathedral was provided with grandiose choir screens." * Examples are those at Bourges and Amiens, twenty feet high, by Slodtz (page 106).

* Gardner, "Ironwork," II.

LOUIS XVI (1774–1793)

The excavations at Pompeii and Herculaneum awakened a renewed interest in the Classic, and extended a restraining hand on the exuberant spirit of the iron work of the reign of Louis XV. The influence told on Paris before 1750, but the new style is termed "Louis XVI." Churches and châteaux were already provided for; the smith could but turn his hand to iron for occasional public buildings and lesser private homes. One of the best examples is the courtyard grille by Bigonnet in the Palais de Justice (page 107). It appears more like cast than wrought iron—a process soon to be introduced in both Europe and America.

L. Ollivier

FIG. 118.—LOWER PART OF A PAIR OF GATES, ROUEN. (FOUR REPEATING SQUARE UNITS TO TOP)

Figs. 119 and 121, courtesy of F. Contet

FIG. 119.—THIRTEENTH-CENTURY DETAIL FROM GRILLE IN SAINT-ÉTIENNE, BEAUVAIS

FIG. 120.—UPPER TWO-FIFTHS OF A PAIR OF THIRTEENTH-CENTURY CHANCEL GATES

FIG. 121.—THIRTEENTH-CENTURY GRILLE NOW IN CLUNY MUSEUM, WITH STAMPED TERMINATIONS

These illustrations typify early French fondness for beating dies into the hot metal to form terminations, and for reeding enclosing stiles

FIG. 124.—FIFTEENTH-CENTURY FRENCH GOTHIC GRILLE
DETAIL, NOW IN NATIONAL MUSEUM, FLORENCE

Les Archives Photographiques d'Art et Histoire

FIG. 123.—FOURTEENTH-CENTURY
GRILLE DETAIL, CLUNY MUSEUM

Courtesy of F. Contet

FIG. 122.—TWELFTH-CENTURY GRILLE DE-
TAIL. CATHEDRAL OF LE PUY-EN-VELAY

Fig. 125, Les Archives Photographiques d'Art et Histoire; Fig. 126, courtesy of F. Contet; Fig. 127, from a photograph by Alinari

FIG. 125 (ABOVE AT LEFT).—NORTH DOOR; FIG. 126 (ABOVE AT RIGHT).—DETAIL AT JAMB, EAST DOOR;
FIG. 127 (BOTTOM).—DETAIL OF RIGHT DOOR, MAIN FAÇADE
WROUGHT-IRON HINGE DETAILS OF CATHEDRAL OF NOTRE DAME, PARIS

Courtesy of Victoria and Albert Museum

FIG. 128.—CHEST HINGES—LEFT, WITH THIRTEENTH-CENTURY STAMPED TERMINATIONS (21¼ BY 15 INCHES), AND RIGHT, WITH FOURTEENTH-CENTURY REPOUSSÉ LEAVES

Courtesy of F. Contet

FIG. 129.—PRE-RENAISSANCE WROUGHT-IRON ESCUTCHEONS, FROM THE BIRET COLLECTION, CALVET MUSEUM, PARIS

"Anciens Chateaux de France," F. Contet

Fig. 130.—Porte de la Nymphée, Châteaux de Wideville. (Louis XIII)

Fig. 131.—Porte de la Galerie d'Apollon, Louvre. (seventeenth century)

Figs. 132 and 133, courtesy of F. Contet

FIG. 132.—GRILLE IN THE CRYPT, CATHEDRAL OF BEAUVAIS

FIG. 133.—GATES TO THE CHÂTEAU, OISILLY

The sixteenth-century grille to the left and the Louis XIV to the right, give a general idea of the changes in design and craftsmanship during a century and a half

FRENCH WROUGHT IRON: ILLUSTRATIONS

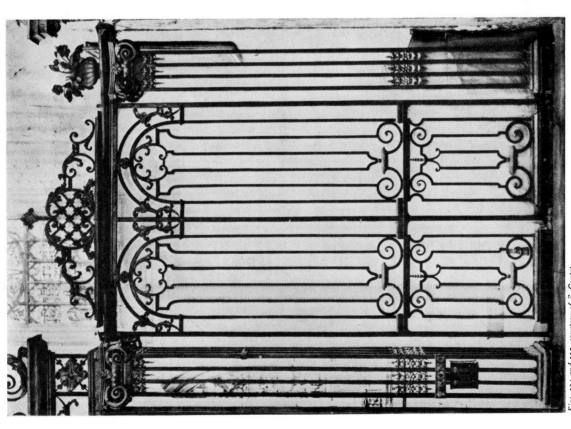

Figs. 134 and 135, courtesy of F. Contet

FIG. 134.—CHOIR GRILLE IN THE CHURCH OF S. ETIENNE, BEAUVAIS

FIG. 135.—DETAIL OF GRILLE AT THE *PLACE STANISLAS*, NANCY

These Louis XV baroque grilles indicate the range which restraint, and lack of it, attained. The more logically structural a design, the more satisfactory it is in any style

Courtesy of F. Contet

FIG. 136.—ENTRANCE GRILLE TO CHOIR, CATHEDRAL OF NOTRE DAME, AMIENS. (1761)

This is considered one of the best examples of Rococo smithing; it was designed by Michel-Ange Slodtz, architect to Louis XV

FIG. 137.—GRILLE TO THE COURT OF THE PALAIS DE JUSTICE, PARIS, BY BIGONNET. (LOUIS XVI)

Some of the traits of the Rococo still cling to the cresting, and in the use of swags and acanthus, but the restraining influence of the Classic is clearly evident in the general *parti* when compared to the Rococo screen on the page opposite

WROUGHT IRON IN ARCHITECTURE

FIG. 138.—HOTEL D'ARGOUGES, 16 RUE SÉGUIER, PARIS. (1695)

FIG. 139.—FRENCH DESIGN, MILITARY BARRACKS, BRAGA, PORTUGAL

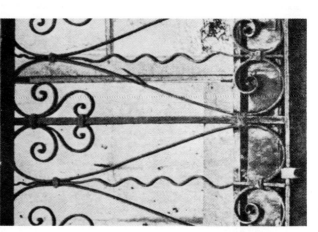

FIG. 143.—20 QUAI DE BÉTHUNE, PARIS

FIG. 142.—20 QUAI D'ORLÉANS, PARIS

FIG. 141.—24 QUAI D'ORLÉANS, PARIS

SEVENTEENTH-CENTURY BALCONY DETAILS

Figs. 138, 140, 141, 142, 143, courtesy of F. Contet

FIG. 140.—16 QUAI DE BÉTHUNE, PARIS

IRON WORK *of* BELGIUM *and* HOLLAND

AUTHORITIES with one accord agree that wrought iron work of the Netherlands during the fifteenth century was the equal, and in many ways the peer, of contemporary craftsmanship in other countries. Yet a curious fact is that there are scarcely any extant traces of preceding work. That there were notable examples of thirteenth- and fourteenth-centuries' smithing cannot be questioned in the light of the marvellous achievements of the succeeding century, but what they were or may have been like is written on one of the several lost leaves in the history of iron work. Charles ffoulkes in his "Decorative Ironwork" opines that the earliest iron of the Netherlands was generally strong, practical, and often purely protective in purpose, like that in the treasure chambers of Bruges, of C- and S-scrolls.

FIFTEENTH CENTURY

Hedged in geographically and politically as were the Netherlands, it would seem but natural that the iron work should be a confused assortment of borrowed mannerisms lacking individuality. The contrary is true. While there are noticeable traits pointing southward toward France, there is enviable originality pervading the craftsmanship of this period, and a decided influence emanating to England across the Channel. Gardner states that the vine was given a new interpretation, that "leaves were symmetrically cleft like those of the thistle, and grapes were oval in shape like the prickly pear." Hinge terminations were apt to be partial to the fleur-de-lis. The outstanding craftsmen were of the Matsys family of Louvain (also spelled Massys or Metsys), the most talented being Quentin.

Existing examples of this century are widely scattered. The great church at Breda, Holland, has an interesting railing with twisted, woven iron bands to imitate basket work. Liége and Louvain in Belgium enjoyed particularly fine craftsmanship, some of the best examples being the treasury door of the Cathedral (page 110), and some presses in the Church of St. James, both at Liége. Hinges of the church of Notre Dame, Hal, are also noteworthy (page 110). Moulded constructive iron work beautifies spires of Bruges, Ghent, and Antwerp. The iron work of St. George's Chapel, Windsor, having its main features of perpendicular Gothic with flamboyant details and not even approached by any similar English work, is thought to have been executed in Belgium. Tradition credits it to Quentin Matsys for Edward IV. It is one of the richest achievements of the century, in full relief and most minute in detail, comprising principally two gates about 7 feet high, flanked by two much higher hexagonal piers (page 115).

SIXTEENTH CENTURY

As in every country, the history of wrought iron was dependent upon the whimsies of politics. The progress for the first half of the century continued without interruption. What summits it might finally have scaled is problematical, but a turn of fate delivered the Netherlands to Philip II of Spain in 1555. The extreme cruelty of the barbarous Duke of Alva with his 20,000 troops, leading to the revolt of the United Netherlands in 1568, started warfare which lasted for eighty years. The tortures of the Inquisition drove hundreds of artisans into foreign countries. The effect on the Lowlands was to stamp out the crafts, while the results in England were to change the nature of iron work because of the large number of Flemish workmen there employed, and thus to produce the mannerisms characterized by the so-called Jacobean style.

Before the Spanish domination and oppression there had been diversified employment for decorative iron: protective grilles for doors, windows, and chapels, often in fleur-de-lis patterns; window gratings of vertical bars, frequently octagonal in section, with crudely moulded caps and bases; or interlacing bars producing patterns of rectangles or lozenges. Not many great monuments still exist, but examples of smithing may be found in some lunettes of the Hôtel de Ville of Brussels; a tabernacle grille from the Chapel of the Counts of Flanders and a window grille from St. Bavon, both from Ghent and now in the Victoria and Albert Museum (page 111); hinges at the Hôtels de Ville of Bruges and Ypres; and some of the Matsys chandeliers, as of Louvain, St. Bavon, Ghent, and St. Peter's, Bastogne. Only rarely has a screen of the Renaissance survived. Sign and lantern brackets became numerous, and although only a few remain, they indicate magnificent and picturesque forging. After the beginning of the century wall anchors became characteristic, recording date, trade-mark or initials. These were sometimes influenced by tracery or fleur-de-lis designs, and usually bound from ten to twelve courses of brick. Fascinating chandeliers, fire-dogs, gridirons, and cooking utensils were forged. Not only English smithing was affected, but German as well. For a time

armor made an enviable reputation for Flemish smiths. The gates to Bishop West's Chapel at Ely (1515-1530) were probably by Flemish workmen.

After the Spanish occupation but little iron work was produced; what still remains is quaint and full of interest. Design was influenced by the Italian Renaissance as adapted to suit northern conditions, as well as Spanish fondness for rich ornamentation. Cranes were conspicuous until the seventeenth century, as at Hal, Breda, Bois-le-Duc, Zutphen, Ypres, and Dixmuiden. Candelabra in Belgium churches were more or less of a type composed of a tripod foot and angular step, interrupted by a hoop or moulding, and supporting circles or sometimes rows of lights stepped one above another. Lecterns boasted simple legs with well-fashioned mouldings, supporting leather tops.

SEVENTEENTH CENTURY

Spanish domination virtually ended all smithing of indigenous character in design. Not many crestings of the sixteenth or seventeenth centuries survive of the relatively few executed; the oldest are openworked crosses. In Holland roof ridges and gables were sometimes ornamented by finials or crestings, while in the fa-

mous Vleeschal (Meat Market), Haarlem, even dormer ridges were frilled with richly worked scrolls. National individuality had run its course with the turbulent century or more of war, so that by the middle of the seventeenth century and after, French precedent in the main was followed.

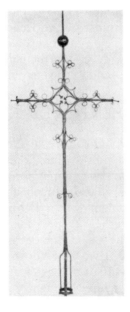

Figs. 144 and 146, courtesy of Charles ffoulkes

Fig. 145, courtesy of Victoria and Albert Museum

FIG. 144.—DETAIL OF TREASURY DOOR, S. PIERRE, LIÉGE. (THIRTEENTH CENTURY)

FIG. 145.—FLEMISH GABLE CROSS. (SIXTEENTH CENTURY)

FIG. 146.—DETAIL OF CHURCH DOOR, NOTRE DAME, HAL. (FIFTEENTH CENTURY)

Height, 8 feet 11 inches; width, 3 feet 7 inches

Courtesy of Metropolitan Museum of Art

FIG. 147.—DUTCH-FLEMISH RAILING.
(SIXTEENTH CENTURY)

Courtesy of Charles ffoulkes

FIG. 148.—HÔTEL DE VILLE, BRUS-
SELS. (THIRTEENTH CENTURY?)

Courtesy of Victoria and Albert Museum

FIGS. 149 (LEFT) AND 150 (RIGHT).—TABERNACLE DOOR FORMERLY IN CHAPEL OF THE CASTLE OF THE
COUNTS OF FLANDERS, GHENT. (SIXTEENTH CENTURY)

Fig. 152, courtesy of Victoria and Albert Museum

FIG. 153.—S. PIERRE, LOUVAIN. (SIXTEENTH CENTURY?)

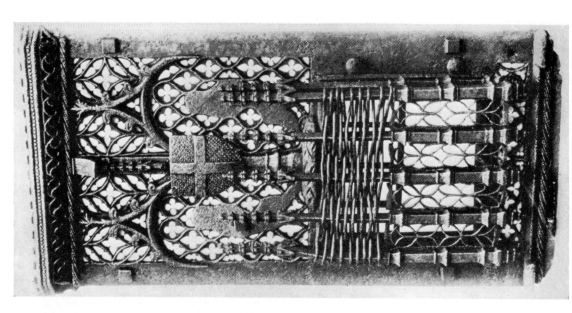

FIG. 152.—FLEMISH, END OF FIFTEENTH CENTURY. (8½ BY 17 INCHES)

Figs. 151 and 153, courtesy of Charles ffoulkes

FIG. 151.—HÔTEL DE VILLE, LOUVAIN. (FIFTEENTH CENTURY)

ENGLISH WROUGHT IRON

I T must be granted to the credit of English iron work that it maintained a higher general average and national individuality, from the eleventh to the nineteenth century, than did that of perhaps any other country. Although Flemish workmen in the early seventeenth and Tijou in the late seventeenth century left their impress on English work temporarily, the foreign influence is as nothing compared to French flavor in iron work on the entire Continent. After the sixteenth century iron was unfortunately worked much as wood or cast bronze, it is true, yet never to the degree as in French Baroque or Rococo. English iron was not always inspired, but neither was it trivial nor undignified. At its best it may not have climbed the dizzy heights of the fourteenth- and fifteenth-century Spanish, but at its worst neither did it descend to the latter's unworthy French imitations of the seventeenth and eighteenth centuries.

In recent years there has been considerable justification for emulating English seventeenth-century precedent in American work, the architecture of which invited it. In too many instances, however, it unfortunately is not inspired by the best of the English craftsmen—Robinson, Partridge, Buncker, or Warren—but by an imitation of an imitation. The result is that the most flagrant carpentry faults, which exist even in the best English work to some extent, are copied with a gusto as though they were the most desirable qualities. True iron craftsmanship had ceased to confine itself to the natural forms of the metal by the fifteenth century in England; thereafter more and more artificial forging methods were relied upon to assemble the various members. The natural consequences were that the inferior designers resorted more to mortising and tenoning, after the manner of woodworking, than to using welding and piercing; this in turn led to frankly unstructural compositions with vertical bars seemingly heavy enough to support a weight, but which instead weakly meet scrolls amidships. A modern designer about to employ English precedent does well to investigate the vocabulary of the best craftsmen, whose work seldom if ever looks illogical and unstructural. There need be no limitations placed on the freedom of the design, but rather a nicer discrimination in the combination of *motifs*. It is interesting in our American Colonial work to notice occasional evidences that the craftsman who was accustomed in England to working with more mechanical aids than he had at his disposal over here, was forced to run vertical bars from top to bottom members without interruption, and to fill in between them with the scrolls or what-nots which he might have allowed to intersect the verticals had he had more tools. The danger of the present age, when anything which the client can pay for *can* be made, is that the designer forgets that he is supposedly designing in a metal which is forged at an anvil with a hammer when hot, and that he is not prescribing a design to be cast from molten metal or constructed of easily worked white pine. "English" iron work can be made no less charming if it be logical, structural, and inspired by the best antecedents; in fact there is scarcely hope of its being satisfactory to a discriminating eye if it is not the product of serious study.

ELEVENTH AND TWELFTH CENTURIES

Although the usage of wrought iron dates from dim antiquity, the earliest known protective iron work is the so-called "St. Swithin" grille at Winchester Cathedral, probably of 1093. Its revered and healthy remains, made up into four panels, now serve as a gate in the nave. C-scrolls are collared and welded to produce an interesting show. Undoubtedly this surviving veteran must have had similar cronies, less lucky in withstanding rust, change of fashion, and disregard for old age.

Up to the introduction of the pointed arch, France exerted but minor influence on English architecture or its accessories. The earliest English characteristics of iron were "strength, independence of architectural style, designs dictated by necessity or derived from symbols, embellished with ornament taken almost exclusively from the animal world." * Such peers were the Saxon smiths, that Norman workmen supplanted native ones in all the building trades except in forging decorative iron.

The hinges of the Normanesque period are of two general types: (1) Long iron straps with single or diverging scrolls foliated so as to unite the various planks as well as to serve as hinges,

* Gardner, "Ironwork," I.

and (2) crescent-shaped forms welded at the base of the main strap, and preferred because of great strength. The surfaces generally could boast only the zigzag pattern of chisel-mark decoration which has always been an international favorite (page 22).

Except for occasional church grilles, not much twelfth-century work survives. A grille consisting of gate and four panels still exists at St. Anselm's Cathedral (1093–1109); it is composed of C-scrolls placed vertically.

THIRTEENTH CENTURY

By this period French smiths had discovered the closely guarded secrets of ornamenting iron by beating prepared dies into the hot metal, and were using the process successfully and extensively. English smiths apparently used the method but sparingly; at least the only extant example is the Eleanor grille or "hearse" in Westminster Abbey by Thomas de Leghtone (spelled variously) of Leighton Buzzard in 1294 (page 119), costing £13 or about $600 in modern money.

Grilles of this century are too few and scattered for grouping by definite characteristics. Lincoln Cathedral has a simply designed one (with unfortunate modern gas-lights added). Grilles and rails were unashamed to borrow ideas freely from the trailing vine.

Hinges have a better longevity record than any other class of thirteenth-century iron work. No startling innovations were devised, but the calibre of smithing was advanced several degrees. The vine is grown on a grand scale on the Litchfield Cathedral doors, but the original work has been lamentably harrowed (supposedly "restored") in a foreign manner. The older crescent design is the basis for notable hinges of the Buttery, Merton College, Oxford, by Thomas de Leghtone. The hinges to the entrance of the Worksop Priory were peers among their fellows, exerting influence as distantly as Burford, Oxfordshire, and Abbey-Dore, Herefordshire. The increased expertness of the smith multiplied decoration at the expense of utility. Much strap-work of this period is purely ornamental, serving to unite vertical planks which composed the door but being quite independent of the actual business hinge. The flowing tracery and vine *motif* acquired a certain sense of grace. Forms taken from Nature were conventionalized with the aid of steel dies or stamps but not, however, after Leghtone.

FOURTEENTH AND FIFTEENTH CENTURIES

The focus of the smith's attention shifted from doors to church grilles. Such hinges as were forged showed less retrogression than was the case in France. The great hinge really expired with the close of the thirteenth century. The old virility had departed, never again to return to door hardware. Strap-hinges, such as they were, ended in the fleur-de-lis or the "double-dragon," long a favorite in German work. Workmanship was more akin to that of the locksmith than that of the blacksmith.

Changes in iron work followed those in architectural forms; consequently the tomb rail began where the hinge left off in usurping the smith's attention. Protective grilles made their

début with the increased value of effigies, which the vogue changed from flat reliefs in stone to full-round figures in alabaster. The majority were frankly utilitarian and simple, composed of plain massive bars. "The marble effigy of Queen Philippa, made for Westminster Abbey by Hawkin of Liége in 1367, appears to have been the first in England protected by a rail of vertical bars. These supported a heavy moulded cornice and battlements with massive standards at the angles, also battlemented and with prickets," * probably by the smith to the Abbey, Peter Bromley. At Canterbury Cathedral, surrounding the tomb of the Black Prince,

* Gardner, "Ironwork," III.

are "plain vertical bars set diagonally under a battlemented cornice, bearing stamped lion's heads and fleur-de-lis, and six battlemented standards with buttress supports," * serving as candle-holders. It is one of the oldest tomb rails, probably succeeded by many similar simple ones which have since been removed for a supposed lack of decorative value. At the beginning of the nineteenth century almost all the tombs in Westminster Abbey boasted grilles, but wholesale quantities were removed in 1820.

The fifteenth-century architect seems to have usurped much of the design which had previously fallen into the undisputed realm of the iron-worker. This marked the beginning of the end of genuine forge craftsmanship, a condition which unfortunately was to repeat itself in every country. When the smith permitted the architect to dictate designs in a material with which he was unfamiliar, sooner or later the demands forced upon iron violated the natural limitations of hammer and anvil with casting-like results. The cloud which was later to darken all genuine craftsmanship appeared on the horizon in the fourteenth century: there was less *blacksmithing* and more *locksmithing*, less individuality and more repetition of the same idea. The tendency was to forsake the tools of the smith for those of the carpenter—the saw, file, drill, and chisel. A bar instead of "threading" or piercing another, was "halved," mortised and sometimes even dovetailed! The chief features in design still included the quatrefoil divided by two diagonal members crossing in the centre, so that the interstices are trefoil in shape. Window grilles of square bars set diagonally, or round bars, terminated their vertical ends in forked fashion, or otherwise as spear-heads or arrow-points. Flowers were geometrically inclined, and crestings enamoured of the fleur-de-lis.

Tomb rails were destined to become more decorative early in the fifteenth century. Vertical bars were carried higher than previously, terminated in points and arrow-heads. Color too was introduced—the tomb rail of Duke Humphrey of Gloucester in St. Albans Abbey (1446) was entirely blue, while others preened themselves with gold, vermilion, and blue in combinations. A fifteenth-century grille formerly in the Snarford Church, Lincolnshire (now in the Victoria and Albert Museum, London), is an unusual type, having a base band of pierced quatrefoil *motif*, twisted bars, leafy

* Gardner, "Ironwork," III.

finials, and a cresting bearing an inscription. Its vertical supports have since been detached; to a degree it recalls Spanish design. The Fitz-Alan tomb railings of plain vertical bars at Arundel (1415) have superimposed strips of fretted sheet metal to form a crowning horizontal band of battlemented caps. The tomb grilles of Sir

Courtesy of Victoria and Albert Museum

FIG. 154.—ST. GEORGE'S CHAPEL, WINDSOR.
(END OF FIFTEENTH CENTURY)

Thomas Hungerford at Farley (c. 1415) and Doctor Ashton's in St. John's College, Cambridge (1522), have similar ornamental horizontals and vertical standards. A part of the grille at the left of the altar in St. George's Chapel, Windsor, is an excellent example of iron carpentry, and illustrates how a supposedly forged metal should *not* be used. There is not an indication of a single hammer mark, and when gilded it must have appeared to be wood. It was probably done during the last half of the fifteenth century; all details are Perpendicular.

Henry V was the first king to have a tomb grille built excelling those of prelates and nobility. In Westminster Abbey it marked the high point in monumental work up to its period, and, like its immediate predecessors, had bars "halved" together at points of intersection. The tomb grille of Edward IV at Windsor in turn surpassed all prototypes; it was most probably by Master John Tresilian, and took six years to complete. "The work for the actual monument comprises the pair of gates, 5 feet 6 inches high, between two half-hexagonal piers, surmounted by eight open cressets or lanterns, 9 feet high in all." *

Under the reign of the Tudors the craft in decorative iron deteriorated. German and Flemish workmen were given preference over native smiths and there was neither the patronage nor the demand for iron there had been. An interesting point, however, is that Henry VIII probably first introduced the use of iron for constructive purposes in England in the palace of Nonesuch.

* Gardner, "Ironwork," III.

THE RENAISSANCE—QUEEN ELIZABETH (1558–1603)

The decree of Elizabeth prohibiting further deforestation in the districts south of London decreased the production of iron materially; timber was adjudged more necessary for building and ship construction than for iron ore refining, especially since Spanish iron was cheaper than the native product. The iron craft had already hinted of retrogradation and by the end of the sixteenth century the evidences were clearly marked. It was not that the execution of the work was faulty but that iron was treated more and more like wood or a cast material. The architect dictated his designs to the craftsman who was constantly compelled to forge unnatural forms. English iron work in this and the following periods assumes mannerisms of cast work, and only on inspection can qualities of wrought work be discerned. The manner of construction changed for the worse: whereas pre-fifteenth-century grilles were frankly assembled by piercing, welding, and collaring component parts, after the Renaissance the woodworker's screws and mortises were relied upon.

More specific characteristics of Elizabethan iron work are illustrated in some of the tomb rails of the period. One of the earliest, Lord Wil-lyam's tomb in the Thame Church (1557), is chiefly interesting for spike terminations formed into well-modeled fleurs-de-lis, made perhaps with the aid of a steel matrix. These reach up 11 feet above the cornice and are used alternately with shorter bars bluntly pointed. Definite changes began to appear, as in the railing to Dean Wotton's monument (1560) in Canterbury Cathedral: the cresting is forged from a single flat bar, and angle standards are reduced to acanthus leaves 7 inches high. The railing to the Jennings Monument in Curry Rivell Church in Somerset (1593) has alternating plain and twisted bars, central parts hammered flat on edge, a border of S-scrolls above, and cresting composed of flat fleurs-de-lis alternating with flattened spikes. Many of the tomb rails have hollow box-like cornices embellished by "cable" mouldings and armorial bearings in relief. The first part of the period favored high standards erected at the corners holding banners or balls, while later ones subsided to about the average height of fleurs-de-lis and spike cresting. The use of heraldry with touches of color and gilt was not uncommon. Archbishop Parker introduced hour-glass stands about 1559; for a century or so they enjoyed a fairly popular existence.

JAMES I (1603–1625)

Monument railings did not differ from the Elizabethan ones. Mediæval traits were continued and exaggerated. The most notable example surrounds the tomb of Montague, Bishop of Westminister, in Bath Abbey, erected after his death in 1618. The cresting or cornice-plate is "moulded with an escalloped ornament"; a crowning staff standard is twisted and terminated in a ball and open fleur-de-lis, which is in turn surmounted by the bishop's arms under a cross; spikes are moulded; finials rise 4 feet in height; vertical bars pass through horizontals and have moulded caps and bases.

At the outset of iron working in the eleventh

century the English smith had devoted his main efforts to church screens; later, in the twelfth and thirteenth centuries, he shifted to door hardware; and in the fourteenth and fifteenth centuries to tomb rails; he was soon to turn to gates and fences after the sixteenth.

During the period of James I the forecourt was introduced, affording an opportunity for gates. These were the wooden forerunners of the great iron masterpieces by Tijou, Robinson, and Partridge, forged in the seventeenth and eighteenth centuries.

CHARLES I (1625-1649)

There are but few existing examples of the iron work of this period. Tomb rails adhered to precedent. Some innovations, however, were introduced in 1639 in the Duke of Richmond's Monument in the Henry VII Chapel of Westminister Abbey. It has a "pierced canopy of rich arabesque design in moulded frames, four-sided, and domed to support a winged figure of Fame. The four curving panels are of stout sheet iron, rivetted together, pierced and richly gilt, introducing different mottoes under coronets, crests and monograms." * It may have been suggested by Flemish work.

* Gardner, "Ironwork," III.

Iron work diversified its subject-matter more than in the previous period. Flemish influence grew more marked as the Spanish Inquisition drove ever increasing numbers of dissenters across the Channel. A font-crane in St. Alphege, Canterbury, is strictly Flemish. Iron became the mode for stair rails, brackets, scrapers, chests, and particularly weather-vanes. Inigo Jones seems to have introduced iron balconies in England at Kirby Hall, Northants (1636); later he used them at Thorpe Hall, Peterborough, and Hutton-in-the-Forest. They are characterized by extreme simplicity of plain or twisted bars, with a pair of twisted standards at the angles.

CROMWELL—COMMONWEALTH (1649-1653); PROTECTORATE (1653-1660)

Under Cromwell the craft lay dormant. For ten or twelve years scarcely anything was produced. Under the Protectorate iron work was again fanned into some semblance of its old popularity. Balconies became the order of the

day. By 1659 it is said they graced every house in Covent Garden. In fact, before the system of numbering houses became general, balconies served for identification in London by their gilding or coloring.

DOOR HARDWARE—RENAISSANCE THROUGH JACOBEAN

The great hinge had surrendered its spotlight rôle at the end of the thirteenth century, but with the Renaissance it made a modest re-entry. It was less pompous, but at the same time more useful in being practical as well as decorative. There were interesting H-types of great variation, particularly twin vertical plates, silhouetted at the ends in the profile of eastern domes or with the same profile reversed and pierced in the horizontal ends. A second device, even more a favorite, varied curving, twin cock's-heads into numberless designs. Some hinges were content with jav-

Courtesy of Victoria and Albert Museum

Fig. 155.—Chandelier Suspension-Rod (c. 1700)

elin points, while others boast scrolls, tridents, trefoils, fleurs-de-lis, leaf points, animal heads, etc. Diverging and recurving scrolls were useful in affording ample space for screws and bolts. Jacobean handles became specialized in being comparatively slender loops, ellipses, rings, and stirrups. The oldest and most popular knockers were forged in the guise of knightly rowel-spurs and, to a lesser degree, prick-spurs.

Window latches became agreeably attached to every house and household alike, and were probably as general a form of wrought iron as ever existed within a single country.

CHARLES II (1660–1685)

The Restoration is characterized by iron balconies on London houses, brought about by one of the Rules of Building after the Fire. The best of the period are in the High Street, Guilford, composed of "alternating plain and twisted bars, cressets over the heavy angle standards, and a central panel of two horizontal bars terminating in large thistle heads, crossed diagonally by bars ending in scrolls and spirals, with a small bird-like head between tulip leaves."*

Outdoor railings were inclined to be severe. The best known are those of the Sheldonian Theatre, and of the Quadrangle, Christchurch College, Oxford. The former is made up of short-length bars on a low wall, with spikes half the rail height, and two C-scrolls near the apex

* Gardner, "Ironwork," III.

of the central standard which rises higher. A most interesting fragment of the forecourt railing to the Lindsay house, London, by Inigo Jones, still survives. Of tomb rails only a few of the seventeenth century remain after the depredations of "restorers." One, of Archbishop Frewen's tomb (1664), consists of round bars with "standards javelin-pointed and twisted." The tulip was the favorite wrought-iron form from 1650 to about 1675, partly perhaps because of simple forging. After the Restoration it was rivalled by the oak, thistle, and rose with many petals (therefore no longer Tudor). Crestings were unostentatious and were usually made by extending vertical bars through the top horizontal member and terminating them with javelin-points or fleurs-de-lis.

TIJOU AND THE EIGHTEENTH CENTURY

The greatest single influence in English iron work from 1688 until the Adam Brothers, arrived from Paris in the person of William Tijou. Foreign workmen had been favored in the past by the Stuarts, and under Charles II and James II the French influence was making marked headway. It was not strange, therefore, that Queen Mary should take a strong personal interest all her life in Tijou's work, particularly since she was overseeing the new gardens laid out at Hampton Court. The great French craftsman was commissioned to create the enclosing gates and railings. Within a year of his arrival Tijou had set up forges at Hampton Court and started work on frankly French designs.

Tijou's iron, in the light of twelfth- to fourteenth-century craftsmanship, is difficult to consider as the product of anvil and hammer (page 125). If similarly designed in the twentieth century it would be better sent to a foundry for execution, than to a forge. However, whether or not one agrees with its fitness for expression in wrought iron, there is a "novelty and charm in Tijou's work due to his masterly ability in designing and embossing masks, garlands, diapers, acanthus, etc., of sheet iron, and using them in discriminating profusion, combined in the French manner with smith's work." * ffoulkes expresses profound admira-

*Gardner, "Ironwork," III.

tion for the technique of the Hampton Court screen, but comments that the vertical bars have no meaning or function. The original work has been so altered and removed that it is unfair to judge Tijou's ability by its present state. On the other hand, his iron under Wren in St. Paul's, London, has survived unadulterated. The ground floor windows, the lower tier, and those above in the choir, transepts and west front, as well as all the work in the choir, are still intact. The window frames were made from 1691 to 1697; the gates to the apse in 1697.

Tijou is more or less a mysterious figure in the history of English iron work. The interval between his sudden arrival and equally sudden departure to Paris reveals only a short period in his remarkable career. Apparently in England he basked in the favor of royalty and nobility, yet died penniless in Paris in 1710. His textbook on iron work is fanciful, including designs which baffle modern execution in wrought iron.

The period following Tijou, the eighteenth and nineteenth centuries, is renowned most for its iron gates. Particularly is this true at Oxford and Cambridge, in such colleges of the latter as Clare, St. John's and Wren's Library loggia of Trinity. Among the most prominent craftsmen were Thomas Robinson, Partridge of London, Warren, and George Buncker, who established most of the traits now credited as characterizing the eighteenth century. The best work of the post-Renaissance period was confined principally between 1700 and 1730.

The Puritans undid in a few years what smiths had laboriously worked for centuries to achieve in the pre-Reformation churches, by destroying metal work on a vandalistic scale. As proof, many chandelier rods alone remain where once there were suspended magnificent fixtures.

Work by the Adam Brothers became the architectural fashion about the third quarter of the eighteenth century. Their taste was accepted as law and the metal artisans were compelled to work accordingly. From a designer's view-point most of the results are charming, but certainly do not appear structural or wrought; they sometimes resorted to a combination of cast with wrought work.

Concerning the general characteristics of seventeenth- and eighteenth-century English iron work, D. J. Ebbets finds an "exuberance of invention displayed in its design and gracefulness and lightness of its detail, so surprising in such a stubborn material as iron, as well as the wonderful perfection of its execution." A distinctive characteristic of the period was the framework of panels connected by mortises and tenons, a feature introduced in the sixteenth century. Welding was employed for combining scrolls, for inserting minor panels into the principal frame, and for attaching leaves and husks, although this function was often performed by concealed countersunk rivets. "In the framework the joints were carefully set up while hot, to produce the sharp edges at junctions and to conceal the joint, the file being but rarely used to clean up the work." * Swage work diminished as time went on. Large mouldings were bent from sheet iron. Rivetting became popular for commercial reasons and replaced welding, so that by the end of the eighteenth century iron work was coarse and clumsy.

* D. J. Ebbets, "Examples of Decorative Ironwork of the Seventeenth and Eighteenth Centuries."

NOTE:—For a comprehensive survey of this period see "English Ironwork of the Seventeenth and Eighteenth Centuries," by J. Starkie Gardner. (B. T. Batsford, Ltd.)

Figs. 156 and 157 courtesy of Victoria and Albert Museum

FIG. 156.—LOWER PART OF CHOIR GATES, FORMERLY IN CHICHESTER CATHEDRAL. (LATE FOURTEENTH OR EARLY FIFTEENTH CENTURY)

FIG. 157.—REPRODUCTION OF LOWER PART OF GRILLE, ST. SWITHIN'S SHRINE, WINCHESTER CATHEDRAL. (1093 ?, OR EARLY TWELFTH CENTURY)

FIG. 158.—ELEANOR GRILLE, WESTMINSTER ABBEY, BY THOMAS DE LEGHTONE. (1294)

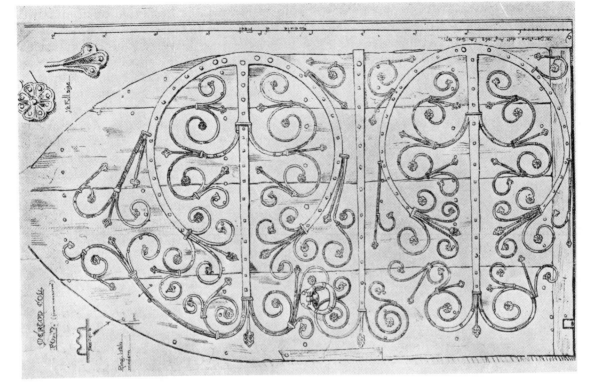

Fig. 160.—Door of Merton College, Oxford.
(middle thirteenth century)

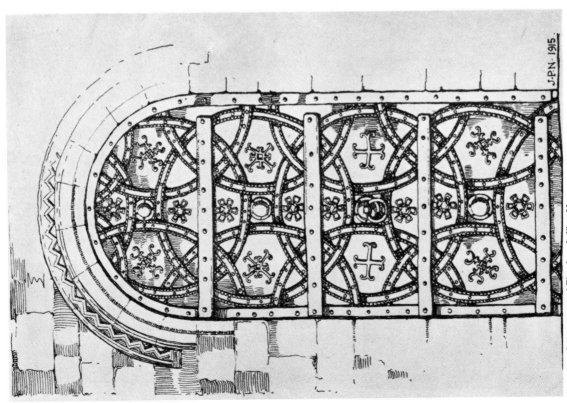

Figs. 159 and 160, courtesy of Victoria and Albert Museum

Fig. 159.—South Door, Skipwith Church, Yorkshire.
(twelfth century)

ENGLISH WROUGHT IRON: ILLUSTRATIONS

FIG. 164.—CHASTLETON CHURCH

FIG. 168.—BAMPTON CHURCH

FIG. 163.—CONDICOTT CHURCH

FIG. 167.—ST. ALBAN'S ABBEY

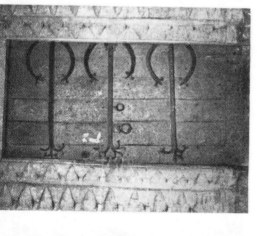

FIG. 162.—BARFORD. (NORMAN)

FIG. 166.—BROUGHTON CHURCH

FIG. 161.—STANTON HARCOURT

FIG. 165.—GOUDHURST CHURCH

Figs. 161, 162, and 168, from photographs by Percy Simms, Fig. 167, courtesy of Victoria and Albert Museum

The English countryside still abounds with a limitless variety of pre-fifteenth-century hinges of all types and terminations

Courtesy of Pennsylvania Museum, Memorial Hall, Philadelphia

Photographs on lower half of page, courtesy of Victoria and Albert Museum

FIG. 169.—ENGLISH STAIR-RAILING AND BALUSTRADE UNITS. (EIGHTEENTH CENTURY)

FIGS. 170 (ABOVE) AND 171 (BELOW).—EIGHTEENTH-CENTURY BALCONY AND DETAIL

According to the Museum catalogue, this balcony was "originally gilded and probably used inside, afterward painted green and used outside." It is more patently French in character, but shows in detail how the forging of leaves and flowers was accomplished and how assembled by rivetting and welding

FIG. 172.—FIREPLACE ADJUNCTS, MOSTLY ENGLISH, OF THE SEVENTEENTH AND EIGHTEENTH CENTURIES

At the left on the wall is an eighteenth-century gridiron from Sussex; next on the wall a seventeenth-century Italian gridiron; in the centre at the top an eighteenth-century English pierced grate-front; below it on the wall a Scottish toaster of the eighteenth century; and at the right on the wall, two gridirons of the seventeenth and eighteenth centuries. On the floor the andirons at the extreme left and right are eighteenth-century ones from Sussex; those in the centre are English of the seventeenth, while the cradle-spit supported on the latter is English eighteenth-century

125

Courtesy of Victoria and Albert Museum

FIG. 174.—SANCTUARY SCREEN
PANEL, ST. PAUL'S, LONDON

FIG. 173.—PART OF WROUGHT-IRON SCREEN, HAMPTON COURT PALACE, LONDON;
FROM THE DESIGNS BY JEAN TIJOU. (C. 1695)

These examples of the design and craftsmanship of Jean Tijou, executed at the end of the seventeenth century, are indicative of his manner, described
more in detail on page 118. He introduced an entirely new series of French forms into England which more or less influenced all subsequent work

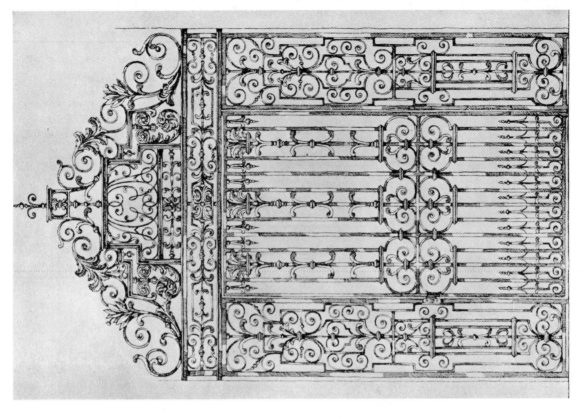

FIG. 176.—GATE AT FENTON HOUSE, HAMPSTEAD. (C. 1706)

The owner's initials, Joshua Gee, are worked into the design; the house was Wren

Figs. 175 and 176, courtesy of Victoria and Albert Museum

FIG. 175.—EIGHTEENTH-CENTURY GATE. (12 FEET HIGH)

When English work of this period is imitated, seldom is it as logically constructed as this

ENGLISH WROUGHT IRON: ILLUSTRATIONS

Figs. 177 and 178, from "English Ironwork of the XVIIth and XVIIIth Centuries," by J. Starkie Gardner. (B. T. Batsford, Ltd.)

FIG. 177.—GATES IN DULWICH VILLAGE

These gates are by George Buncker, one of the best eighteenth-century craftsmen

FIG. 178.—GATES TO TEWKESBURY ABBEY

These gates were made for Lord Gage, in 1734, by William Edney

Courtesy of Victoria and Albert Museum

FIG. 179.—SCREEN IN TEMPLE CHURCH, BRISTOL. (BY WILLIAM EDNEY, 1726)

Tijou's influence is more strongly marked in Edney's work than in that of any other contemporary smith. In this
example there is an admirable structural use of verticals which produce a stability not usually present in Tijou's work

From "English Ironwork of the XVIIth and XVIIIth Centuries," by J. Starkie Gardner. (B. T. Batsford, Ltd.)

FIG. 180.—GATES TO ETWALL HALL, MELBOURNE, DERBYSHIRE. (BY ROBERT BAKEWELL)

Courtesy of Victoria and Albert Museum

FIG. 181.—SCREEN FROM ST. JOHN'S CHURCH, FROME. (C. 1700. 15 FEET 10 INCHES LONG)

Modern imitations of this style of iron work generally fail to reproduce the fineness, delicacy, and variety of this screen, thought to be by Paris of Warwick. It is between the Lady Chapel and pews belonging to the lord of the manor

From "English Ironwork of the XVIIth and XVIIIth Centuries," by J. Starkie Gardner. (B. T. Batsford, Ltd.)

FIG. 182.—GARDEN ENTRANCE TO EXNING HOUSE, NEAR NEWMARKET. (BY WARREN)

FIG. 183.—SCREEN IN ALL SAINTS' CHURCH, DERBY. (BY ROBERT BAKEWELL, 1723–5)
This is considered by Gardner as the best example of Bakewell's work; it formerly extended across the east
end of the church enclosing the Cavendish Chapel, but is now partly altered and changed in its position

FIG. 184.—FANLIGHT FROM DRAPER'S HALL, LONDON.
(DESIGNED BY ROBERT ADAM, LATE EIGHTEENTH CENTURY)

GERMAN WROUGHT IRON

I T might not be amiss if across the face of all illustrations of German iron work the parcel-post admonition were stamped: *Handle with care*. From the earliest forging the craftsman's manipulation has been of the first order, often *too* good, in that his prowess at the anvil encouraged striving to achieve the impossible with iron instead of allowing it to follow its natural bent, and designing for it accordingly. Then too, if the designer be seeking so-called design inspiration he can more profitably turn to the originals rather than to Teutonic interpretations. The earliest examples of German work of the thirteenth century strove to imitate the French method of beating dies into the heated metal, but with no success comparable to such French masters as Biscornet. In the following century the French Gothic forms also were imitated, while at the time of Louis XIV and thereafter the work executed might to all appearances have been forged in Paris or, more accurately, the French provinces.

It is doubtful whether the modern designer will elect to imitate any of the characteristics which stamp iron as being German, in lieu of the other possibilities which display the strength and virility commonly associated with the material. Microscopic realism is never art, and least of all in such an untractable medium as iron. German work can always be distinguished by naturalistic forms which, when painted, might very well be the genuine article; by thin sheets of metal surface-scored, having the appearance of being worked cold and not displaying the spontaneity of Italian or Spanish chisel-mark decoration; and by the fondness for employing round bars instead of square ones. In terminating scrolls in imaginative animal heads, the German smiths contributed a genuine bit of artistry which is capable of admirable variety in a design by concentrating interest at definite points (pages 137 and 139). For the most part, it would seem wisest to follow French or Italian precedent first-hand, rather than an intermediate state of foreign interpretation.

ELEVENTH, TWELFTH, AND THIRTEENTH CENTURIES

The Romanesque in Germany preferred bronze to iron, so that the experimental beginnings of the latter are of later date than in either France or England. Scarcely any evidence remains to trace early characteristics. In Austria early iron work was purely decorative.

By the end of the thirteenth century the pointed arch had established itself in architecture and demanded the accompaniment of wrought iron. The first versions of grilles were inaccurate French translations, based on vertical bars filled between with C-scrolls ending in leaves and rosettes. The French usage of beating dies into the heated iron was not understood as the imitations indicate; a hammered and not stamped example in the Hildesheim Cathedral is composed of C-scrolls curling up in small leaves and flowers. At St. Michael's, Lüneberg, is a grille similar in the main to French and English examples of early origin but distinctive for scrolls terminating in small leaves, and a cresting consisting of bold trident spikes.

Hinges of this period, when they can be found, are not without interest or merit. Doors at Kaisheim and St. Magnus Church, Brunswick, are examples of a century when meagre demand offered few opportunities to the smith. Those of St. Elizabeth's Church, Marburg, with a curious cross in the middle, are good examples of the end of the period. Among other towns having contemporary iron work are Wahren (near Leipsig), Eisdorf, Magdeburg, and Schmalkalden (near Coburg).

In Germany the same tendency which carried Gothic architecture beyond the "limits of restraint and refinement imposed in France" was reflected in iron work, leading gradually to a general deterioration. Natural foliage was the basis of smithing throughout the Gothic period, and although it illustrated ability on the anvil, it failed to show a corresponding conception of good iron design. Had there been the same feeling for iron design as in Italy and Spain, the work of both might have been equalled.

FOURTEENTH CENTURY

The craft continued developing along the same lines as the previous century, deriving its main characteristics from the French Gothic school. Hinges usurped most of the smith's efforts; extant examples of this century are rare, but indicate that the vine which hitherto had been the only *motif* for rich hinges, shared honors with flat, lozenge-shaped leaves, deeply cut so as to form distinct quatrefoils. Among notable examples the best is at Schloss Lahneck on the Rhine, where the iron work almost entirely covers the doors. Other examples have spirals springing from the main member, more or less elaborate; fleur-de-lis often supplanted the cinquefoil; wheat-ear designs were used as in France. The inside faces of doors were often covered by decorated sheet iron.

Iron grilles of the period are particularly rare; there are probably but two according to ffoulkes.* One at St. Mary's, Wismar, is a cable pattern and knotwork of horizontal bars; another exists in the Chapel of the Cross at St. Mary's, Schloss Karlstein, near Prague.

* Charles ffoulkes, "Decorative Ironwork."

FIFTEENTH CENTURY

Grilles became more popular in this period and gave testimony that the smith was now able to diversify his attentions creditably. One of the best examples is in the Chapel of Bishop Ernst, Magdeburg Cathedral (c. 1498); there is elaborate Gothic tracery, nine pillars and a cornice—a *parti* general on the Continent at this time—but the workmanship smacks of wood joinery. At St. Ulrich's, Augsburg (1470), is a flamboyant grille with light and brilliant tracery constructed by welding and skilful collaring, surmounted by a simple cresting. Two good examples are by the hammer of Peter von Straelen (c. 1463) at Kempen and Straelen. Tabernacle grilles were a popular exercise in smithing; examples flourish at Vienna, Pressburg, Heiligenblut, Vordenberg, and König-grätz. One of the best came from Ottoburg, Tyrol, and is now in the Victoria and Albert Museum; it is excellent technically but is delicate after the manner of locksmithing.

Various changes developed in hinge work. By the fifteenth century the cinquefoil displaced the quatrefoil, as at Orb, Oppenheim, and Magdeburg. Notable hinges enrich the entrance of Erfurt Cathedral, having the vine pattern interpolated with rosettes and escutcheons of arms. Domestic door hinges were inclined toward the strap type, either plain or ornamented by superimposed pierced sheet iron; often these ended in a variety of arabesques. Pierced sheet iron work became common as in the rest of Europe, fashioned into tracery of a semi-architectural nature much like Gothic windows. Pierced ornament was often bounded by twisted rods which were applied along the edges and then beaten out at their extremities into complicated foliage forms. Door handles were crescent in form, "solid or richly pierced," the horns of the crescent being formed into dolphins, dragons, snakes, etc. Plain and twisted ring-handles continued into the Renaissance. Larger pierced handle-plates and escutcheons were modeled in the form of warriors. The thistle, later to become the most courted form of Nature, made its début.

German smiths were noted for armor from the fourteenth through the sixteenth centuries.

SIXTEENTH CENTURY BEFORE 1550

Door hardware for the most part continued as in the preceding century. Hinges were smaller and less impressive perhaps, but the usage of sheet metal remained unchanged. The strap was richly fretted, composed either of a single thickness of sheet iron or of superimposed sheets on a thicker plate, as in box- and cupboard-hinges. Earlier hinges had left the main strap unmolested but invited ornamental crescents or scrolls to spring from it; in this period the main hinge itself took to frolicking ways and spent its energy composing circular or leaf-shaped discs with no scroll appendages. Working the metal cold in this period exacted the same price it always has and always will, in producing results sadly lacking in spontaneity. It became common practice to line the inside of doors with pierced or embossed plates having iron straps at their junctures. Erfurt has a good example, although the best is said to be the Priory door of Bruck-an-der-Mur; the painting of panels in black, white, red, blue, and gilt has left traces which even yet are merry revelations. This inner ornamentation of doors spread to Bohemia, Poland, and Austria, maintaining a vogue in the latter country until well after the Renaissance.

According to ffoulkes* the craft at the beginning of the century lacked strength, virility, and spontaneity. Most of the screens of the period were painted, one of the best being at Hall, Tyrol, decorated in green and gold. However, by the middle of the century craftsmen of outstanding merit began to assert themselves, such as Jörg Schidhammer, Prague, an inventive soul who forged his iron in a graceful yet re-

* Charles ffoulkes, "Decorative Ironwork."

spectful manner. Examples from his anvil exist in the Cathedral of Prague; his railings around the tomb of the Emperor Maximilian I at Innsbruck are far better than the average contemporary work and even earn a high rating in the next period of the craft—the Renaissance. The thistle supplanted the vine as the parent symbol for decoration, and seems to have so impressed itself upon the imagination of the smith that without faltering he forged it into every composition. The plant sometimes had but a single termination, as in the hinge at Hagenau, or in the grille of vertical bars at the Cathedral of Freiburg im Breisgau (1538). If the thistle could not be coaxed into the iron whole-heartedly, a design was adapted from it. By mid-century designs were too often inclined to have meaningless members which cannot even be hailed as excellent decoration.

RENAISSANCE

The work executed from about 1550 to 1625 is with difficulty tagged by definite dates and clearly defined characteristics. The legend that a drop of the Virgin's milk fell on a thistle and turned its veins white, gained such credence that the plant became the foremost decorative form of Nature. It usually certifies sixteenth-century workmanship. Gothic tracery was widely used in this period, either plain or ornamented with the holy thistle; screens were often trellises with rectangular bars threaded diagonally; crestings were of scrolls or tracery. Threading or piercing one set of bars by another series at right angles was a favorite exercise to display the smith's skill, made more difficult by the introduction of complicated figures. More interest was often displayed in the braggadocio of the workmanship than in the sincerity of the design; pride was taken in welding several parts together without any undue swelling where the juncture would naturally show, as where leaves or stems sprouted from a parent branch. Plate metal was scored with lines in the manner since so beloved by the Teutonic smith, usually establishing his authorship beyond a shadow of a doubt (pages 137 and 142). From sheet metal were forged masks, heads, armorial bearings, angels, cherubs, etc. Much iron found itself shaped into well-

heads of fantastic, playful *motifs* (page 138), sometimes beautiful, otherwise curious, but always of interest. Church screens secured considerable attention, among the most important being those of the Fugger Chapel, St. Ulrich's, Augsburg, 1588 (page 140), and Maximilian's cenotaph of deep red and gold at Innsbruck (1580–'85).

The decreasing inventiveness of the smith changed his status and, naturally, the character of his work. Up to the Renaissance he had represented the most impressionable and popular of the crafts; for a century and a half smithing was and had been the outlet of the people's art; designs were made and executed by unsophisticated workers. But withal the sum total was not too encouraging. By the end of the Renaissance the smith was designing less as he was fettered more, by being given definite designs by the architect. He was less affected by the Renaissance than by the Reformation. Although some of the craftsmanship was technically excellent, the love of "manipulative skill" seems to have paralyzed the smith's sense of design and left him satisfied to repeat hackneyed forms *ad infinitum:* round bars were woven or threaded and their terminations coiled up as scrolls, leaves, and flowers, in stereotyped patterns.

SEVENTEENTH (AFTER 1625) AND EIGHTEENTH CENTURIES

Up to this period German work had a distinctive flavor readily distinguishable not only in traits of craftsmanship but in design as well. However, with the mounting of French political power went the influence of court entourage, to such an extent in fact, that in Germany not only did her princes ape French dress and mannerisms, but the designers of iron were well content to import Louis XIV *motifs*. German iron work of this period might easily be mistaken for provincial French. The Thirty Years War had badly handicapped the German smiths, so that when they again turned to decorative iron work, it was in a cramped vocabulary of mediæval phraseology. It was only to be expected that the feeble designs of the smith would fall victim to the prevailing popularity of French influence. After the middle of the century the smith relinquished his claims as a designer and accepted the dictates of whatever he was asked to execute. It must be said for Baroque and Rococo technique, however, that in perfection of detail it exceeded that of the mediæval or Renaissance. Much though it left to be desired in restraint and good taste in design, at least what it forged was amazingly executed; some of the volutes and scrolls almost baffle modern reproduction.

Late-seventeenth-century architectural design changed iron work for the worse by decreasing the already slim existing margin of restraint, and by needlessly complicating forms still further. Round rods were beaten out to imitate floral growths; large panels were unified by welding, no collars or rivets being employed; over-elaborated *motifs* toiled with increasing restlessness. The smith's own designs were confined to such minor exhibitions as wall-anchors, weather-vanes, sign-brackets, and finials, with an occasional domestic balcony or screen. A new departure in iron design, by Meister Johann Reifell of Constance, introduced the effect of perspective in grilles, arcades, balustrades, etc., by designs which converged to vanishing points; this idea was enthusiastically received by German and Austrian smiths of the Baroque and Rococo, although in other countries it was never used. Products of the less meritorious eighteenth century are more nu-

FIG. 185.—REALISTIC IRON SPRAY OF ROSES

merous and consequently better known than those of the seventeenth. The work of the latter century was often as magnificent as any in provincial France, expressed in rails and gates to parks or palaces, stair rails or balconies, and ecclesiastical screens. The railing in St. Mary's, Danzig, surrounding the tomb of Simon Bahr (c. 1620), is remarkable for the manner in which the vertical bars are split near the top into branching horns and become intermeshed with a series of rings. Prague has a rich assortment of iron of the seventeenth century. At the borders near Italy the Teutonic mannerisms were not pronounced; in fact, the excessive interlacing which was so generally popular was not present in screens, such as in Campo Santo of Salzburg, as far back as 1570.

The time limits of the German Baroque are sometimes placed as late as mid-eighteenth century, which would crowd the Rococo into the reign of Louis XVI. The Rococo should more nearly correspond with the reign of Louis XV; the style of Louis XVI had but little effect on Germany, because the French Revolution came too soon after the inception of the new restrained manner to allow it time to percolate across the Rhine. It may be said, concerning the differences between French and German Rococo, that the latter made "freer use of armorial bearings, cornets and ciphers,"* and that leaves were more crisp, shredded, curled, and veined, than in the French. The cartouche and similar shapes were used lavishly on a background of diagonal trellis straps with rosettes at their intersections. It has well been termed the "most sumptuous period of German iron work,"* although that very quality acted as a boomerang in defying restrained employment.

Smiths made merry with iron as though it were a plastic substance and used extravagant forms wherever feasible.

Vienna is everywhere rich in the forging of this period. The nine pairs of gates to the Belvedere Gardens, the gates and balcony at Schönbrunn erected by order of Maria Theresa, and the window gratings at the entrance of the Chapel of St. John Nepomuk (1744), are representative of German work as well as Austrian.

* Gardner, "Ironwork," II.

FIG. 187.—GOTHIC DOOR IN THE CHURCH OF MARIA-STIEGEN, VIENNA

FIG. 186.—"SACRAMENT-HOUSE" DOOR, KLEIN-ZELL, AUSTRIA. (FIFTEENTH CENTURY)

Both doors are built up of successive sheets of iron pierced and rivetted together; the one at the left is particularly vigorous and full of suggestion

FIG. 190.—BAROQUE SCREEN AND GATE, JOHANNESKAPELLE, VIENNA. (1758)

FIG. 189.—GATE IN CHOIR, PETERSKIRCHE, VIENNA. (SIXTEENTH CENTURY)

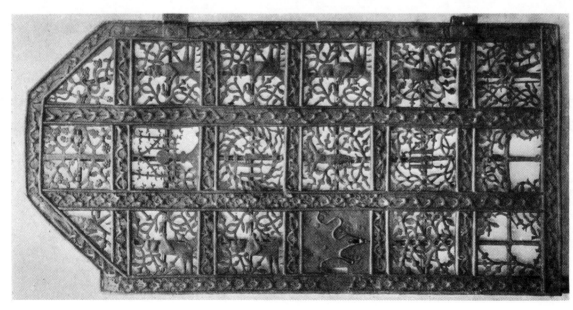

FIG. 188.—TABERNACLE DOOR, SPITALKIRCHE, KREMS. (FIFTEENTH CENTURY)

GERMAN WROUGHT IRON: ILLUSTRATIONS

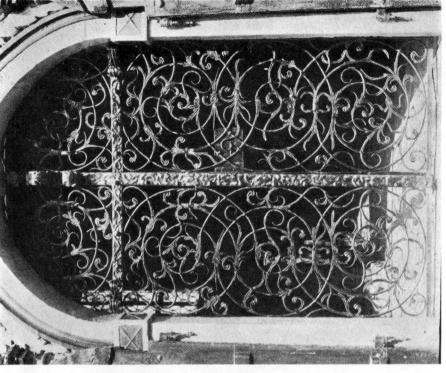

Fig. 192 (above).—Chapel Grille in Kalvarienberg near Gratz, Austria. (Seventeenth Century)

Fig. 193 (left).—Wrought-Iron Panel, Late Seventeenth-Century German

Height is 2 feet 7 inches

Courtesy of Victoria and Albert Museum

Fig. 191 (above).—Grille in Augustine Abbey, St. Florian, Austria. (Sixteenth Century)

The terminations as heads are amusing caricatures, and comprise the significant feature of the composition; the woven bars show the forging ability of the smith but not his good taste

WROUGHT IRON IN ARCHITECTURE

Fig. 194 (Left).—Entire View, and Fig. 195 (Right).—Detail, of one of twelve Railing Panels,
Well-Head at Bruck an der Mur, Austria. (By Hans Prosser, 1626)

While modern taste in design may not find application for this creation in its entirety, there are potential flower-boxes, lighting fixtures, and decorative panels

GERMAN WROUGHT IRON: ILLUSTRATIONS

FIG. 197.—ARCADE-FANLIGHT, ST. PETERS-FRIEDHOF, SALZBURG. (SIXTEENTH CENTURY)

FIG. 196.—LEOPOLDS-KAPELLE, KLOSTERNEU-BURG, NEAR VIENNA. (SIXTEENTH CENTURY)

FIG. 199.—PALACE FANLIGHT, PRAGUE, CZECHOSLOVAKIA. (8 FEET 10 INCHES BETWEEN STONE JAMBS)

Courtesy of Victoria and Albert Museum

FIG. 198.—SIXTEENTH-CENTURY GERMAN FANLIGHT WITH TYPICAL FORGING. (HEIGHT, 3 FEET; WIDTH, 7 FEET 10 INCHES)

Courtesy of Victoria and Albert Museum

FIG. 200.—SEVENTEENTH-CENTURY GERMAN FANLIGHT

FIG. 201.—GRILLE FROM THE FUGGER CHAPEL, ST. ULRICH, AUGSBURG

FIG. 202.—GATE TO THE CLOISTERS OF THE SALESIAN NUNNERY, VIENNA. (1720–30)

FIG. 203.—GERMAN WROUGHT-IRON HINGES

While this collection is labelled as dating to the end of the seventeenth century, it follows the traditions of work as early as the fourteenth.   The metal is scored in a manner never to be mistaken for anything but German workmanship; other countries used the punch and chisel mark as decoration, as on pages 8, 58, and 99, but with an entirely different effect

AMERICAN WROUGHT IRON

PRE-TWENTIETH CENTURY

IT would be of interest to know whether America came to be termed the "melting-pot" of the world because of her iron work. After reviewing existing examples it seems plausible to apply such a craft-term from Colonial to modern iron. While European precedent was followed only so far as the immigrant-craftsman could render existing favorites which were within the more limited means of forging at his command over here, yet the completed work has all the peculiar qualities which any product might be expected to have on being "melted down."

After a fortnight's excursion through Kent, Sussex, and Surrey one wonders if there be any originality whatsoever in the so-called "American Colonial" style; yet the iron work, although inspired in a measure by British tradition along the upper Atlantic seaboard, is in no sense as indebted to England as is the architecture. The building operations carried on by English settlers seem to have incorporated less iron work, at least in the New England states, than those by any other colonists. Boston, New York, and Philadelphia have a certain amount of early iron work, but scarcely any in comparison with the quantity produced by French and German smiths in New Orleans, Mobile, Savannah, Charleston, and the German settlements in Pennsylvania. Iron work which dates to the Revolution and the quarter century thereafter is fairly well confined to a narrow fringe along the coast, and then only the larger towns which seem to have been able to afford the luxury of importing smiths and iron.

Although early American iron of the North has all the hammered "ear marks" of foreign parentage, such characteristics do not readily condense themselves into well-defined design forms. During the seventeenth and early eighteenth centuries the work was of a simple, practical nature, as strap hinges; door hardware and knockers; fireplace necessities and conveniences, as fire dogs, cranes, skewers, toasters, kettle-warmers; cupboard, chest and wagon hinges, etc. Weather-vanes were not backward in appearing nor were footscrapers (pages 157 and 162), but more ornate forms—balconies, railings, fences, gates or grilles—were a development of the late eighteenth century, when the

worries of too much Indian and too little corn had been mitigated. When the first railings were forged they lacked the tortuous convolutions which were the vogue in Europe at the time, perhaps because of the puritanical tastes of their owners, but more likely because of the simple tools and apparatus available for their forging. That the iron was light and delicate may not have been so much a radical departure from what the smiths had been accustomed to forging in Europe at the time, as it was more likely one of those happy necessities which have so often contributed to superior design in diverse fields. Lightness of the metal stock probably indicates a frugal usage of an expensive import rather than any dislike for heavy members. English traits in design were more confined to ornamental features such as scrolls and the manner of employing them, rather than in the refined severity of top and vertical members of a railing.

After the Revolution when the northern states became less English in their constituents, French and German craftsmen affected the iron work. The former imported baroque roller-coaster curves in balcony panels or gate crestings, while German hardware in Pennsylvania duplicated favored forms of the *vaterland*, not only in silhouette but in scoring the metal's surface, as has been a Teutonic delight ever since the fourteenth century. Before the introduction of cast-iron ornaments in conjunction with wrought members, another change was brought about by the use of lead. Mr. Charles Kemp of Philadelphia has made this a matter of investigation for some time past, and has found that lead rosettes and sometimes even half scrolls were "sweated on" the iron (page 153). Not only on the Octagon House, Washington, D. C., is this usage of lead found to exist, but in many of the characteristic railings of Philadelphia, which have been painted over and considered cast iron as a matter of course. The design of iron in the North, even after the introduction of cast-iron ornaments, remained for the most part a severe *parti* of vertical bars for railings, balconies, and gates, softened by double or single C-scrolls back to back, or S-scrolls enlivened by additional smaller scrolls at the point of tangency to the vertical bar. Horizontal bands of scrolls at the top were not uncommon.

In gates an additional festivity was a series of scrolls and curves pyramiding up in the centre of the cresting.

The employment of wrought iron during the first half of the nineteenth century, including the period of cast iron addendas, did not greatly vary from the usages already mentioned for the last quarter of the eighteenth century. Lighting on a humble scale utilized wrought iron for the small "betty" lamps and candlesticks; iron standards for candles, very similar to modern "floor lamps," were of refined and delicate proportions which might well deserve modern adaptation to electricity (page 186); lanterns were principally of tin, while chandeliers were of brass or even silver, but rarely of iron.

In the North there seem to have been no eminent craftsmen specializing in smithing whose names have been recorded. Much of the forging, of course, was done as a matter of practical necessity in the age when a man with cultured taste could build his own house (often superior to that of the present-day architect), and could execute or direct the iron work to be made. No one thus far seems to have busied himself with the task of uncovering what history there is yet traceable concerning the outstanding craftsmen who must have been responsible for the work in Boston between the State House and the Charles River Basin, or Salem, New York, or New Castle, in addition to the hundreds of lesser towns whose iron must have been on a par.

In the South the iron work differs from that of the North both in its quantity and playfulness. Cities like Charleston and New Orleans still are the wealthy inheritors of balconies, railings, fences, gates, lamps, etc. Not only that, but even the names of craftsmen are known.

CHARLESTON

During the first half of the nineteenth century Charleston welcomed a number of craftsmen from Germany, chief among them being Werner (arrived 1828), who did perhaps more iron work than any other single person in that city. One Dothage worked for him from 1849 to '60, and is supposed to have been almost as capable as his employer; iron was also cast in their shop. The reputation of a colored man, "Uncle Toby" Richardson, who worked for Werner, gives him credit for being exceedingly gifted at executing work which was previously designed and laid out. Tunis Tebout, in the first quarter of the nineteenth century, is responsible for some of the finest city gates, railings and fences, characterized by simple bars large in section; associated with him was his partner, William Johnson. In 1820 Justi came from Germany to Charleston; one of his best-known achievements—and at the same time a good illustration of the effect of America on a foreign smith—are the gates to St. Michael's church (page 149). Although the metal is almost ribbonlike in thinness of section, the extreme delicacy is offset by structural members bounding the four panels, and the strong rosette accents at the corners. When Italian smiths of the seventeenth century employed ribbon wrought iron it looked decadent and entirely unsatisfactory, yet these gates by Justi, particularly in the lower half, are nothing short of inspired design. It is preferable to think that some one else added the scrolls of different scale above; it is curious to note that by this date Justi was apparently far more influenced by local work than by his *vaterland* training. Julius Ortmann, another prominent smith, came from Baden-Baden in 1847. Swedish iron was almost exclusively used in Charleston on account of its resistance to moisture and its superior malleability.

NEW ORLEANS

The city which has pawned least of its invaluable Colonial iron inheritance, and has at the same time the largest natural outdoor museum of diversified smithing, is New Orleans. For the information and photographs relative to it, we are indebted to Richard Koch, who is well versed in a subject which has always been of great interest to him.

The iron work of New Orleans traces a development through successive stages of European adaptation to the climatic and practical conditions of America, first by French and Spanish settlers, and later, after the purchase of Louisiana by the United States in 1803, by colonists from further north. The character of the iron work changed with the controlling factors of the various régimes, as well as with the varied purposes for which it was employed. It may be roughly divided into three stages and classes: first, the forged iron of the French and Spanish settlers with strongly marked European characteristics; second, or transitional period, of wrought structural members and cast ornaments in the Directoire and Empire manner of France, with a sprinkling of American innovations; and, third, entirely cast designs which continued until the present century. In the old French Quarter the extant work dates chiefly to the second period, while the entirely cast designs are found principally above Canal Street in the section occupied by the American colony after the 1803 purchase. Of the old iron work the best was done under the Spanish Governors using French designs, not only because that was the nationality of many of the workmen, but because of the universal influence of French taste at the time. It is curious that at Palma de Mallorca (page 91) railings were not radically different from certain ones in New Orleans, such as the Cabildo and others in its vicinity. Courtyards were more French than Spanish in character, and, strangely enough, rarely employed iron except in an occasional lantern or in hardware.

The principal use of iron was in balconies, and it is this unfailing characteristic which typifies the old streets even as they exist to-day. The railings usually show some simple repeated form of ornament with an elaborate centre panel, as a monogram flanked by variously shaped scrolls; these centre features gradually became popular in other forms of iron design. Designers did not hesitate to carry balconies around corners, and they were usually supported by double scroll brackets (page 147). Open balconies did not give sufficient protection from the rain and hot sun, so in many cases they were extended to the street's edge and supported on cypress posts. Examples may still be seen where part of the building is a balcony supported on brackets, while other portions are carried to the street's edge, reposing on cypress posts or iron columns which replaced them. As added protection from the sun and rain, balconies sometimes were surmounted by slender wrought-iron columns which supported a curved copper canopy above. In some cases additions are obvious, while in others the *ensemble* was designed as a unit, as in the courtyard at 920 Chartres Street—one of the rare examples where wrought iron is a part of the original design. The advent of cast iron encouraged a form of balcony extending to the street's edge and with a roof overhead; although the ornament was cast iron, the structural members which supported the roof and tied together the interlaced ornament were wrought.

Another distinctive iron usage was a wrought frame for copper lanterns on cypress supports. These served as the original street lights of the city, while to-day there are only very elaborate cast-iron ones for the use of gas. A sketch in George W. Cable's "Creoles of Louisiana" shows a wrought-iron bracket of Louis XVI design supporting an oil lamp which could be lowered by a cord attached to the building.

Of intrinsically fine old iron work but comparatively little is to be found to-day, and that only in unmolested places where fires and remodelings have not taken their toll. Very little is markedly of Spanish character, with the exception of the gateway of the Cabildo, which shows mouldings beaten from solid bars as in some of the old *rejas* of the Spanish cathedrals. There must have existed a market for cheap iron work, as is indicated by many extant pickets with ornamental castings which were easily duplicated and furnished in quantities. These early castings are restrained, some having mouldings that might be from Spanish grilles while others are adaptations of Louis XVI iron work. The use of cast ornament became more frequent in the second quarter of the nineteenth century, leading in the following quarter to the florid development after the mid-century.

Little is known of the artisans who created the early iron balconies, but there is a tradition that many of these were made in the blacksmith shop of Jean and Pierre La Fitte, the famous pirates. Other forges are associated with the names of Devault, Malus, Marre, Rouli, and Urtubise. It is known that many of the early French settlers were forcibly brought to New Orleans and there is a legend of such a visit of Manon Lescaut. Cast iron foundries of Shakespeare and Leeds are known of, and to-day the grandson of Mangier can relate how his grandfather cast the little ornaments to the pickets of many a familiar street front, and that the shop of Pelaine and Moret executed the fence around Jackson Square.

Fig. 204.—Gate Detail,
917 N. Rampart Street

Fig. 205. — Gate from
the Patio Royal

Fig. 206.—Seat in Jackson Square

*The photographs on this page are by
Richard Koch*

In Fig. 209 the gate is old but
the balcony and lamp were designed by Armstrong & Koch,
architects

Fig. 207.—Courtyard
Gate, Royal Street

Fig. 208.—Typical Street Balconies,
St. Peter Street

Fig. 209.—Lamp and Gate,
730 Esplanade Street

Wrought Iron of New Orleans

FIG. 210.—MONT DE PIETE, ROYAL AND CONTI

FIG. 211.—CHARTRES STREET (NOW DEMOLISHED)

FIG. 212.—ORIGINAL BUILDING, "LITTLE THEATRE"

FIG. 213.—CABILDO, OR TOWN HALL

Photographs on this page by Richard Koch

FIG. 214.—715 HOSPITAL STREET

FIG. 215.—HOUSE ON DAUPHINE STREET

WROUGHT–IRON BALCONIES OF NEW ORLEANS

FIG. 216.—WASHINGTON SQUARE. (PARTLY CAST)

FIG. 217.—47 EAST BAY. (HOUSE BUILT 1765)

Photographs of Figs. 216, 217, and 219 by George W. Johnson

FIG. 218.—12 LEGARE STREET   FIG. 219.—63 MEETING STREET

GATES OF CHARLESTON, SOUTH CAROLINA

FIG. 220.—36 LEGARE STREET. (SWORD GATE)

FIG. 221.—23 LEGARE STREET

Photographs of Figs. 220, 221, 222, 223, by George W. Johnson

FIG. 222.—68 SOUTH BAY

FIG. 223.—ST. MICHAEL'S CHURCH

GATES OF CHARLESTON, SOUTH CAROLINA

FIGS. 224 (ABOVE) AND 225 (BELOW).—BALCONIES FROM BROAD STREET, CHARLESTON, S. C.

Neither of these balconies leaves much to be desired in delicacy of feeling, nimbleness of design, harmonious variety, and suitable lightness of members. The average modern "Colonial" railing is put to eternal shame by examples such as these

FIG. 226.—DETAIL OF RESIDENTIAL BALCONY, SAVANNAH, GEORGIA

Although the circular *motif* repeats the same unit, there is a lively grace and lack of monotony which modern inventiveness generally misses

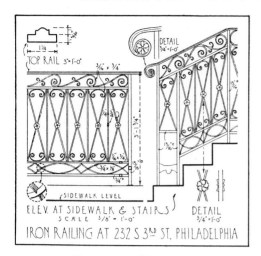

FIG. 227.—RAILING AT 232 SOUTH THIRD STREET, PHILADELPHIA. (CAST ROSETTES)

FIG. 228.—BALCONY AT 23 KING STREET, CHARLESTON, SOUTH CAROLINA

FIG. 229.—WROUGHT-IRON BALCONY, CHARLESTON, SOUTH CAROLINA

FIGS. 230 (TOP), 231 (LEFT ABOVE), AND 232 (RIGHT ABOVE).—THREE BALCONY DETAILS FROM THE OLD
STEPHEN GIRARD WAREHOUSE, NORTH DELAWARE AVENUE, PHILADELPHIA

FIG. 233.—BALCONY, CONGRESS HALL, SIXTH AND
CHESTNUT STREETS, PHILADELPHIA

FIG. 234.—RESIDENTIAL BALCONY, LAMBOLL STREET,
CHARLESTON, SOUTH CAROLINA

FIG. 235.—CIRCULAR BALCONY, AND FIG. 236.—DETAIL, "THE OCTAGON," WASHINGTON, D. C.

Both the ornaments on the bars and the ovals between them are of lead, although they pass for wrought iron; note the bent oval at the left

FIG. 237.—GENERAL VIEW OF STAIR RAILING, AND FIG. 238.—DETAIL OF SAME RAILING,
"THE OCTAGON," WASHINGTON, D. C.

The horizontal part of the railing is the original, the remainder restored.   The detail shows the manner of leading in the verticals securely

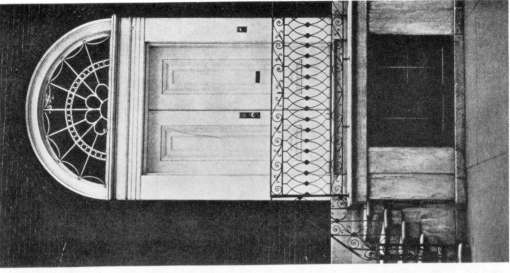

Courtesy of Essex Institute

Fig. 241.—Wrought-Iron Railing, Eighth and Spruce Streets, Philadelphia

From a photograph by George W. Johnson

Fig. 240.—Balcony on Russell House, 51 Meeting Street, Charleston, South Carolina

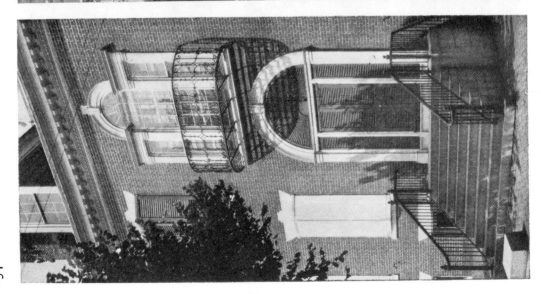

Fig. 239.—Balcony and Stair Railing, Reed House, New Castle, Delaware

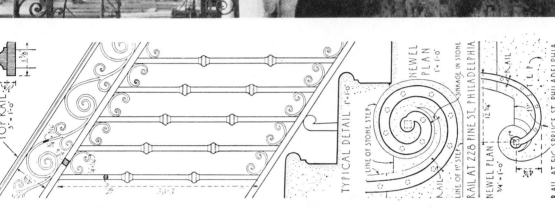

FIG. 243.—DRAWING AND PHOTOGRAPH OF STAIR RAILING, 516 SPRUCE STREET, PHILADELPHIA

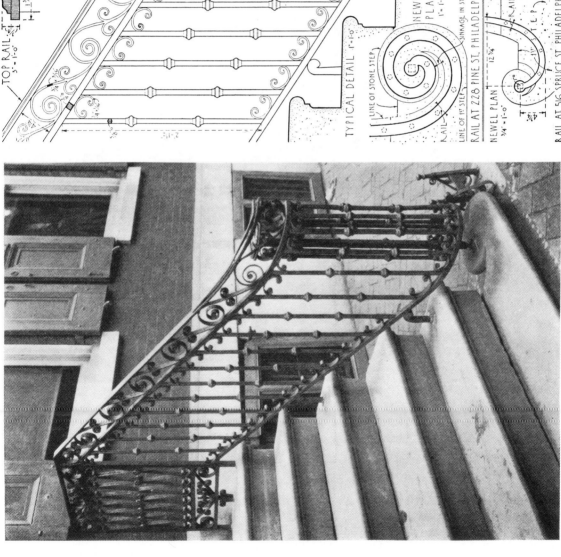

FIG. 242.—STAIR RAILING, 228 PINE STREET, PHILADELPHIA

These illustrations are typical for scores of railings in the old quarter of the city, all with the same *parti*: verticals with cast neckings, a band of scrolls sometimes at the top or bottom, and often both

FIG. 244.—PENROSE HOUSE, 700 SOUTH WASHINGTON SQUARE, PHILADELPHIA

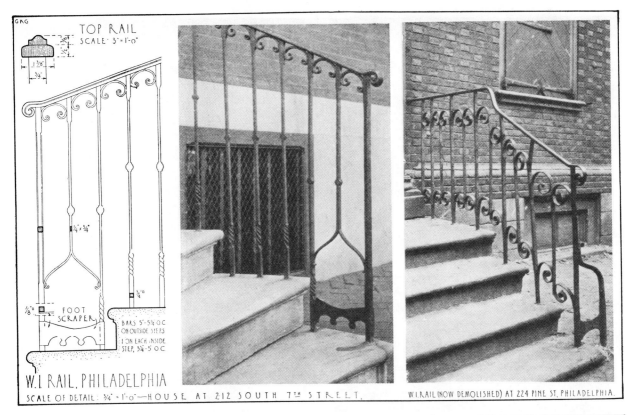

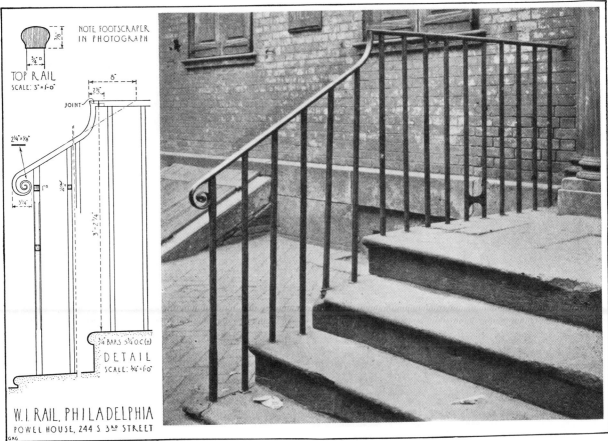

FIGS. 245 (ABOVE) AND 246 (BELOW).—THREE SIMPLE TYPES OF PHILADELPHIA RAILINGS

The tact with which foot-scrapers are included is of interest

Courtesy of Essex Institute

FIG. 247.—RAILING, 59 CHESTNUT STREET, BOSTON

FIG. 248.—272 S. AMERICAN STREET, PHILADELPHIA

Photographs of Figs. 249 and 250, by George W. Johnson

FIG. 249.—KING MANSION, CHARLESTON, S. C.

FIG. 250.—CHARLOTTE STREET, CHARLESTON, S. C.

The grace of curving railings such as these is justly to be admired, but is not readily to be obtained in modern reproductions

FIG. 251.—WROUGHT-IRON AWNING FRAME, CHARLESTON, SOUTH CAROLINA

FIG. 252.—RAILING DETAIL SHOWING SPIRAL TERMINATION, MOUNT PLEASANT. (c. 1761)

This close-up of a simple top rail shows the frank manner in which the spiral end was spliced to the long straight portion of the ramp; the usual manner of securing the vertical bars to the rail was to pierce the latter and rivet the ends of the bars

FIG. 254.—REAR HALL
DOOR, VAN DEUSEN
HOUSE, HURLEY, NEW
YORK

Courtesy of Metropolitan
Museum of Art

FIG. 253.—MID-EIGH-
TEENTH-CENTURY FIRE-
PLACE ACCESSORIES,
BROOKLINE, MASS.

FIG. 255.—EIGH-
TEENTH-CENTURY
AMERICAN ANDIRONS

AMERICAN WROUGHT IRON: ILLUSTRATIONS

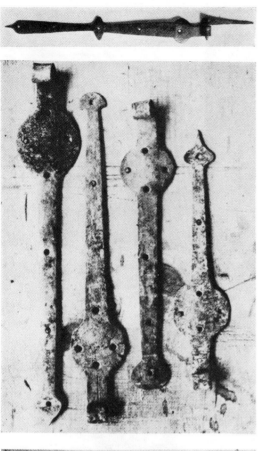

FIG. 256.—PENNSYLVANIA-
GERMAN STRAP HINGE
(C. 1710)

FIG. 257.—DUTCH FLAT HINGES
FROM HURLEY, NEW YORK

FIG. 258.—FOUR STRAP HINGES
FROM HURLEY, NEW YORK

FIG. 259.—PENNSYLVANIA-
GERMAN STRAP HINGE
(C. 1710)

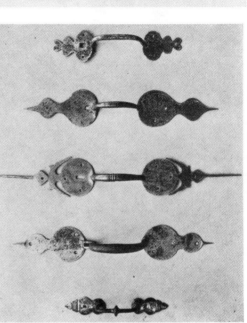

FIG. 262.—DOUBLE-DRAGON HINGES,
PENNSYLVANIA-GERMAN. (C. 1710)

FIG. 261.—WROUGHT-IRON AND BRASS
DOOR LATCHES

FIG. 260.—HINGES AND HASP ON LID OF CONESTOGA
WAGON, PENNSYLVANIA-GERMAN. (C. 1710)

Figs. 256, 259, 260, and 262 by courtesy of Pennsylvania Museum, Memorial Hall, Philadelphia; Fig. 261 by courtesy of Metropolitan Museum of Art

Fig. 263.—Philadelphia Foot-Scrapers

The middle one at the top and the one at the right of the second row are cast, the
others wrought; the rosettes of the middle one of the second row are obviously cast

TWENTIETH-CENTURY WROUGHT IRON

PRESENT–DAY iron work speaks many tongues, both academic and patois. There is the school that conscientiously studies the historical vocabularies with an eye to adapting them to modern parlance and, vice versa, occasionally seeks to find modern usage for historical forms. Opposed are the so-called "modernists," stimulated by imagination rather than avowed precedent. We shall not become embroiled in the constant controversy as to which is the better craftsmanship and which the wiser "policy," for, after all, the grounds of dissension are not so great as superficially seems the case. The best craftsmanship of the "moderns" is thoughtful, sincere, and to definite purpose, having antecedents not always traceable to prototype forebears, yet indicating a lineage sometimes springing from the East and Far East, or possessing the qualities in form, modeling and simplification akin to Babylonian and Egyptian bas-reliefs. If the bone of contention seems to be a matter of having or not having historical precedent, then we are tempted to term the adherents of the "conservative" school as the "post-Greek Empire" and the "moderns" the "pre-Greek Empire." Offhand this may seem paradoxical, but on analyzing sculptures, paintings, and even much iron work of the "modern movement," the student of archæology could trace them to parent bas-reliefs or textile designs native to the banks of the Nile, Euphrates, Bramaputra or Yangtze, with the same facility as the "conservative" craftsman can lay claim to forebears indigenous to the meanderings of the Tiber, Seine, Rhine or Thames. It must occur to many that the term "modernist" is either a misnomer or else a fulfilment of the prophecy that "the first shall be last, and the last shall be first," together with the Old Testament's sage observation that "there is no new thing under the sun."

In addition to the disagreement as to the design of form, there is the argument concerning the introduction of color into wrought iron work. Until lately the "orthodox-historic" school—let us call them—refrained from using any other metal in conjunction with iron, as though it were anathema, and yet lately even some of the chief citadels of opposition have capitulated to the extent of introducing color in applied brass, copper, or enamelled ornaments.

It is small wonder that there is such a variety of influences and periods existent in present iron work. Knowledge of foreign styles has become widely disseminated through the lessening expense of documents; facilities for travel have multiplied the numbers of designers studying abroad; demands of the public have increased to include every known style; the designer has been forced to accept the mandatory requirements of the client, instead of being able to dominate the situation as a czar-architect; easy transportation has placed every material at the disposal of the entire world, whether or not it be extravagant or inappropriate. New iron work at Paris in the *Exposition des Arts Decoratifs Modernes* (1925) was broadcast to the world and imitated overnight; in the fifteenth century a series of new grilles in Paris might not have affected Rouen for a century. Whether or not this universality of design and puddling of all the periods of all the countries is beneficial to us, and whether it will be provocative of a distinctive and distinguished period worthy of emulation in the future, is a much mooted question. At all events the dust of the gallant battle is too thick about us now to predict anything. Certainly we are giving the laymen a world-range of iron forms to behold, and if they are not well informed in every tendency and cross-breeding of styles, it cannot be blamed upon our designers for lack of untiring sleuthing through documents in the hunt for new and unexploited styles. If the Canary Islands or the deepest recesses of Abyssinia want League-of-Nations publicity, there could scarcely be a more successful manner of obtaining it than to intrigue the world with a new "trend in thought" which may be embodied in the iron work of our homes and offices.

When iron historians grimly survey us a century or two from now they may not observe the wide divergence between the "historic" and "modern" schools which we ourselves feel existing. To them it may seem rather a battle of the patient with the impatient during a period when the styles of all countries were assimilated in the development of what we consider to be a "new" manner, and which may after all be but a grand recapitulation of the twentieth century. By that time too, the nineteenth-century origin of the *Art Nouveau* may be more certainly established, as well as its debit and credit accounts in its curious influences for good and evil. Its lack of appreciation of iron as iron, insecure knowledge of historic modes and uncalled-for extravagances of forms, are in contrast with a worthy stimulation of the imagination which to some extent may have nurtured the roots of the present movement. Whether to France or Germany goes the palm for the *Art Nouveau* of the last quarter of the nineteenth century is of little intrinsic value; the greater issue at stake is whether or not craftsmen of the present will profit by its lessons. The overindulgence of the *Nouveau* movement was followed in Europe by the pendulum's swinging back to the lifeless rigidity and coldness of the unpoetic decade or two preceding the World War, and, in America, the emerging from our national adolescent age into the first period of timid creativeness since the second quarter of the nineteenth century.

During the nineteenth century not only the political disturbances and slow transportation were responsible for the divergence of American iron work from European, but also the more limited economic resources and greater mixture of nationalities in craftsmen, on this side of the Atlantic. As illustrated in the chapter on "American Wrought Iron, Pre-Twentieth Century," the trend of design in the United States was commendable almost until the outbreak of the Civil War. The aftermath of that conflict seems to have temporarily blighted all national sense of design and good taste, and not until the end of the century was there assertive in the public mind a renaissance in things beautiful.

Such work as was produced in America in the two decades preceding the World War, in general lacked all the inventiveness and naïveté of the Colonial days and succeeded in being commendable only in so far as it imitated European forms. The architectural stimulus and inspiration furnished by the work of McKim, Mead & White, which frankly drew its inspiration from classic application of *motifs* and compositions, beneficially affected metal work as well. Also, the great number of American architects who received their education at the Ecole des Beaux-Arts, Paris, or who were influenced by it, accounts for the boulevard balconies all over the United States. Much of

this work, frankly designed in imitation of European precedents, is splendid forging and is entirely to the credit of the craftsmen, but is scarcely indicative of any inventiveness on the part of architectural designers. It was all very well to have learned copiously from the French, but why we found it needful to import their designs from coast to coast with such shameless plagiarism, is anything but complimentary to ourselves. All the world, except the United States, was imitating French iron work from the reign of Louis XIV through the Napoleonic régime; a century later we seem to have awakened with fervid enthusiasm to the apparent need for duplicating this same work. Many reproductions illustrate the technical abilities of American forges, although, in so far as some designs are concerned, the architects often seem to have troubled no further than to furnish a plate number in a book, much as though they were ordering so much structural steel. By the beginning of the World War (1914) public taste had developed by leaps and bounds, so that the iron work took on a semblance of sensible, logical design, well executed under the guidance of the better architects.

It was not for some time after the cataclysm of 1914–18 that anything like normalcy was restored in both building and the arts either in Europe or America. It is miraculous that by 1925 Paris assembled, at the *Exposition des Arts Decoratifs Modernes*, metal work not only of sterling merit in craftsmanship, but with decided emphasis on color, imaginative forms, and freedom from stifling traditions. It would be sadly inaccurate to make such a sweeping statement regarding all the metal work there exhibited, but on the whole, although it took days really to observe it, one could not help feeling (to see published works of the Exposition only verifies the impression) that there was a vigorous, genuine attempt to add a new interpretation to iron by increasing its scope and encouraging its natural qualities in variety of surface and form. Modern work which seems most satisfactory takes on no unbecoming traits which are at variance with the natural strength of iron. By a long stretch of the imagination it may be decorative to treat iron as silken garlands but whether or not it be in character with the material seems rather evident. Geometric forms have been happily combined in designs ever since man first made records, and there is no legitimate reason why the modernist should not use them at the anvil. But here again, with a material possessing evident strength, most satisfactory results are produced when iron is not used in a trivial manner without consideration for structural composition. The human mind, accustomed to logic and reason, will not sympathetically acclaim as a great work of art any unreasonable muddling of forms which begin at random and end in confusion, be it on canvas, in stone or with iron.

The fact that in the "modern" school there are no standards of perfection yet crystallized in the public's estimation, provokes a hardship for the gifted artist who expresses himself with the tools and palette of the new movement. It means that whereas in the "conservative" manner his abilities could be rated according to comparison with accepted masters, in the "new" expression there may be one hundred impostors and dilettantes who, for social or other reasons, may "succeed" with inferior work better than he. The iron artisan who is a serious student of his craft and modern design, must find it a heart-rending task to carry on the best traditions only to witness the merits of new ideas being discounted and discredited by the antics of inferiors who at best are but commercial copyists. Certainly the way of the craftsman pursuing the beaten path is by far the more pleasant and lucrative, for he has but to follow and adapt what Europe since the thirteenth century has done for him; true, the "adaptation" process requires no little discrimination and experience, but at least it is not navigating by "dead reckoning" without a dependable compass.

However, the lot of the "conservative" iron-worker is by no means an enviable one. His artistic reputation is at stake in whatever he does, which entails the necessity of refusing to do certain work dictated by the uninformed architect, even at a loss of future business. Only few architects know wrought iron intimately enough to design it with inveterate certainty, and it is not surprising therefore that sometimes on a building outspokenly Georgian there should be a Sienese pre-Renaissance grille. Worse than that is the predicament of the smith when given a grille to be executed "exactly as shown," with composite parts of varying scale in decidedly poor taste. The architect who resents having a client dictate what the design should be, most often acts the czar toward the iron-worker, whether or not he knows the historical or practical precedents of the case.

If, several hundred years hence, the iron work of the present and that of the fifteenth century be contrasted, it is to be hoped that the differences under which the iron was forged will be taken into account. In the mediæval work there were no time-contracts. No inflated land values demanded that day and night shifts speed up construction so that no loss in rentals ensue. The wealthy patron of the arts or the bishop of a cathedral allowed the workmen to dream and live with their tasks over a period of years. The problem could be studied at leisure at the spot where it was to fit. The rough "pigs" were hammered into bars square and round so that they naturally acquired a personal appearance of being lived with. Now it is quite a different story. Work, which would take three years to produce artistic results, must be delivered and erected in three months. In place of the patron of the arts, or the bishop, has come the hard-fisted "realtor," to whom iron work is not an expression of art but an income-producing asset to attract tenants; he countenances no dawdling or dreaming but demands that the iron be erected as soon as constructional progress permits. Iron forged in one city is shipped to another without the smith having the slightest opportunity to know any of the building conditions whatsoever. Stock bars and plates are rolled out in such a variety of shapes and sizes that they can be used in the design without a hammer blow being necessary to make them the right size, and as a natural result they look as mechanical as the mill made them. This however is preferable to the haphazard mutilation of dents which certain smiths of the poorest order think necessary to produce the visible guarantee of "hand-hammered" workmanship (refer to "Wrought Iron Craftsmanship," page 11).

These and many other differences should mitigate criticism of present-day work compared to that of the Renaissance. Given time, and left to their own devices, without having to be concerned with the financial worries of business overhead and payroll expenses as well as with driving the wolf from their own thresholds, probably a corps of the best modern metal craftsmen could turn out work on a par with the revered historic examples. For rich inventiveness of compositions and originality in texture approaching beaten silver, probably no modern craftsman exceeds Edgar Brandt of Paris (pages 180–1). No one's work is perfect and Brandt would make no claim that his is; there are examples no doubt which are not always equal to his usual refreshing achievements. But he is responsible in a great measure for much splendid, virile work by other iron-workers which had otherwise not come into being for want of an impetus. He has affected not only many craftsmen in Europe and this country, but architects as well. Smiths executing work as they are directed by an architect who has borrowed freely from Brandt-*motifs*, are sometimes embarrassed by the criticism that the design is plagiaristic; such censure reflects on the architect, of course, not the smith.

As to what the tendencies of the present century thus far may be, and what the most notable achievements are, we hesitate to say. Where historic examples are followed, the characteristics pursue those of the original as conscientiously as the designer knows them, as ably as the smiths can forge them, and as thoroughly as the client can afford to pay for them. Work of the "modern" order has too recently come

into being for analysis by traits, except that it seems to show a fondness for geometric forms; a simplification of modeling; a fanciful introduction of flowers, fruits, animals, etc.; a surfacing like beaten silver; and the introduction of various other metals to add color. There is no reason to feel discouraged over the progress of twentieth-century iron work, although at the present writing there are so many possible developments which may lead from the multifarious mannerisms of a hundred styles and periods churned up with modern tendencies, that the goal for which we are heading is by no means certain. It is to be hoped that the increased interest on the part of the public, and a gradual elevation of professional and lay taste, will be of growing importance in the improvement of both design and craftsmanship. Perhaps by the middle of the century the loose fringes and divergent tendencies may be gathered up into concerted progress of virility, imagination, sincerity of purpose, and wisely controlled ability.

FIG. 264.—ENTRANCE GRILLE, RESIDENCE OF E. T. CANNON, ESQ., CHARLOTTE, N. C.

Wm. H. Peeps, Architect   Executed by The Iron-Craftsmen (3 feet 8 inches wide by 7 feet high)

FIG. 265.—GATE IN BARKER BROTHERS' FLOWER SHOP, LOS ANGELES, CAL.

Designed by Kem Weber
Executed by the Atlas Ornamental Iron Works

Fig. 266.—Wrought-Iron Hardware for the Wurzburg Residence, Bronxville, New York

The wide variety of form, ornamentation and texture possible in wrought iron are indicated in these handles, pulls
and knocker. All the types are perfectly suited to the material, a virtue which makes the results doubly effective
H. T. Lindeberg, Architect   Executed by The Iron-Craftsmen

FIG. 268.—DETAIL OF TYPICAL *MOTIF* AT LOCK

HARDWARE MUTUAL INSURANCE BUILDING, STEVENS POINT, WIS.

Various hardware symbols are artfully incised at the centres of the repeating motif

Samuel Yellin, Craftsman

FIG. 267.—VIEW OF ENTIRE DOOR

Childs & Smith, Architects

FIG. 269.—MAIN ENTRANCE, STATE BANK AND TRUST COMPANY, EVANSTON, ILLINOIS

Childs & Smith, Architects   Samuel Yellin, Craftsman

Fig. 270 (above) Entire View, and Fig. 271 (below) Detail; Wrought-Iron Fanlight in Residence of F. King Wainwright, Esq., Bryn Mawr, Pa.

H. Sternfeld & J. Bright, Architects   (10 feet wide)   Executed by The Iron-Craftsmen

FIG. 272.—FANLIGHT IN RESIDENCE OF F. KING WAINWRIGHT, ESQ., BRYN MAWR, PA.

H. Sternfeld & J. Bright, Architects   (30 inches wide)   Executed by The Iron-Craftsmen

FIG. 273.—FANLIGHT IN RESIDENCE OF F. KING WAINWRIGHT, ESQ., BRYN MAWR, PA.

H. Sternfeld & J. Bright, Architects   (5 feet wide)   Executed by The Iron-Craftsmen

In the fanlight on the page opposite the artistry with which the craftsman has interpreted the feeling of flowing water is accentuated by the verticality of the branches and birds' necks; with the problem solved, it is evident that without the massing of birds and branches, an over-all pattern as in Fig. 272 would have been lifeless and flimsy. In Fig. 272 the scale of the ornament has been suited to the small size of the fanlight, while in the illustration below it the impression of fluttering leaves is remarkable in such a stubborn material as iron. In all three fanlights forms of nature have been freely translated according to the personality of the craftsman, not foolishly copied atom for atom

FIG. 275.—TYPICAL TELLERS' WICKETS IN COUNTER-SCREEN

FEDERAL RESERVE BANK, NEW YORK CITY

Samuel Yellin, Craftsman

FIG. 274.—DOOR IN COUNTER-SCREEN

York & Sawyer, Architects

FIG. 276.—TELLER'S WICKET IN COUNTER-SCREEN, SOCIETY FOR SAVINGS, HARTFORD, CONN.

FIG. 277.—DOOR IN COUNTER-SCREEN, MUTUAL TRUST COMPANY, PORT CHESTER, N. Y.

FIG. 278.—DETAIL OF DOOR (SEE FIG. 277), MUTUAL TRUST COMPANY, PORT CHESTER, N. Y.

For all three illustrations: Dennison & Hirons, Architects, and Renner & Maras, Craftsmen

FIG. 280.—PART OF RADIATOR GRILLE IN RESIDENCE OF F. G. ACHELIS, ESQ., GREENWICH, CONN. (3 FEET HIGH)

FIG. 279.—RADIATOR GRILLE IN RESIDENCE OF K. E. WOMACK, ESQ., HOUSTON, TEXAS (2 FEET SQUARE)

For both illustrations: H. T. Lindeberg, Architect.   Executed by The Iron-Craftsmen

TWENTIETH-CENTURY WROUGHT IRON: ILLUSTRATIONS

Fig. 282.—Radiator Grille in Residence of H. V. Newhous, Esq., Houston, Texas (4 feet wide by 2 high)

Executed by The Iron-Craftsmen

Fig. 281.—Grille in Residence of H. C. Martin, Esq., Glen Cove, N. Y. (17 by 23 inches)

For both illustrations: H. T. Lindeberg, Architect

FIG. 283.—INNER VESTIBULE DOOR IN RESIDENCE OF F. G. ACHELIS, ESQ.,
GREENWICH, CONN.

H. T. Lindeberg, Architect   Executed by The Iron-Craftsmen
(Note the texture of the outer stile)

FIG. 284.—BALCONY RAILINGS, MEZZANINE OF LOBBY, LINCOLN HOTEL, NEW YORK CITY

FIG. 285.—CASHIER'S COUNTER-SCREEN

FIG. 286.—RADIATOR GRILLE

LINCOLN HOTEL, NEW YORK CITY

Designed and executed by Renner & Maras, Craftsmen

Courtesy of Metropolitan Museum of Art

FIG. 288.—DECORATIVE PANEL
By Edgar Brandt

FIG. 287.—GATES TO MODERN EUROPEAN GALLERY,
DETROIT INSTITUTE OF ARTS, DETROIT
Paul P. Cret, and Zantzinger, Borie & Medary, Architects   Samuel Yellin, Craftsman

FIG. 290.—RADIATOR GRILLE, SOCIETY FOR SAVINGS, HARTFORD, CONN.
Dennison & Hirons, Architects   Renner & Maras, Craftsmen

This is also all wrought iron except for small accents of brass

FIG. 289.—RADIATOR GRILLE, FEDERAL TRUST COMPANY, NEWARK, N. J.
Dennison & Hirons, Architects; George E. Jones, Associated Architect
Renner & Maras, Craftsmen

This is all wrought iron except for the centre panel, which is cast

FIG. 292.—"LES PLUMES"

FIG. 291.—"LA BICHE"

WROUGHT-IRON FIRE-PLACE SCREENS BY EDGAR BRANDT

From photographs by F. Contet

From a photograph by F. Contet

FIG. 293.—TWO WROUGHT-IRON GRILLES BY EDGAR BRANDT

These were displayed in the *Exposition des Arts Decoratifs Modernes*, Paris, 1925, in the *Cour des Métiers*

Fig. 295.—Entrance Gate, British
Medical Association, London
Sir Edwin Lutyens, Architect   The Birmingham Guild, Ltd., Craftsmen

Fig. 294.—Entrance Gates, Residence
of S. M. Spaulding, Esq., Los Angeles
Hunt & Burns, Architects   City Ornamental Iron Works, Craftsmen

LIGHTING FIXTURES *and* KNOCKERS

ONLY rarely does the fascinating problem of designing lighting fixtures or knockers present itself to the architect. When it does it may only require an approximate indication of what is wanted, to be followed later by detailed study of a specialist. Unfortunately the lighting fixture illustrations of this chapter are too few to serve adequately as design inspiration for all problems, but they may at least pique the architectural designer's interest and prompt him to investigate other sources further. Not infrequently it happens that stock wrought-iron fixtures are not only unimaginative in design, poor in execution, but entirely too high in price to elicit a client's enthusiasm. In such a case the architectural designer, by accepting the challenge, letting his fancy roam without constraint, and inviting the aid of a genuine craftsman, may achieve a notable success.

In the design of lighting fixtures several factors must be taken into account which do not prominently figure in the usual architectural problem. Among them is the consideration of whether or not the electric bulbs are to be frosted and exposed or, on the other hand, enclosed within glass, mica, parchment, etc. A hanging lamp which may be perfectly in scale with a room, having its frosted bulbs exposed and arranged in tiers, is likely to appear twice the size if glass or mica encloses them. Another problem is that of properly distributing the bulbs within the glass enclosure (a matter for a lighting consultant), so that there will result an equal distribution of light and not an evident concentration anywhere from top to bottom, unless such an excess of light be an asset and not the usual detriment to the design. Perhaps the most difficult feature for the architectural designer is the departure from the usual four-sided solid he is accustomed to visualize, and instead, the provision for circular, octagonal, and irregular shapes designed to be seen from below. Not only do numerous or curved sides complicate things, but the nature and suspended position offer vistas through the fixture, enlarge the importance of the decoration underneath, and, unless carefully considered, will even exclude the top part from appearing when viewed from below.

FIG. 296.—PALAZZO STROZZI, FLORENCE FIG. 297.—PALAZZO GAUDAGNI, FLORENCE

TWO LAMPS ON BRACKETS BY NICOLÒ GROSSO, CALLED *IL CAPARRA*

183

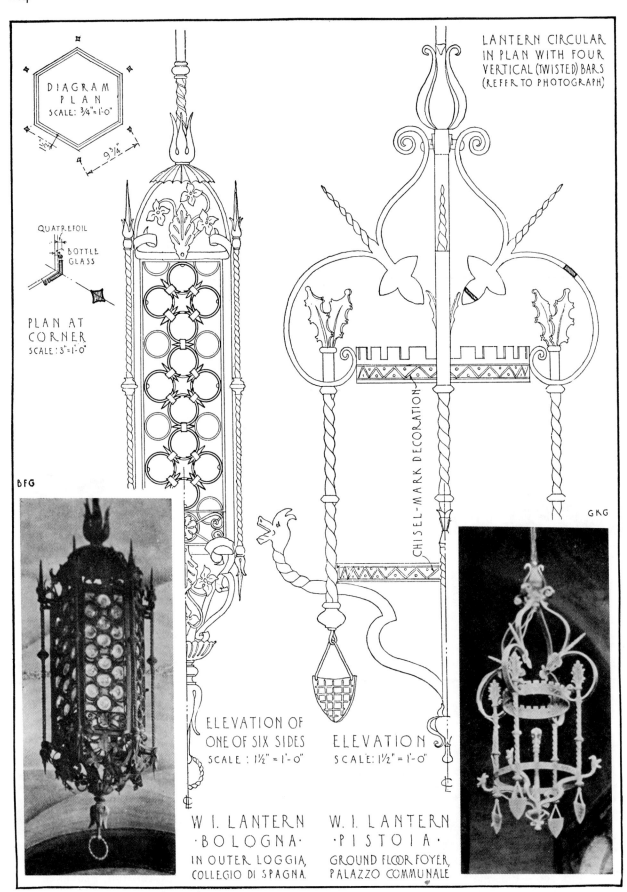

DIAGRAM
PLAN
SCALE: 3/4" = 1'-0"

QUATREFOIL
BOTTLE
GLASS

PLAN AT
CORNER
SCALE: 3" = 1'-0"

BFG

LANTERN CIRCULAR
IN PLAN WITH FOUR
VERTICAL (TWISTED) BARS
(REFER TO PHOTOGRAPH)

CHISEL-MARK DECORATION

GKG

ELEVATION OF
ONE OF SIX SIDES
SCALE : 1½" = 1'-0"

ELEVATION
SCALE: 1½" = 1'-0"

W. I. LANTERN
·BOLOGNA·
IN OUTER LOGGIA,
COLLEGIO DI SPAGNA.

W. I. LANTERN
·PISTOIA·
GROUND FLOOR FOYER,
PALAZZO COMMUNALE

FIG. 298

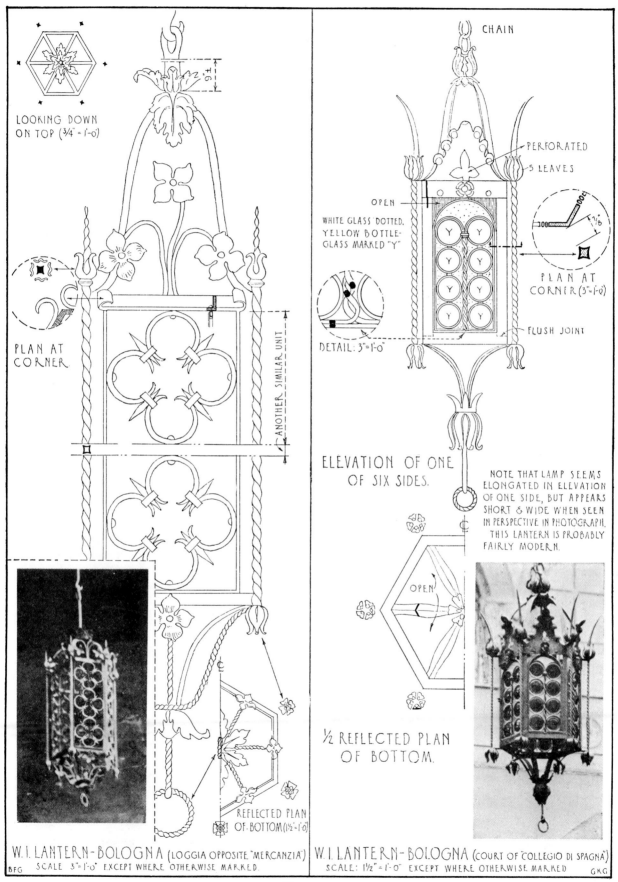

LOOKING DOWN
ON TOP (¾"=1'-0")

PLAN AT
CORNER

ANOTHER SIMILAR UNIT

CHAIN

PERFORATED

5 LEAVES

OPEN

WHITE GLASS DOTTED.
YELLOW BOTTLE-
GLASS MARKED "Y"

PLAN AT
CORNER (3"=1'-0")

FLUSH JOINT

DETAIL: 3"=1'-0"

ELEVATION OF ONE
OF SIX SIDES.

NOTE THAT LAMP SEEMS
ELONGATED IN ELEVATION
OF ONE SIDE, BUT APPEARS
SHORT & WIDE WHEN SEEN
IN PERSPECTIVE IN PHOTOGRAPH.
THIS LANTERN IS PROBABLY
FAIRLY MODERN.

OPEN

½ REFLECTED PLAN
OF BOTTOM.

REFLECTED PLAN
OF BOTTOM (1½"=1'-0")

W.I. LANTERN-BOLOGNA (LOGGIA OPPOSITE "MERCANZIA")
BFG   SCALE: 3"=1'-0" EXCEPT WHERE OTHERWISE MARKED.

W.I. LANTERN-BOLOGNA (COURT OF "COLLEGIO DI SPAGNA")
SCALE: 1½"=1'-0" EXCEPT WHERE OTHERWISE MARKED   GKG

FIG. 299

WROUGHT IRON IN ARCHITECTURE

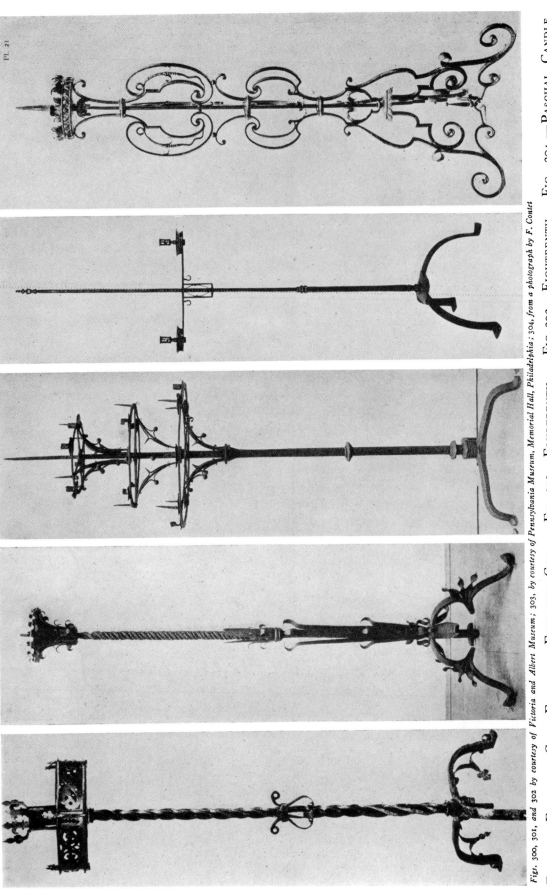

Figs. 300, 301, and 302 by courtesy of Victoria and Albert Museum; 303, by courtesy of Pennsylvania Museum, Memorial Hall, Philadelphia; 304, from a photograph by F. Contet

FIG. 300.—FIFTEENTH-CEN-
TURY SPANISH GOTHIC
CANDLE-HOLDER

FIG. 301.—FIFTEENTH-CEN-
TURY ITALIAN CANDLE-
HOLDER.

FIG. 302.—FOURTEENTH-
CENTURY FRENCH
CANDLE-HOLDER

FIG. 303.—EIGHTEENTH-
CENTURY AMERICAN
CANDLE-HOLDER

FIG. 304.—PASCHAL CANDLE-
HOLDER, CHURCH OF SAINT-
BÉNIGNE, DIJON

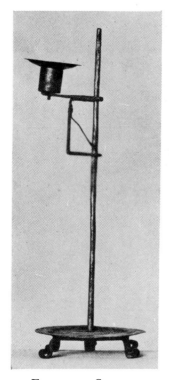

FIG. 305.—SPANISH
CANDLESTICK
Note the simple height-adjust-
ment device, and the sensitive
curves of the holder-flange and
base

FIG. 306.—HANGING CANDLE-HOLDER CHANDE-
LIER, CASTELLO DI VINCIGLIATA, NEAR
FLORENCE

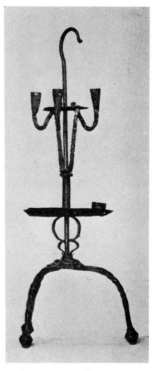

FIG. 307.—SPANISH-
GOTHIC CANDLESTICK
The hook at the top permits
hanging up like a "betty" lamp;
the general form is an unexploited one

From a photograph by F. Contet

FIG. 308.—FIFTEENTH-CENTURY
HANGING RING FOR SUSPEND-
ING FOOD, BUT SUGGESTIVE
FOR A LIGHTING FIXTURE
(FRENCH)

FIG. 309.—LATE-FIFTEENTH-
CENTURY GERMAN GOTHIC
CHANDELIER
(Height, 3 feet 1½ inches; width, 19½
inches

Courtesy of Victoria and Albert Museum

FIG. 310.—HANGING SPANISH
CANDLE-HOLDER, PROBABLY
THIRTEENTH CENTURY, NOW
IN MUSEO EPISCOPAL,
BARCELONA

FIG. 311.—SIXTEENTH-CENTURY ITALIAN CRES-
SET AND BRACKET (Height 5 feet 6 inches)

FIG. 312.—SEVENTEENTH-CENTURY CRESSET,
PALAZZO BARONI NEL FILLUNZO, LUCCA

Figs. 311 and 313 by courtesy of Victoria and Albert Museum

FIG. 313.—SIXTEENTH-CENTURY FLORENTINE
CRESSET AND BRACKET (Height 4 feet 2
inches, width 3 feet 2 inches)

FIG. 314.—SIXTEENTH-CENTURY CRESSET,
PALAZZO BOCCELLA (FORMERLY "CONTI"),
LUCCA

FIG. 315.—KNOCKER WITH CHISEL-MARKS, SPRINGING FROM FOUR LEAVES WITH GILT SUN IN PIERCED CENTRE

FIG. 316.—GERMAN KNOCKER WITH CHARACTERISTIC LOOP FORM HAVING DIVERGING SCROLLS (C. 1600)

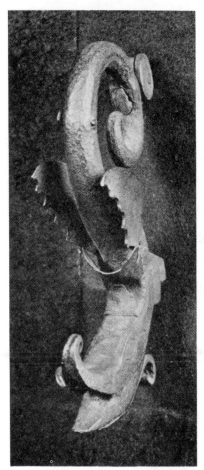

FIG. 317.—WINGED HERALDIC LIZARD, ABOUT 20 INCHES HIGH

FIG. 318.—FRENCH KNOCKER, SECOND HALF OF EIGHTEENTH CENTURY

The "catafalco" above the pin is characteristic of many Bordeaux knockers

FIG. 319.—FIFTEENTH-CENTURY FRENCH KNOCKER

Fig. 321.—Knocker and End of Strap-Hinge

Fig. 320.—Key-Plate and Two Types of Studs

Photographic Details of Main Exterior Door, Casa del Conde de Toledo, Toledo

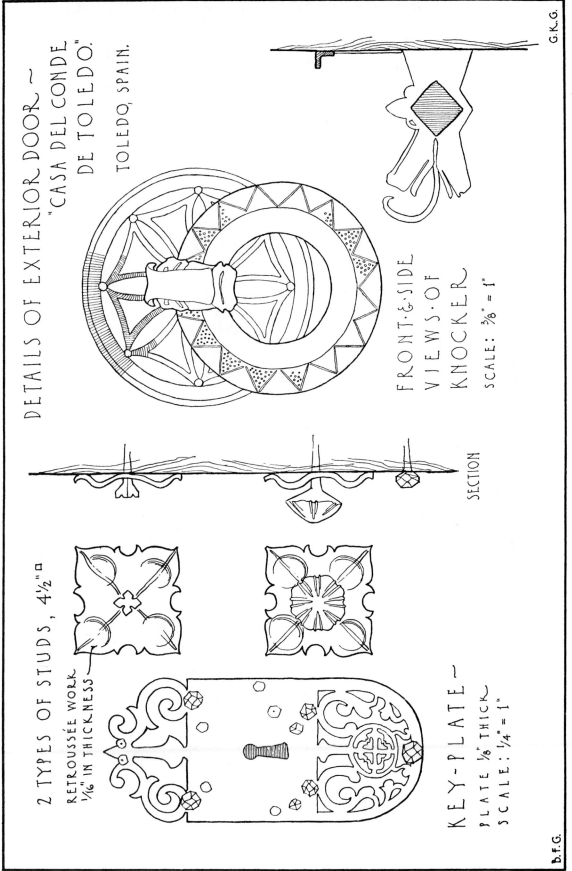

DETAILS OF EXTERIOR DOOR ~
"CASA DEL CONDE DE TOLEDO."
TOLEDO, SPAIN.

FRONT·&·SIDE VIEWS·OF KNOCKER
SCALE: ³⁄₈" = 1"

SECTION

2 TYPES OF STUDS, 4½"□

RETROUSSÉE WORK ¹⁄₁₆" IN THICKNESS

KEY-PLATE ~
PLATE ⅛" THICK
SCALE: ¼" = 1"

G.K.G.

B.F.G.

Fig. 322.—Measured Drawing Details of Main Exterior Door, Casa del Conde de Toledo, Toledo. (see page opposite)

ELEVATION

SECTION
KNOCKER
SCALE . 1½" = 1'-0"

HALF ELEVATION

SECTION
DETAIL OF
STUD
SCALE : 3" = 1'-0"
- GKG

FIG. 323 (ABOVE).— DETAILS OF KNOCKER AND STUDS OF MAIN EXTERIOR DOOR, CASA DE IL GRECO, TOLEDO

FIG. 324 (LEFT).— VARIOUS TYPES OF SPANISH STUDS OR BOSSES, USED PRINCIPALLY ON WOOD DOORS

WROUGHT IRON SPECIFICATIONS

THE architectural specification writer usually finds himself in the same predicament with each succeeding job—that of starting on it when it was supposedly complete a month previous. If the first page is finished only a week later than the date when the last page should have been completed, he thinks himself fortunate. Constant inquiry as to when the typed copy will be ready drives the harried writer to making the best he can of a tardy situation, resorting to ambiguous phrases instead of enumerating definite conditions, and substituting "etc." where there should be detailed lists of required items.

The effect on the estimators of hastily written specifications is to make them dubious as to how to figure. To take seriously all the phrases which the specifications include as "protective measures" for the architect, would mean certain loss of the contract because of the high estimate submitted; on the other hand, to disregard them entirely would cause certain loss of money if the work were awarded and enforced as described. The bid must lie somewhere between what the architect actually specified and what is covered by ambiguous clauses and a wholesale sprinkling of the too familiar "etc."

The net result imposed on the client by ambiguous specifications is that he pays for what contractors have come to assume as so much "overhead." What is lost on one job because of indefinite wording must be made up on another. Occasionally a client may be fortunate in getting more than he has paid for—but not if the contractor can help it! Indefinite specifications cost the client more money, as a rule, than all the items of decoration which he considers "unnecessary trimmings." When there is to be a "cut" on a building operation after the estimates have been too high, unfortunately for the metal craftsmen it is their work which can be dispensed with most readily (according to the client), and the ambiguous specifications which have caused excessively high bids in all lines reduce the amount of their work.

The problem of writing accurate requirements for a building operation, to supplement the plans, is one which has always been a thorn in the flesh of metal craftsmen. Among other organizations the Allied Building Metal Industries of New York City has long been waging a campaign for definite specifications; we are indebted to them for a number of suggestions, and duplicates of pamphlets and letters which they have sent out from time to time toward the attainment of that goal. It is a problem of the vicious circle: the client unreasonably demanding completed plans and specifications; the architect attempting to meet these demands by rushing the specifications at the expense of their accuracy; the estimator being at a loss to give an accurate bid and consequently adding a certain percentage to protect himself against the *implied* wishes of the architect; the client having to pay "extras" and higher prices compared with a definitely specified job. If the architect could impress upon the client the necessity of adequate time allowance for the proper preparation of his plans and definite specifications, it would seem that the problem would be largely solved, for no architect purposely makes conditions more difficult for the contractors. But a client is not readily impressed by the fact that a certain length of time is necessary for efficient specification writing and that he will eventually profit by being patient; too often the land rental or a completion date for the building seems too grotesquely important to allow the architect adequate time. Sometimes, however, the specifications are indefinite and riddled with ambiguous terms solely because the architect has not previously informed himself of general conditions, the scope of work, the manner of working the metals, or the qualities of craftsmanship.

In the ideal specification the contractor will not have to search through all the plans, examining each square inch minutely, in order to determine what he is expected to furnish. Blueprints are variable vehicles at best. What may have been distinct pencil lettering on an original drawing when it was first made, may, by the time it was sent out for estimate, have blueprinted indistinctly; after the blue-print has been used by several estimators and been exposed to the sun, it is not to be wondered at if important items may be skipped in the unsatisfactory and unfair hide-and-seek system of estimating. The architect prefers not to list the work which is required, for fear of omitting something, yet assuredly that should be no one's responsibility but his own. Moreover, it is not unfair to either client or craftsman if an item be omitted in the specification list, for the client has not paid for anything which he will not receive. Absence of a definite list often results in the most careless estimator's being the successful bidder, for by counting short the items to be furnished he naturally lowers the amount of his bid. When shop-drawings, or lack of them, bring attention to the items not figured, it becomes the contractor's problem so to skimp on materials and workmanship as to prevent there being a loss to himself. The client is by no means then getting more than he paid for, and both the architect's reputation and the building suffer.

A not infrequent clause in specifications is that "the contractor shall do his work in accordance with the plans and full-size details which will be issued *later*." It is needless to repeat, in addition to what has preceded under "Architects' Drawings" (page 27), that such a clause is in order only if the estimate drawings include details at no less than ¾-inch scale; if they are less than that in scale, estimating becomes a competition of relative mental guesses between the estimators as to what the architect may eventually demand.

Excerpts compiled by the Allied Building Metal Industries typifying the ambiguous character of many specifications, may be illustrated by the following:

The work under this heading includes, generally, the furnishing of . . . (brief list of items) etc., and other miscellaneous iron work as shown on drawings or herein specified.

All miscellaneous iron work hereinafter specified or required by the drawings, shall be furnished and erected as per plans and details, except such portions as are definitely specified to be furnished by the steel contractor and set by others.

The work under this heading includes generally . . . (brief list followed by "etc.").

The contractor shall furnish all labor, materials, tools, apparatus, equipment, etc., as required to fully complete this branch of work, as indicated on the drawings, herein specified and in general including the work and materials under the following headings . . . (list of headings in which "etc." is frequently used); also, all other necessary and incidental work in connection with the above and all such as is required by actual conditions at the premises.

This contractor shall furnish all the materials and perform all the work that may be required to fabricate and erect all the ornamental and miscellaneous iron of any description throughout the entire building and such other work as may be specified herein.

Sometimes specification writers fall into the habit of employing certain terms which are not quite sufficiently obsolete to be taken as a ritual of trumpeting which may be disregarded, and yet so indefinite as to make for guess-work estimating. Among them are such phrases as: in general; as required, or, as may be required; as indicated; necessary and incidental; in connection with; required by actual conditions; includes generally; other miscellaneous items; hereinafter specified or required; as specified or indicated; "etc." (at the end of all lists of items or conditions).

In compiling items to be covered in specifications, the architect often has some sort of list he skims over to remind him of possible omissions. Any such method is of material help. For ornamental metal work specifications one of the most useful lists of the kind is issued by the Allied Building Metal Industries, 18 West 34th Street, New York City, called, "Work of the Contractor for Ornamental and Miscellaneous Iron, Bronze and Wire Work."

In the methods of modern competition the honest craftsman often finds himself at a disadvantage because of the unfair, dishonest practice of certain competitors. It is becoming a regular trait, for which certain business men (not craftsmen) are known, to "go over the architect's head" and make business deals directly with the owner. This consists in convincing the client that the architect is incompetent to judge the merits of substitute materials, and that thousands of dollars can be saved by awarding the contract for workmanship and materials which are "just as good" as those specified. If such a contractor be sufficiently wily, he may even prove to the client's satisfaction that inferior materials and an uncertain quality of workmanship are superior to what the architect had specified. If such tactics are not resorted to before the work is estimated upon, they often follow the opening of bids if the unscrupulous business-getter has not been awarded the contract. Only recently the work for a large bank was won in fair competition by a reputable craftsman, and while the architect was drawing up his contract one of the unfair competitors talked the owner into another contract without the architect's knowledge. There was nothing in the architect's agreement with the owner which might have prevented this, even though the work as executed will be a blot on the architect's reputation. The remedy for this situation lies more in the architect's contract with his client than in the specifications. In the former it should be clearly understood in case one bidder is successful by virtue of his estimate's being the lowest, that the client gives the architect full and sole power to award a contract for such work, and also, *in the event that it seems advisable to substitute cheaper materials, all estimators shall have the privilege of submitting new bids.* It takes no great intelligence to understand that if one contractor can save money by using less superior material, another bidder can do likewise, and that the client, in awarding a contract on a new basis, is doing so without the competition which would assure him of lowest prices.

As a matter of fact almost more important than the specifications, in high-class wrought iron work, is the list of bidders. There is only a limited number of forges capable of craftsman-like artistry, yet for public work the architect cannot usually designate who shall and who shall not be permitted to estimate. His only recourse then is to make conditions so definite as regards quality of workmanship, that even the contractor who is endeavoring to palm off discreditable products is rigidly held to execute the work as specified, and is compelled to complete it sufficiently far in advance so that if rejected either he or another contractor has time to execute acceptable work without delaying the final completion of the building. The architect who has not previously awarded contracts in wrought iron work does well to investigate the reputations of all prospective bidders before allowing them to estimate, and, if the ornamental metal contract be under a so-called "general contract," to name a list of craftsmen from whom general contractors may receive bids. This should always be insisted upon if the architect wishes a creditable job, executed by honest bidders who will play fair with him and his client. He will find certain business enterprises in existence with whom he will never care to deal.

Probably the most difficult of all ornamental metals to specify is wrought iron. The craftsman is usually given to scoffing at the architect's attempts to do so, but when confronted with the problem of writing what *he* would consider a definite, binding, descriptive specification, which could safely be used for open competitive work where the lowest bidder is awarded the contract, he finds it no easy task. When the architect can designate only those craftsmen who shall be permitted to estimate (the one certain way to be assured of first-class work), the specification may condense itself into merely

a single sentence that "all work shall be done in the most craftsmanlike manner." But open competition compels more specific diction.

Obviously, to specify by words any material which is as personal a creation as artistic wrought iron, would require books rather than pages. It is impossible so to describe the *feeling* which an artisan should beat into his iron, and make so definite the quality of craftsmanship, that the money-making business-getter can be held by law to executing a first-class job. It seems more sensible to depend mainly upon submitted samples, or a sample on view at the architect's office comprising a part of the specifications, rather than attempt to describe voluminously how a rod should be beaten at the anvil. If the contract is to be of great value and is open to all contractors, then the advisable method seems to be similar to that employed by York & Sawyer in securing estimates on the wrought iron work for the Federal Reserve Bank, New York City, where not only the estimate was taken into consideration, but the quality of a required sample as well. For a lesser contract it seems satisfactory that the architect should have a sample on view at his office, which is considered "par" for all work to be executed, and from which estimators can by one moment's examination determine more clearly what is expected than they could gain by reading volumes. The alternate, if the architect has no sample on hand, is to designate a building or a specific part of it which is to be taken as the standard for estimating.

As new conditions arise in each building operation it would be advantageous if some index record could be kept, so that when the same problem again presents itself it will not be necessary for the architect's organization to determine anew how it is best specified. For example, a subject—"Entrance Grille"—could be placed at the top of a card (which in a card index would be listed under "Wrought Iron"), and below it the names of the jobs specifying one, followed by the page number in the specification.

The best craftsmen are always willing to be of help to the architect, and in no way can they be of greater service than in the matter of specifications. In specifying his initial wrought iron work, if the architect were to invite an expert craftsman to look over the plans—particularly the special conditions—he would invariably receive excellent suggestions that could advantageously be incorporated.

It is realized that it is impossible adequately

to specify wrought iron in skeleton form for all conditions, yet the material which follows should be helpful to the architect who has not previously used the material, or to any who has felt that his specification would bear improvement and comparison. Conditions are so variable for each building that, when consulted, many craftsmen frankly intimated that it was impossible to formulate an ideal specification which would assure the best of craftsmanship. However, it is better to begin with something than never to begin at all; as time goes by revisions and additions can be made by the architect in his practice, eventually resulting in a thoroughly useful and satisfactory form, as much so to him as to the craftsman.

Various craftsmen were requested to aid in the compilation of what would approach being a specification which would make difficult, if not impossible, competition between the inferior workman or business-getter and the conscientious craftsman who has the architect's and client's interests at heart. The general opinion was that it is impossible to specify the artistic standard which a product should attain, and that if the architect cannot exclude all but craftsmen whom he knows by reputation and workmanship, it is unlikely that a specification can exclude inferior products. However, the architect is often confronted with the problem of open competition, and must do the best he can with writing a stringent specification which will empower him to reject faulty work, and make it clear to all estimators that only the highest type of workmanship will be acceptable.

Under "Materials," specifications have used endless terms and phrases which have meant little if anything—except to amuse the craftsman. To state the number of required hammer-marks per square inch has not been uncommon. It is usually demanded that the iron be "hand hammered while hot," which is of course the only way it should be done, yet certain craftsmen have found that expression amusing. Sometimes beating of the iron is demanded until all the carbon content has disappeared—rather a strenuous chemical problem. Actually it should be enough to specify under "Materials" that for the best work "Swedish," or "Norway," iron be used, that all work be forged hot and never worked cold, that all welding be done at the anvil by beating (not by a blow torch—see page 16), and that the texture correspond to that of a designated piece of work.

One craftsman suggests that under "Ma-terial and Craftsmanship," the following sentence be included: "The best obtainable iron shall be employed and worked at the forge with the care and in the spirit of the old masters; there is to be no attempt made to produce artificial surfacing by random hammer marks, but there should be a natural hand-worked appearance imparted as ornamental features are fashioned from bars or rods."

Some idea of a craftsman's abilities could be obtained from observation and photographs of previously executed work, and the requirement that some clear prints be submitted might be embodied under the conditions of "Workmanship."

The following paragraphs are suggestions for "Notice to Bidders," "Workmanship," "Samples," and "Scope" which could be used in connection with wrought iron specifications; specific conditions should be inserted where they are necessary.

Notice to Bidders.—It must be fully realized by all contractors before estimating on these specifications that the owner and architect are expecting and will pay for the artistic execution of the work, to be carried out according to the best traditions and methods of the craft. The interest of the metal craftsman in the execution of this work must be that of an artist taking personal pride in his craft, and not merely a commercial undertaking to reap as profitable a harvest as possible. The architect will rigidly enforce both the word and spirit of these specifications, so that if the contractor is not artistically capable of executing the highest quality of wrought iron work, it will only result in a financial loss to him to undertake this contract, because *any and all work which does not come up to the artistic standard set by the architect will be rejected and will under no circumstances be paid for.*

Quality of Workmanship.—It is the intent of these specifications to make it clearly understood that none but the highest type of craftsmanship will be accepted by the architect, who will be the sole judge as to the artistic merits and execution of the work. Bids will be accepted only on condition that the contractors submitting them acknowledge that the architect has the right to reject any and all work which does not come up to the quality of the craftsmanship of . . . [designate a sample submitted, a sample on view at the architect's office, or an executed piece of work in a certain building]. The architect will accept no excuses whatsoever for the faulty or inferior execution of any of the work.

Samples.—The estimate for this work shall be accompanied by a sample of an executed piece of work done by the contractor submitting the estimate (or information concerning where his work may be examined not too far distant), which will indicate clearly the capabilities of the contractor in the execution of this type of craftsmanship. If it does not measure up to the artistic standard established by the architect, who alone shall be the judge, the estimate will not be considered. When the contractor is awarded the contract for this work, all items not of equal or superior quality compared with the sample submitted [or like that of a designated building] shall be rejected and immediately replaced by the contractor at his own expense. If however he cannot execute the work satisfactorily, it will be awarded to another contractor. Such work which in the architect's opinion must be replaced in this way will not be paid for. In submitting an estimate the contractor automatically acknowledges that he clearly understands that *he will be paid only for such work as is accepted by the architect, who shall be the final judge in all matters of this nature.*

Scope of Work.—The work included in this section comprises the following items: [definite list follows, accompanied by reference to sheet numbers of plans and details, with no use of "etc."]

The specifications for the ornamental wrought iron work of the Federal Reserve Bank, New York City, by York & Sawyer, architects, are given below because of their completeness. With a few changes made to fit particular conditions, the architect should find them a helpful guide.

Shop Drawings.—This contractor shall prepare shop drawings and details for all work included herein, and shall submit same in triplicate (through the general contractor's office) to the architects for approval or correction, together with full-size studies of the special ornamental work. These shop drawings and sketches shall be altered by this contractor as required by the architects, and, upon approval, sufficient copies of the shop drawings and sketches shall be issued to the general contractor for distribution.

Models.—This contractor shall prepare and submit, for approval or correction, full-size models or patterns of all ornamental work included herein. These models or patterns shall conform to the approved full-size details, supplemented by the verbal directions of the architects. The architects reserve the right to make such changes as they consider advisable.

Sample.—Each bidder shall submit, with his bid, a sample of a complete section of banking screen, taking in pilaster at each end, which shall be wrought, incised and finished complete, as per details, to enable the architects to judge the qualifications of the bidder for this type of work. The sample submitted by the successful bidder shall be used as the standard of workmanship for all wrought iron work, subject to such modifications as the architects may require.

Materials and Workmanship.—All work included herein shall be executed of special grade of wrought iron, except where otherwise specified herein or indicated on drawings.

All wrought iron shall be best quality forged iron, tough, ductile and fibrous in character, of even texture, fulfilling the conditions required by all standard tests. All work shall be executed by craftsmen skilled in the trade.

All ornamental iron work shall be carefully forged, hand wrought and incised where and as required to produce the design and effect desired.

All parts of the work shall be substantially framed together as shown, and closely fitted. All joinings shall be neatly and strongly tenoned and rivetted together, or welded. All dowels and rivets shall be counter-sunk flush, or be finished as indicated or required. All spindles shall be forged; collars, where required, shall be welded onto spindle. All leaves, rosettes, or other free ornament shall be forged from substantial iron and welded where connecting with stems or other iron work. All welding shall be done at the forge, and all shall be clean and perfect. No cast parts will be accepted. All solid ornamental work shall be worked and incised as required by approved design.

All hinges, pivots, handles, knobs, escutcheons, plates, and other hardware shall be ornamented, incised, worked or otherwise finished, as required by the architects to correspond to the design for each particular item; all locks shall be provided with special cases, and where lock guards are required they shall also be provided.

Anchors.—This contractor shall include all anchors, stays, and supports required for securely fastening in place all work included herein. All anchors shall be subject to the approval of the architects as to sizes, shapes, quantity required and method of application. All built-in anchors or supports shall be furnished to the general contractor in ample time for building in, while the masonry is being built.

Cutting and Fitting.—This contractor shall do all necessary cutting, drilling, tapping, and fitting as required for securing his work in position, and shall also do all necessary cutting, drilling, and tapping of the work furnished by him to accommodate the work of other contractors.

Painting and Finishing.—All wrought iron shall be given an approved finish (by this contractor) which will prevent rust, and which will not mar or impair the craftsmanship or texture of the material.

On completion of the building all work included herein shall be carefully examined, all defective portions removed and replaced with perfect work, all work shall be thoroughly cleaned, touched up or refinished as required, and all left in an approved condition.

All structural steel supporting, bracing, or stiffening members, and all concealed portions, shall be painted two coats of an approved metal preservative paint, one coat at the shop before delivery and the other after erection. All portions which will be inaccessible after being assembled or placed, shall be given the two coats of paint before erection.

In order to preserve the natural texture of wrought iron we are indebted to a New York craftsman for the prescription which follows. The surface of the iron should be coated at least once every three months with wax, but before new wax is applied all rust spots should be removed by rubbing with emery cloth, aided by a few drops of turpentine if the rust be heavy.

Following this the entire surface should be rubbed with almost any liquid floor wax, or beeswax with just enough turpentine to dissolve it. After about fifteen minutes, when the turpentine has evaporated and the wax has "set," the surface should be lightly rubbed with a soft cloth. It may be found where the iron comes in constant contact with people's hands, as for example a stair rail, that, due to the wax wearing off and the action of the acid in perspiration, the wax application may have to be applied oftener than every three months. However, considering the fact that it takes considerably less time to apply the wax than a coat of paint, and that the effect is incomparably superior, there should be no question as to the value of maintaining the natural finish of wrought iron as compared with painting it and obscuring all evidences of fine craftsmanship (refer to pages 26–7).

BIBLIOGRAPHY

THE following list of books does not attempt to state every possible source for wrought iron information. It is primarily intended to give the interested reader first a series of three books which will afford a general review of the entire realm of iron work in Europe, followed by those books of illustrations of the various countries which seem to provide the best starting point for either cursory study or building up a library. Where anything of special interest or any specific qualification marks the contents, it is stated within parenthesis; where only special plates deal with iron they are sometimes enumerated. The historic styles are readily referred to in books widely known, but the *moderne* movement is being reflected in new publications being brought out almost continuously. Since most of the latter are foreign, the list given under the heading "The *Moderne*" is no doubt deficient even as it goes to press because of the length of time necessary for books to reach American libraries, and thus resulting in the author's regretted ignorance of their existence. However, for the interested student of the *moderne* he should find the selected five books listed of intrinsic help in design, providing he discards the mediocre.

WROUGHT IRON TECHNIQUE

Handbook of Art Smithing, by Franz Sales Meyer; introduction by J. Starkie Gardner in the English edition. New York: B. Hessling, pre. 1896.
Plain and Ornamental Forging, by Ernst Schwarzkopf. New York: John Wiley & Sons, Inc., 1916.

GENERAL SURVEY

Decorative Ironwork, from the XIth to the XVIIIth Century, by Charles ffoulkes. London: Methuen & Co., Ltd.; 1913. (Excellent for historical review, illustrated by many famous examples.)
Das Eisenwerk, called also *An Encyclopædia of Ironwork*, with an introduction by Otto Hoever. Berlin: Verlag Ernest Wasmuth, 1927. (A few pages of historical matter—which are not to be compared with the texts by ffoulkes and Gardner—are followed by illustrations of European countries only, with a heavy predominance of late German work.)
Ironwork, from the Earliest Times to the End of the Eighteenth Century, in Parts I, II, and III, by J. Starkie Gardner. London: Victoria and Albert Museum Art Handbooks. (Invaluable for a complete historical survey of all European countries.)

ITALIAN

Enciclopedia delle Moderne Arti Decorative Italiane, II—Il Ferro Battuto, under direction of Guido Marangoni. Milan: Casa Editrice Ceschina, 1926. (Work executed since the Renaissance; has much of interest in design.)
Il Ferro nell' Arte Italiana, by Giulio Ferrari. Milan: U. Hoepli, 1910. (An Italian text illustrated with many of the best examples of Italian craftsmanship.)
Lavori Artistici in Ferro. Torino: C. Crudo & C., 190-. (Illustrates the French influence on Italian work after the Renaissance, the blending of French and German styles, and some *moderne* examples.)
Northern Italian Details, by Walter G. Thomas and John T. Fallon. New York: The American Architect, 1916. (Mostly examples of the late Renaissance and after; plates 82, 83, 85, 88, 90, 114, 118 to 125.)

SPANISH

Architectur und Kunstgewerbe in Alt Spanien, by August L. Mayer. Munich: Delphin-Verlag, 1920.
Arte y Decoración en España, vol. 1 to 7. Barcelona: Casellas Moncanut h^{nos}, 1917–19.
Catálogo de la Exposición de Mobiliario Español, 2d Edition. Joaquin Enriquez. (Examples of furniture usage, from fifteenth century to mid-seventeenth.)
Exposición de Hierros Antiguos Españoles; Catálogo por Pedro Miguel de Artiñano y Galdácano. Madrid: "Mateu," 1919. (Small specimens of interior usage from page 49 to end.)
Hierros Artísticos, by Luis Labarta. Barcelona: F. Seix, 1902. (Lithograph drawings of many types of iron usage; other European examples besides Spanish.)
Materiales y Documentos de Arte Español, by Mira Leroy, in 10 volumes. (A scattering of photographs of iron work of all periods in vols. 7, 8, 9, and 10, some being of great interest and value; not as many in vols. 3, 5, and 6, and still less in vols. 2 and 4.)
Minor Ecclesiastical, Domestic and Garden Architecture of Southern Spain, by Austin Whittlesey. New York: Architectural Book Publishing Co., 1920.
Provincial Houses in Spain, by Byne and Stapley. New York: William Helburn, Inc., 1925. (Excellent as reference for informal use of wrought iron.)
Rejería of the Spanish Renaissance, by Byne and Stapley. New York: The De Vinne Press, 1914. (One of the outstanding books on the subject.)
Renaissance Architecture and Ornament in Spain (1500-60), by Andrew N. Prentice. London: B. T. Batsford, Ltd., 1893. (A considerable number of the plates deal with wrought-iron *rejas* of the cathedrals, some being reproduced in this book in the chapter on "Spanish Iron Work.")
Renaissance Architecture of Central and Northern Spain, by Austin Whittlesey. New York: Architectural Book Publishing Co., 1920. (A scattering of photographs throughout dealing with wrought iron, but chiefly toward the end.)
Spanish Interiors and Furniture, Volumes 1 and 2, by Byne and Stapley. New York: William Helburn, Inc., 1921-25. (Excellent as reference for use of iron in interior settings, furniture, lighting fixtures, etc.)

Spanish Interiors, Furniture and Details, 14th to 17th Centuries, with an introduction by Harold Donaldson Eberlein. New York: Architectural Book Publishing Co.

Spanish Ironwork, by Byne and Stapley. New York: Hispanic Society of America, 1915.

FRENCH

Documents de Ferronnerie Ancienne: Époques Louis XV et Louis XVI (1re, 2e, 3e, et 4e Séries); *Périodes du XIIe au XVIIIe Siècles* (5e et 6e Séries). Paris: F. Contet, 1908–22. (A most exhaustive collection of well reproduced examples of the periods covered.)

La Ferronnerie Française, aux XVIIe et XVIIIe Siècles; Décoration Ancienne, 3e Séries. Paris: Vve Charles Schmid, 1909. (An excellent reference guide, particularly for balcony railings.)

Monographie du Musée de Cluny, Part 2. Paris: Armand Guérinet. (Plates 150, 151, and from 295 to the end.)

Musée le Secq des Tournelles a Rouen; Ferronnerie Ancienne; Séries I et II, by H. R. d'Allemagne. Paris: J. Schemit, 1924.

Recueil de Ferronnerie Ancienne et Moderne. Paris: Armand Guérinet.

Le Style Louis XV, published by E. Rümler. Paris: Librairie de la Construction Moderne, 1914.

FLEMISH

Belgian Ironwork, by Charles ffoulkes. "Connoisseur," London, 1915; vol. 41, pages 143–153.
(See also *Decorative Ironwork*, by the same author, referred to under the preceding heading "General Survey.")

ENGLISH

Decorative Ironwork, by Charles ffoulkes. (See preceding heading "General Survey"; excellent reference illustrations for early work, particularly hinges.)

English Homes, by Henry Avray Tipping. New York: Charles Scribner's Sons, 1920. (Published in 6 periods; Period IV, vol. 1, has a large number of photographic illustrations of iron work incidental to the general exterior architectural views.)

English Ironwork of the XVIIth and XVIIIth Centuries, by J. Starkie Gardner. London: B. T. Batsford, Ltd., 1911. (No better source can be referred to for either historical matter or exhaustive illustrations for the period covered.)

English and Scottish Wrought Ironwork, by Bailey Scott Murphy. London: B. T. Batsford, Ltd., 1904.

Examples of Decorative Iron Work of the 17th and 18th Centuries of England, by D. J. Ebbets. London: B. T. Batsford, Ltd., 1879. (The illustrations include drawings by the various craftsmen.)

Georgian Details, by Francis Rowland Yerbury. London: E. Benn, Ltd., 1926.

Ironwork, I, II, and III, by J. Starkie Gardner. London: Victoria and Albert Museum Art Handbooks. (Although including a general historical survey, particular attention is given to England, and the relation of its craftsmen to those of other countries.)

The Practical Exemplar of Architecture, by Mervyn E. Macartney, Series I–IV. London: Westminster (London) Architectural Review, 1908–13. (The illustrations are mostly English although some are Italian, dealing with smaller gates, railings, etc.; vol. 1, pl. 71–75; vol. 11, 70–81; vol. 111, 22, 32, 55, 56, 59, 61–66; vol. 1v, 73–91; vol. v, 67–74.)

A new booke of drawings invented and designed by J. Tijou. . . . For the use of them that work iron in perfection and with art; 1693, reproduced with a description of the plates by J. Starkie Gardner. London: B. T. Batsford, Ltd., 1896.

GERMAN

Deutsche Schmiedearbeiten aus Fünf Yahrhunderten, by Hans Bösch. Leipsig: Baumgärtner, 1920 (?).

Deutsche Schmiedeeisen-Kunst: I–Mittelalter, II–Renaissance und Frühbarock, by Ferdinand Stuttman. Munich: Delphin-Verlag, 1927.

Geschichte der Metalkunst, by Lüer & Creutz. (A general history in German, illustrated by examples of all periods.)

Geschmiedete Gitter des XVI–XVIII Yahrhunderts aus Süddeutschland, by Adalbert Roeper. Leipsig: A. Schumann's Verlag; Munich: J. Albert, 1895 (?).

Die Kunstschlosserei, by Professor Max Metzger. Lübeck: Verlag Charles Coleman, 1927.

Ornamente Alter Schmiedeeisen, by Martin Gerlach. Vienna: Gerlach & Schenk, 1895. (Consists of 50 plates of photographs ably taken and well reproduced.)

Die Schmiedekunst, seit dem Ende der Renaissance, by Adolph Bruening. Leipsig: H. Sumann, Nachf., 1902.

AMERICAN

Colonial Lighting, by Arthur H. Hayward. Boston: B. J. Brimmer Co., 1923.

Early American Hardware, by Wallace Nutting. "Antiques," August, 1923. (Series of photographs of latches.)

Early American Wrought Iron, by Albert H. Sonn. New York: Charles Scribner's Sons, 1928. (Three vols., illustrated with over 1,000 pencil drawings.)

Examples of Colonial Architecture in South Carolina and Georgia, by Edward A. Crane and E. E. Soderholtz. New York: Hessling & Spielmeyer, 1895. (Plates 1–3, 29–34, 43–45.)

Gateways and Doorways of Charleston, South Carolina, in the Eighteenth and Nineteenth Centuries, by Elizabeth Gibbon Curtis. New York: Architectural Book Publishing Co., 1926.

The Georgian Period, in 6 volumes, by William Rotch Ware. New York: U. P. C. Book Company, Inc., 1923. (Drawings and photographs occur incidentally in views which primarily illustrate architectural features.)

Iron Work in Charleston, South Carolina, a collection of photographs by George W. Johnson, in the Art Room of the New York Public Library.

THE MODERNE

Le Fer à l'Exposition Internationale des Arts Decoratifs Moderne, 1re et 2e Séries, by Guillaume Janneau. Paris: F. Contet, 1925.

Le Fer Forgé dans la Décoration Moderne. Paris: Ch. Massin & Cie, 1925.

La Ferronnerie, Exposition des Arts Decoratifs, Paris, 1925, with an introduction by H. Martinie. Paris: Albert Lévy, 1926.

I Ferri Battuti di Alessandro Mazzucotelli. Milan: Casa Editrice Bestetti & Tumminelli.

Geschmiedetes Eisen von Jaroslav Vonka. Breslau: Ostdeutsche Verlags-Anstalt, G. M. B. H., 1927. (Illustrating the work of a modern craftsman who applies historic forms in a modernistic manner; the modeling is simple, clever, and excellent throughout, offering however more suggestion for details than *parti*.)

INDEX OF ILLUSTRATIONS

(Author's Note: The "List of Illustrations," which is usually included in the front matter of a book, has been omitted here because there seemed to be no useful purpose served by a series of 324 titles. It seemed sufficient to have only the following index, which classifies the illustrations according to subject-matter; when the book is being used as a design reference guide illustrations can be found under subject headings, e. g., "Balconies," "Hinges," etc. If the work of any particular country alone is desired, the Contents pages clearly designate where it is to be found. Unless otherwise specified, all the items in the ensuing list are of wrought iron.)

NOTE: ALL NUMERALS REFER TO *Figure* NUMBERS, UNLESS OTHERWISE NOTED.

Dover Books on Art

PINE FURNITURE OF EARLY NEW ENGLAND, R. H. Kettell. Over 400 illustrations, over 50 working drawings of early New England chairs, benches, beds, cupboards, mirrors, shelves, tables, other furniture esteemed for simple beauty and character. "Rich store of illustrations . . . emphasizes the individuality and varied design," ANTIQUES. 413 illustrations, 55 working drawings. 475pp. 8 x 10¾. 20145-7 Clothbound $15.00

BASIC BOOKBINDING, A. W. Lewis. Enables both beginners and experts to rebind old books or bind paperbacks in hard covers. Treats materials, tools; gives step-by-step instruction in how to collate a book, sew it, back it, make boards, etc. 261 illus. Appendices. 155pp. 5⅜ x 8. 20169-4 Paperbound $2.75

DESIGN MOTIFS OF ANCIENT MEXICO, J. Enciso. Nearly 90% of these 766 superb designs from Aztec, Olmec, Totonac, Maya, and Toltec origins are unobtainable elsewhere. Contains plumed serpents, wind gods, animals, demons, dancers, monsters, etc. Excellent applied design source. Originally $17.50. 766 illustrations, thousands of motifs. 192pp. 6⅛ x 9¼. 20084-1 Paperbound $3.50

A DIDEROT PICTORIAL ENCYCLOPEDIA OF TRADES AND INDUSTRY. Manufacturing and the Technical Arts in Plates Selected from "L'Encyclopédie ou Dictionnaire Raisonné des Sciences, des Arts, et des Métiers," of Denis Diderot, edited with text by C. Gillispie. Over 2000 illustrations on 485 full-page plates. Magnificent 18th-century engravings of men, women, and children working at such trades as milling flour, cheesemaking, charcoal burning, mining, silverplating, shoeing horses, making fine glass, printing, hundreds more, showing details of machinery, different steps in sequence, etc. A remarkable art work, but also the largest collection of working figures in print, copyright-free, for art directors, designers, etc. Two vols. 920pp. 9 x 12. Heavy library cloth. 22284-5. 22285-3 Two volume set $40.00

SILK SCREEN TECHNIQUES, J. Biegeleisen, M. Cohn. A practical step-by-step home course in one of the most versatile, least expensive graphic arts processes. How to build an inexpensive silk screen, prepare stencils, print, achieve special textures, use color, etc. Every step explained, diagrammed. 149 illustrations, 201pp. 6⅛ x 9¼. 20433-2 Paperbound $3.95

STICKS AND STONES, Lewis Mumford. An examination of forces influencing American architecture: the medieval tradition in early New England, the classical influence in Jefferson's time, the Brown Decades, the imperial facade, the machine age, etc. "A truly remarkable book," SAT. REV. OF LITERATURE. 2nd revised edition. 21 illus. xvii + 240pp. 5⅜ x 8. 20202-X Paperbound $3.50

THE AUTOBIOGRAPHY OF AN IDEA, Louis Sullivan. The architect whom Frank Lloyd Wright called "the master," records the development of the theories that revolutionized America's skyline. 34 full-page plates of Sullivan's finest work. New introduction by R. M. Line. xiv + 335pp. 5⅜ x 8. 20281-X Paperbound $6.00

AN ATLAS OF ANIMAL ANATOMY FOR ARTISTS, W. Ellenberger, H. Baum, H. Dittrich. The largest, richest animal anatomy for artists in English. Form, musculature, tendons, bone structure, expression, detailed cross sections of head, other features, of the horse, lion, dog, cat, deer, seal, kangaroo, cow, bull, goat, monkey, hare, many other animals. "Highly recommended," DESIGN. Second, revised, enlarged edition with new plates from Cuvier, Stubbs, etc. 288 illustrations. 153pp. 11⅜ x 9.

20082-5 Paperbound $6.00

ANIMAL DRAWING: ANATOMY AND ACTION FOR ARTISTS, C. R. Knight. 158 studies, with full accompanying text, of such animals as the gorilla, bear, bison, dromedary, camel, vulture, pelican, iguana, shark, etc., by one of the greatest modern masters of animal drawing. Innumerable tips on how to get life expression into your work. "An excellent reference work," SAN FRANCISCO CHRONICLE. 158 illustrations. 156pp. 10½ x 8½.

20426-X Paperbound $4.50

ARCHITECTURAL AND PERSPECTIVE DESIGNS, Giuseppe Galli Bibiena. 50 imaginative scenic drawings of Giuseppe Galli Bibiena, principal theatrical engineer and architect to the Viennese court of Charles VI. Aside from its interest to art historians, students, and art lovers, there is a whole Baroque world of material in this book for the commercial artist. Portrait of Charles VI by Martin de Meytens. 1 allegorical plate. 50 additional plates. New introduction. vi + 103pp. 10⅛ x 13¼.

21263-7 Paperbound $6.50

HANDBOOK OF DESIGNS AND DEVICES, C. P. Hornung. A remarkable working collection of 1836 basic designs and variations, all copyright-free. Variations of circle, line, cross, diamond, swastika, star, scroll, shield, many more. Notes on symbolism. "A necessity to every designer who would be original without having to labor heavily," ARTIST AND ADVERTISER. 204 plates. 240pp. 5⅜ x 8.

20125-2 Paperbound $4.00

CHINESE HOUSEHOLD FURNITURE, G. N. Kates. A summary of virtually everything that is known about authentic Chinese furniture before it was contaminated by the influence of the West. The text covers history of styles, materials used, principles of design and craftsmanship, and furniture arrangement—all fully illustrated. xiii + 190pp. 5⅝ x 8½.

20958-X Paperbound $4.00

DECORATIVE ART OF THE SOUTHWESTERN INDIANS, D. S. Sides. 300 black and white reproductions from one of the most beautiful art traditions of the primitive world, ranging from the geometric art of the Great Pueblo period of the 13th century to modern folk art. Motives from basketry, beadwork, Zuni masks, Hopi kachina dolls, Navajo sand pictures and blankets, and ceramic ware. Unusual and imaginative designs will inspire craftsmen in all media, and commercial artists may reproduce any of them without permission or payment. xviii + 101pp. 5⅝ x 8⅜.

20139-2 Paperbound $2.50

Dover Books on Art

ANIMALS IN MOTION, Eadweard Muybridge. The largest collection of animal action photos in print. 34 different animals (horses, mules, oxen, goats, camels, pigs, cats, lions, gnus, deer, monkeys, eagles—and 22 others) in 132 characteristic actions. All 3919 photographs are taken in series at speeds up to 1/1600th of a second, offering artists, biologists, cartoonists a remarkable opportunity to see exactly how an ostrich's head bobs when running, how a lion puts his foot down, how an elephant's knee bends, how a bird flaps his wings, thousands of other hard-to-catch details. "A really marvellous series of plates," NATURE. 380 full-page plates. Heavy glossy stock, reinforced binding with headbands. 7⅞ x 10¾.　　　20203-8　Clothbound $15.95

THE BOOK OF SIGNS, R. Koch. 493 symbols—crosses, monograms, astrological, biological symbols, runes, etc.—from ancient manuscripts, cathedrals, coins, catacombs, pottery. May be reproduced permission-free. 493 illustrations by Fritz Kredel. 104pp. 6⅛ x 9¼.　　　20162-7　Paperbound $2.75

A HANDBOOK OF EARLY ADVERTISING ART, C. P. Hornung. The largest collection of copyright-free early advertising art ever compiled. Vol. I: 2,000 illustrations of animals, old automobiles, buildings, allegorical figures, fire engines, Indians, ships, trains, more than 33 other categories! Vol. II: Over 4,000 typographical specimens; 600 Roman, Gothic, Barnum, Old English faces; 630 ornamental type faces; hundreds of scrolls, initials, flourishes, etc. "A remarkable collection," PRINTERS' INK.

Vol. I: Pictorial Volume. Over 2000 illustrations. 256pp. 9 x 12.
　　　20122-8　Clothbound $15.00

Vol. II: Typographical Volume. Over 4000 specimens. 319pp. 9 x 12.　　　20123-6　Clothbound $15.00

Two volume set, Clothbound, only $30.00

THE UNIVERSAL PENMAN, George Bickham. Exact reproduction of beautiful 18th-century book of handwriting. 22 complete alphabets in finest English roundhand, other scripts, over 2000 elaborate flourishes, 122 calligraphic illustrations, etc. Material is copyright-free. "An essential part of any art library, and a book of permanent value," AMERICAN ARTIST. 212 plates. 224pp. 9 x 13¾.　　　20616-5 Paperbound $9.95

AN ATLAS OF ANATOMY FOR ARTISTS, F. Schider. This standard work contains 189 full-page plates, more than 647 illustrations of all aspects of the human skeleton, musculature, cutaway portions of the body, each part of the anatomy, hand forms, eyelids, breasts, location of muscles under the flesh, etc. 59 plates illustrate how Michelangelo, da Vinci, Goya, 15 others, drew human anatomy. New 3rd edition enlarged by 52 new illustrations by Cloquet, Barcsay. "The standard reference tool," AMERICAN LIBRARY ASSOCIATION. "Excellent," AMERICAN ARTIST. 189 plates, 647 illustrations. xxvi + 192pp. 7⅞ x 10⅝.　　　20241-0　Paperbound $6.00

Dover Books on Art

GREEK REVIVAL ARCHITECTURE IN AMERICA, T. Hamlin. A comprehensive study of the American Classical Revival, its regional variations, reasons for its success and eventual decline. Profusely illustrated, displaying the work of almost every important architect. 2 appendices. 59 figures, 94 plates containing 221 photos, 62 architectural designs, drawings, etc. 324-item classified bibliography. Index. xi + 439pp. 5⅜ x 8½.

21148-7 Paperbound $7.50

CREATIVE LITHOGRAPHY AND HOW TO DO IT, Grant Arnold. Written by a man who practiced and taught lithography for many years, this highly useful volume explains all the steps of the lithographic process from tracing the drawings on the stone to printing the lithograph, with helpful hints for solving special problems. Index. 16 reproductions of lithographs. 11 drawings. xv + 214pp. of text. 5⅜ x 8½.

21208-4 Paperbound $4.50

ARABIC ART IN COLOR, Prisse d'Avennes. 50 full-color plates from rare 19th-century volumes by noted French historian. 141 authentic Islamic designs and motifs from Cairo art treasures include florals, geometrics, Koran illuminations, spots, borders, etc. Ranging from 12th to 18th century, these exquisite illustrations will interest artists, designers of textiles and wallpaper, craftspeople working in stained glass, rugs, etc. Captions. 46pp. 9⅜ x 12¼.

23658-7 Paperbound $6.00

THE ALPHABET AND ELEMENTS OF LETTERING, F. W. Goudy. A beautifully illustrated volume on the aesthetics of letters and type faces and their history and development. Each plate consists of 15 forms of a single letter with the last plate devoted to the ampersand and the numerals. "A sound guide for all persons engaged in printing or drawing," Saturday Review. 27 full-page plates. 48 additional figures. xii + 131pp. 7⅞ x 10¾.

20792-7 Paperbound $4.00

THE COMPLETE BOOK OF SILK SCREEN PRINTING PRODUCTION, J. I. Biegeleisen. Here is a clear and complete picture of every aspect of silk screen technique and press operation—from individually operated manual presses to modern automatic ones. Unsurpassed as a guidebook for setting up shop, making shop operation more efficient, finding out about latest methods and equipment; or as a textbook for use in teaching, studying, or learning all aspects of the profession. 124 figures. Index. Bibliography. List of Supply Sources. xi + 253pp. 5⅜ x 8½.

21100-2 Paperbound $4.00

Dover publishes books on commercial art, art history, crafts, design, art classics; also books on music, literature, science, mathematics, puzzles and entertainments, chess, engineering, biology, philosophy, psychology, languages, history, and other fields. For free circulars write to Dept. DA, Dover Publications, Inc., 31 East 2nd Street Mineola N.Y. 11501.